Advance Praise

"Elizabeth Rau's writing style has always reminded me of Raymond Carver's. Like Carver, Rau understands the power of simple, concrete language and closely observed details. She uses her writing chops to illuminate the intricacies of everyday life, from the awkwardness of leaving a Red Sox game before the team makes a startling comeback, to her homesickness for her Midwestern hometown. With humor and uncommon sensitivity, Rau transforms the ordinary into the extraordinary."

— Jonathan Saltzman, reporter for *The Boston Globe* and former reporter for *The Providence Journal*

"This woman knows how to write. Blessed with a sharp memory and an astonishing eye for detail, she takes you by the hand and welcomes you into her world. Enjoy!"

— M. Charles Bakst, retired *Providence Journal* political columnist

"Elizabeth Rau offers proof of what I've always believed: everyone out there in the world is living a compelling story. With her journalist's eye and elegant style, Rau demonstrates that she knows how to suss out the moments in an ordinary life that will move us most. Each essay reminds us how little difference there is between us when it comes to life's big moments: leaving home, losing loved ones, making good in gym class. Rau reminds us that even when we feel alone, we are alone together and that's a great comfort."

— Marybeth Reilly-McGreen, author

"With delightful description and disarming humor, Elizabeth Rau wrote a popular column in our paper, *East Side Monthly*, for over a decade about the joys of raising two irrepressible boys. Her gift though, is that these well-crafted narratives produce smiles of recognition regardless of where one lives. Do yourself a favor and dig in. A great read."

— Barry Fain, publisher, Providence Media

"Elizabeth Rau has written your story, many of them. Writing is about noticing and thinking and learning about what surrounds you. Rau does that with clarity, warmth, wit, humor, and a turn of phrase that captures the moment. Her spirited stories of everyday life experiences will charm you and bring you into her world. There you will find much of yours."

— Dr. Edward Iannuccilli, author of *Growing Up Italian*

"I teared up reading Elizabeth Rau's "Spaghetti Cowboy," a piece about my dad. She captured his personality perfectly. Her collection of essays reads like a Master Class in observation—a welcome reminder to pause and to find meaning and humor in the quirky, familiar details that surround us."

— Georgia Hunter, author of *We Were the Lucky Ones*

The Good Slope

The Good Slope

Elizabeth Rau

Apprentice
House Press
Loyola University Maryland

First Edition

Library of Congress Control Number: 2022950465

Hardcover ISBN: 978-1-62720-442-2
Paperback ISBN: 978-1-62720-443-9
Ebook ISBN: 978-1-62720-444-6

Design by April Hartman
Editorial Development by Natalie Misyak
Promotional Development by Natalie Misyak

Published by Apprentice House Press

Apprentice
House Press
Loyola University Maryland

Loyola University Maryland
4501 N. Charles Street, Baltimore, MD 21210
410.617.5265
www.ApprenticeHouse.com
info@ApprenticeHouse.com

To Peder and Henry

Contents

Introduction

I came with six boxes of books, an old green cardigan, and a childhood keepsake, a wood carving of a ruddy-cheeked man playing an accordion that I found in my shoe on Saint Nicholas Day one winter morning when I was a little girl.

My apartment in Providence was small, but cozy, and anyway, why did I need more? It was just me. I stacked my books in piles on the floor and put my sweater in a suitcase that doubled as a dresser. I put my keepsake on a spice rack in the kitchen.

I'd do my best to make Rhode Island my home. I managed well enough during the day, but at night, alone, I was homesick. I cried so much a neighbor knocked on my door one day and asked if everything was all right.

No, it wasn't. I missed St. Louis, my hometown. I missed our red-brick house with black shutters; Velvet Freeze, where I had my first job scooping ice cream onto sugar cones; and the big clock at Roosevelt Bank that gave the time and temperature—a delightfully suffocating 101 degrees on a summer day.

One year tumbled into the next, and I'm still here, now with my husband and two sons. I've lived in Rhode Island for more than three decades, most of that time in a postage-stamp size community in Providence called the East Side.

I know the state well. Pale-green sea glass washes up at the eastern tip of Goosewing Beach in Little Compton. Steamers live buried in the muck at Fogland in Tiverton. The strongest rope swing hangs from a knobby swamp maple that bends over the Pawcatuck River in Bradford, across from Bill's Barber Shop.

But does a Catalog of Best Places make it home? If you had asked me this question a decade or so ago, when my sons were playing Little League and racing pinewood derby cars as Cub Scouts, I would have said, no: Their home is most certainly Rhode Island—and especially the East Side—but my home is that sweltering Midwestern city.

And then time had its way. My feelings about home—and what that is—started to change in the last few years. That shift might have something to do with getting older, or with seeing my sons, now young men in college, bolt from the family embrace to take a crack at living, to fill their own closets with stuff.

Rambling around my once-noisy-now-still house, I'm trying to figure out, again, what home means to me. It's clear that the pull of home is becoming stronger as my sons fly the coop, and that my instincts are kicking in: preserve the roots, especially in memory, so we all have a place to return to.

If a fact-checker were to ask, this decades-long road trip started in 1984, when I left the familiarity of St. Louis to work for a skiing magazine in Brattleboro, Vermont. From there, I went to a small newspaper in Connecticut and then, in 1986, to *The Providence Journal* to work as a reporter. A few years into the job, I started writing essays for the paper, many of them about my Midwestern childhood. Some of those essays are included in this collection.

I left the newspaper in 2000 to care for my two sons at home and launched a career as a freelance writer. One day, I wrote an essay about my older son's quest to get a college football player's autograph and submitted the story to our neighborhood publication, *East Side Monthly*.

That column led to more than 100 columns that I wrote for the paper over the years, many of which centered on my sons and their friends, and are also included in this book. There was no need to dig. Ideas came along daily: yo-yos, ukuleles, duct tape wallets, fountain pens, clamrakes, birthday blowouts, stargazing, hermit crabs, Little League games, and trips to Fenway and the emergency room.

What I observed from this motley crew of boys who patronized "the yellow house" east of Elmgrove were funny, honest, and touching moments that many adults can relate to and probably miss. Oh, to taste the tart wild mulberries on my school path one more time.

The more I wrote, the more I found myself revisiting my childhood memories in the Midwest and weaving those remembrances into my sons' adventures. Why did I do that? As my sons moved forward with their lives, my thoughts moved back in time. Images of my girlhood became so vivid I felt as though I was watching a series of short films—all in living color.

Home, precious home. We leave it and want to go back and discover that we cannot, ever. We build our own home—and we're happy in it—and yet we still long for the one we left. And then the home we created changes, and we miss that one and the one we left, long ago. An ancient angst, dizzying, but part of being alive.

It shouldn't be a surprise that I still have the accordion player I found more than fifty years ago at my hearth in St. Louis. And it shouldn't surprise that it rests on a bookshelf in my house in Providence next to the 7-inch-long race car that my sons cut, polished, and fitted with wheels for a pine-wood derby race in a church basement in 2009, when they were about the same age I was when the present appeared in my shoe.

There they sit, side by side. I planned it that way. We all circle back in the end.

CHAPTER 1

....

Where the Heart Is
October 1989

Early one morning not so long ago, my sister and I sat in the kitchen of my apartment on the East Side, drinking coffee and eating buttered bagels. Her suitcase lay open next to a dresser she had painted pink and for more than a year had filled with bottles of perfume and paycheck stubs and T-shirts. She would be on a plane to St. Louis in an hour. She was going back home. I wasn't.

I was so nervous my mouth was dry. I got up from the table and kept myself busy doing odd jobs around the apartment—emptying the dishwasher, watering the plants, hanging up blouses—so that I wouldn't think about her departure. But I did think about it. And I thought about mine.

She was still in the kitchen when I told her that maybe I should leave, too—not now, with her, but soon. I would start making plans right away. I would hustle to find a new job. I would be home by winter. Julia thought it was a good idea. The family, she said, wanted me back.

Julia had moved to Rhode Island a year earlier, to keep me company and to start a new adventure in the East, far away from her Midwestern roots. She arrived with two suitcases, an oversize gray purse hanging off her shoulder, and a map of Rhode Island that she bought for a few dollars at an airport kiosk.

I unrolled the futon in my living room, put up a second towel rack in the bathroom, and emptied out my bottom dresser drawer for her things. Within days, she had found a job at The Narragansett, a clothing store a few blocks away. Within months, she had saved enough money to move into her own apartment at Wayland Square, buy a car, and support two cats, Mimi and Sophia—sisters, too.

We saw each other every day. "We're lucky to have each other," she once wrote to me on a birthday card. "Isn't that true?" And when we missed our family—our parents, three sisters, brother, and niece—we talked about them: "Mary Louise cut her hair up to her chin." "Margaret bought Little Emily black pool flippers." "Richard is fishing in the Keys." Our relationship grounded us in this foreign place.

Julia started having second thoughts about her decision to move East about a month before she left. She lost her job, her Subaru was demolished in an accident, and someone broke into her apartment and stole just about everything. One night, she told me that she was tired of struggling. The next day, she got up the courage to tell me she was going home, for good.

But I think she left for other reasons.

My life is defined by my work. I go where the job is. That meant leaving my hometown five years ago for Vermont, then Connecticut, then Rhode Island. Now it means being home-sick. It means being alone, especially in the beginning, and convincing yourself that one day the fever will break.

Things are different for Julia. She missed lunches at the West End with her childhood friends, walks down Wydown Boulevard with my mother, and the feeling at a party of knowing all the people there. Most of all, she missed the constant chatter of a big family, the chaos, the noise.

I wonder if even the toughest people long for their hometowns. And I wonder if that longing grows stronger when you get older, when your children move away, when your spouse or partner dies or departs, and there you are in unfamiliar surroundings—on a strange street, in a strange city, without a map. Is it too late to go home then?

The night before Julia left, we watched mind-numbing sitcoms on television to pass the time. We didn't say much. What was left to say? We both knew her leaving was final and that it would be hard for both of us.

I waited until she fell asleep on the futon, with the blue flowered comforter she had brought with her to Providence and would leave behind, for me. Then I switched off the television and stepped quietly into my bedroom. The next morning, at the airport, I gave Julia a hug at the check-in counter and walked outside to the parking lot, in full view of the plane. I couldn't bear to wait around with her until she boarded. I sat on a concrete divider and conducted my own, private farewell ceremony.

I watched Julia's trunk—the one with the broken lock we'd pried open with a table knife—land in the belly of the plane, and I tried to look for her face peering out from a window, but of course, I couldn't see anything. I knew then—as I may have known all along—that what I had told her about being home by winter was a lie, something I had said to make her departure easier for both of us.

I ran across the asphalt to track the plane as it flew over the terminal and headed west and disappeared. Then I scanned the lot searching for my car, found it, slid behind the wheel, started the engine, and drove away. Julia would be at her home in three hours. I would still be looking for mine.

La Mia Amica
July 1990

My best friend, Cate, has been sleeping on a raft for thirty-five days. I know this because she called one night from her new apartment—the one she moved into after leaving John—to describe her furnishings. I was lying in bed with the phone tucked under my chin, and Cate was sitting in the middle of her bare living room, grading students' papers from her introductory Italian class. It was close to midnight, and she was lonely. "Fourteen years is a long time to spend with someone," Cate said. "John and I had a history."

I suggested that things would get better because they have to, and anyway, they couldn't get any worse. We talked until we both couldn't talk anymore, as we always do, and then, just before hanging up, she gave me a tour of her apartment: My carpet is the color of a celery stick, my shoes are lined up on my bookshelf, my travel alarm clock wakes me up in the morning, and there is my bed, an inflatable raft. I asked if a real bed was in the cards someday. "Forse," Cate said, in Italian. Maybe.

That night, I imagined Cate arranging her shoes in a row, pulling out the stem on her clock to set the alarm, lying back on her pillow of air, staring at the ceiling, hoping the emptiness would pass. It would be a long night for her, but I knew she would call the next day.

Cate and I met in Florence at a small school for foreigners called Dante Alighieri, where we were studying during a college semester abroad. There were too many distractions, and we never took to the books. We spent a lot of time hanging out in a cafe on the Piazza Nazionale, smoking Italian cigarettes called Muratti, drinking cappuccino loaded with sugar, and pretending to read *Corriere della Sera*, the Italian newspaper. At night, we roamed the streets fearlessly, even the dark corners by the swift-flowing Arno. By the end of our first month, we decided "la nostra Firenze" was too beautiful to leave after only a semester. We stayed a year.

We took a leave from our college and found jobs. Cate worked at Ricci, one of the many little shops that cover the Ponte Vecchio, Florence's fabled bridge; she sold silver pocket watches and coral rings and cameos. I sold leather coats and purses and paper-thin wallets at Casini, a shop across from Palazzo Pitti, once home to the Medicis, the great Florentine family of the Renaissance. Our ground-floor apartment on Via Romana was damp and dim and crumbling—plaster fell from the walls every night—but it was close to our shops, the rent was cheap, and we had a shower.

Our workdays were longer than we expected, but the summer light was longer, too, so we continued promenading the streets, a habit we had picked up from the Italians. "Andiamo fuori, Elisabetta," Cate would say, after a dinner of tortellini, her specialty. "Si, Andiamo, Caterina," I'd say, and we'd loop arms and rush down the narrow, bumpy streets to the Ponte Vecchio, where at dusk, after the shops had closed, the free spirits would gather on the cobblestones to sell bangle bracelets and wooden crosses and ruby-red dresses from Pakistan. Then we would cross the span and go past the open market with the bronze boar to the steps of the Duomo, where we watched people pass by or feed the pigeons or play the flute to earn a few lire.

It's been decades since our Italian days, but our friendship is as strong as ever—a miracle, considering we live in different parts of the country. We use the phone to keep things going, calling at least once a week, and, in a crisis, once a day, sometimes twice. Our conversations always start with simple matters and then develop into lengthy, almost philosophical talks. Cate's frustration about flunking a student turns into a talk about kindness. Her news that she's sleeping on a raft, away from John, her one and only, turns into a talk about love.

Lately, Cate and I have been asking ourselves why we got lucky, why we haven't tired of each other, why we expect to grow old together. Could it be our lack of judgment, our readiness to call, day or night? Or how we listen to each other—really listen? The only thing we know with certainty is that our friendship is not a chore: it's a gift. And, of course, we have our history.

Not long after Cate told me about her raft, she called again. This time, she had a different story. She had taken the wrong highway exit on her way to tutor a student in Italian and had gotten lost in an unfamiliar neighborhood. Too stubborn to stop at a filling station to ask for directions, she drove around for an hour and ended up missing her appointment.

Cate was too embarrassed to tell anyone what she had done, except me. I told her not to worry, that I would have kept driving and gotten lost, too.

She said, "I know."

The Thief
December 1990

The morning of the attack, Angela rose, as she always does, at 8 o'clock sharp.

Breakfast was the usual: juice, toast, and coffee. She fed

her two cats, fluffy Persians that hide under the flowered sofa in her three-room apartment; then she read the paper. It was a chilly day, so she dressed in pants, instead of her usual skirt, to keep her warm on her 15-minute walk to St. Joseph Church, where she has been going for most of her 70-plus years.

She selected her most comfortable walking shoes, loafers, and settled on a pocketbook that matched them—the leather one hanging on a hook in her bedroom closet. She filled the pocketbook with the things she would need that morning: tissues, a comb, her keys, her bus pass, and two checks for $10 each, donations for the church. At the last minute, she threw in her black change purse, thinking she would pick up some warm dinner rolls on the way home.

Wearing a khaki raincoat that fit snugly on her petite frame, she left her apartment at 10:35, giving her plenty of time to make 11 o'clock Mass. Five minutes into her walk, the straps of her pocketbook fell off her shoulder, so she wrapped them around her fingers and wrist, and clutched the pocketbook to her chest.

Angela took the same route she had taken every Sunday for the last 12 years. Passing rows of stately houses on the East Side, where she grew up, she reminisced about playing in those houses as a child, running after her childhood friend, Esther, in a game of tag.

Esther, she thought. *You can't catch me.*

She never heard his footsteps.

He came up from behind at the corner of Governor Street and Young Orchard Avenue, wrapped his brawny right arm around her neck, and pinned her to his chest, so she couldn't see his face.

"Give it to me," he said.

"No," Angela said.

He grabbed her pocketbook with his other hand and tried to yank it away but couldn't. The straps were still tangled in her fingers. Now she wanted to let go, open her fingers, and give him what he demanded, but the straps tightened as he pulled harder.

No, she thought.

He pulled again, this time with such force that he ripped the pocketbook from its straps, leaving them dangling on her fingers. As he fled up the street, she begged him to give her back what she needed most.

"Just give me my keys," Angela shouted. "Please."

He was bigger than she had imagined—6 feet tall and 200 pounds.

She ran after him, after her keys, but he was faster and disappeared around a corner.

Too frightened to knock on a stranger's door and ask for help, she rushed to her apartment, seven blocks away, trembling all the while. Near some bushes in the front yard, she dug up the extra apartment key she had buried months earlier in case she locked herself out. She dug in the dirt for what seemed like hours.

Once inside, she called the police. They asked her what he looked like.

He was big, Angela said. He was wearing a red shirt.

They asked her if she wanted to go to the hospital.

No, she said. I'm fine.

But she wasn't.

After the police had left, she knocked on my door, across the way, as she does nearly every day. But this time there was a sense of urgency.

"Open up," Angela said.

She was leaning against the wall, crying. She rubbed her fingers, now a light shade of purple, and held up two thin brown straps: the only thing left of her pocketbook. We went to her apartment and she sat down on her flowered sofa; she was shaking so much when she told me what had happened that I gave her a glass of brandy.

Two hours later, she got a call from the police. They had found her pocketbook on a street about a mile from where it had been snatched. Her tissues, comb, keys, bus pass, and checks were still inside, but her money, $28 and change, was gone. So was her peace of mind.

The next Sunday, she took a different route to church, but kept looking over her shoulder, wondering if he was following her. He could have her address from the checks and watch her as she left the apartment; this much she knew.

She is still looking for him and his red shirt—at the bus stop she goes to almost daily, at the mailbox by the bank, at the crossway near the grocery store.

She can't get him out of her mind, this menacing man, with his broad shoulders and round face. He's hiding behind a dumpster, a bush, a tree. He sees her coming, an older woman, alone, on a deserted street. His eyes are drawn to the pocketbook held against her chest. He waits until she passes, then creeps up behind her.

He's so quiet, and she can't hear him.

Fit

August 1991

Everything President Nixon demanded of me I could do, except the softball throw.

I could leap across a pile of sand, speed down the blacktop, raise my scrawny body from the gym floor dozens of times. But my arms were as thin as broomsticks, too weak to hurl a softball from home plate to the giant oak that shaded our school soccer field and where, on a dare, I kissed David Wall.

I was 11 years old, a kid in Mr. Zeitz's sixth-grade class at Maryland School, a tomboy—and proud of it. My bedroom shelves were stocked with baseball bats and mitts, not Barbie dolls and tea sets. Susie and I competed to see who could get more cuts on her rawboned legs. Abigail and I played soccer, not house, on Sunday afternoons.

One day, Miss Stock, our lanky, white-haired gym teacher, summoned the class to her office to tell us about the Presidential Physical Fitness Award, which Nixon was bestowing on schoolchildren to honor their athletic prowess. We could win it, too, she promised, if we excelled in certain fitness tests.

Getting the award was the only thing I thought about all spring. I had to propel myself several feet in the long jump, run the 50-yard dash lickety-split, muster 100 sit-ups, and shinny up a rope dangling from the ceiling of the school gymnasium. I mastered everything but the softball throw.

Again and again, I'd skip sideways to the starting line, arch my right arm, grunt, and let go. The ball would soar through the air and land with a thump. Miss Stock would mark the spot with chalk, then size up the distance with a measuring tape she kept in the pocket of her powder-blue Bermuda shorts, pressed and with a crease down the middle. At the end of the day, I'd go home broken-hearted; the ball was always a few inches short.

But Miss Stock didn't give up, and neither did I.

She plopped a ball into the palm of my hand and told me to go home and practice. That night I took my baseball mitt off the shelf. For weeks, I played catch with our clunky oak garage door, making so much noise that Mrs. Ellston came out of her house next door and asked what I was doing.

"Throwing," I yelled, never missing a pitch.

During my short breaks, I wondered whether Nixon knew that I was bulking up my arm just for him.

Those days of hard work paid off. One afternoon I ran to the line and hurled the ball with all my might. It seemed that Miss Stock was miles away when she took the measuring tape out of her pocket and then shouted out the good news, cupping her hands around her mouth so I could hear so very far away. I had made it, and she duly recorded my accomplishment on her clipboard.

At my elementary-school graduation, I basked in the applause as Miss Stock presented the presidential certificate and a blue patch to me and my classmate Sylvia Agnew, the only other student in the school to win.

Standing before hundreds of people in my white party dress with bell-shaped sleeves, I remember hoping that everyone would notice my scabby knees: the mark of a true tomboy. It was my last athletic achievement for many years.

I dabbled in other sports but never had the drive to see them through. My career on the swimming team ended abruptly when I stopped in the middle of a 50-yard freestyle event during a meet at the Shaw Park Pool in my hometown, Clayton. Thinking I was drowning, a lifeguard—nicknamed Itchie for the way he scratched his side on the starting block before a swimming race—jumped in to save me. Although I was in the shallow end—and could stand on my own—he held me with his taut arms. "Sorry, Itchie," I whimpered. "I got tired."

Cheerleading kept me on the sidelines in junior and senior high school, an activity that consisted mostly of slapping my hands against my thighs and belting out, "We got a team over here, we got a team over there, but our team's going everywhere." The team might have been going somewhere, but I was off the field.

A stroll to the dining hall was the extent of my exercise in college. I preferred to curl up with a good book—and a few slices of cheesecake—than to swim laps in the college pool. At a decaying bar near campus, I filled my belly with cheap beer and stale peanuts.

And so the years passed, and I came up with lots of excuses not to exercise: I didn't have time; it was boring; I didn't need it. By my thirties, I was so out of shape, a leisurely walk uphill from the office to a restaurant left me out of breath.

The next trek was to a health club.

My first visit to the club's Fitness Room—with its mirrors, shimmering weight machines, and high-tech aerobic equipment—was humbling. Like the straight-backed Miss Gulch in *The Wizard of Oz*, I pedaled furiously on the Lifecycle, trying to make up for those years of neglect. It was a spin to nowhere. Huffing and puffing, after 10 minutes I slid off the bicycle's slippery seat and shuffled to the locker room.

But Miss Stock taught me that persistence pays off, so I went back. I'm still going. Now I can jog 30 minutes on the treadmill, bench-press 40 pounds, climb 20 minutes on the Stairmaster.

Sometimes, as I head into the final stretch of my routine, I feel like giving up and curse the red dots blinking inside the computer console like warning lights.

Other times, exhilarated, I kick up the speed and let'er rip. I'm not good enough to be the pick of the president anymore, but that's okay. Sweat is pouring down my face, dripping onto the handlebars, the pedals, my sneakers, the floor. My legs—fuller now, and smooth—are burning.

And my arms are pumping, again.

Putting up the Ritz
October 1991

One summer afternoon in late August, when I had finished rinsing out my Speedo in the cold tap water after a swim at the public pool, I toured my hometown.

Alone in my parents' car, I drove from one end of town to the other, pulling off to the side of the road now and then so I could take a long look at the places of my childhood.

I drove down Wydown Boulevard, lined with trees so thick you can barely see the sky, then took a right on Big Bend, glancing at the stone arches of Fontbonne College, where my nursery-school teacher, Sister Celine, tried to teach me French. At Davis Place I stopped at Amy's house, remembering her sleepless slumber parties on the back porch; then I drove a mile to the big clock at Roosevelt Bank. It was 4:42.

I took a left on Forsyth Boulevard, checked out my old high school, then cut over to the Posh Nosh delicatessen, where as a teenager I took orders for chopped chicken liver on rye and hot pastrami on a Kaiser roll—hold the mustard.

Off Kingsbury Boulevard, I wondered what had happened to my first boyfriend, Brant, who played Beatles records for me on his Sony turntable in his basement, and I thought about the time I shoveled snow in front of houses on Pershing Avenue for a few dollars to buy my mother fluffy blue slippers for Christmas. Then I went to find my school path, even though I knew it wasn't there.

When people ask me where I'm from, I say St. Louis, Missouri. Nothing could be further from the truth. I'm from Clayton, a two-and-a-half-square-mile city of about 16,000 residents, 15 minutes from the heart of St. Louis, on the banks of the muddy Mississippi River, or as we called it when we were kids, the Missis-sloppy.

Clayton has a few claims to fame. It has Shaw Park Pool, an Olympic-size swimming pool, where teams from all over the country compete. The best barbecued chicken wings are on North Bemiston Avenue, not far from the office of my former pediatrician, Dr. Wissmath, who handed out lollipops along with shots. On sticky summer nights, the crickets begin their steady chorus, and you have to stop what you are saying, stop talking about your friend's baby girl or the neighbor's new blue shutters, and just listen—or you can go inside, where it is quiet, and have a glass of iced tea.

These are the things I like to remember about my hometown. But there are some things I would just as soon forget.

As a kid, I'd stand on the front steps of our red-brick house, on Oakley Drive, and see a skyline of trees, nothing but trees: oaks, sycamores, pines. The city's business district was beyond the trees, but the buildings were so squat you couldn't see them. In the mid-'60s, developers built the first office tower, the

Pierre Laclede, and, sadly, it peaked above the sycamores like a chimney. Neighbors worried that more buildings would follow.

They were right. Developers riding the boom of the next two decades stormed into town, ripping down sturdy houses with wraparound porches and building condominiums with third-story balconies. Steel office towers shot up, while cozy shops like Pam's, where I bought my first pair of brogues, and restaurants like Fitz's, where I could sit in our station wagon and order a burger and a mug of root beer with a foamy top, disappeared. Our city fathers built a new library, with skylights, to replace the old one, a brick building with arched doorways next to the fire station. It wasn't long before 35,000 people were commuting to the city to work; brochures boasted about our 26,000 parking spaces.

And then I lost my school path.

I used to walk it to my elementary school, stopping to pick wild mulberries or draw the juice from a honeysuckle blossom. The passage wound through a forest so thick and dark all it took was the hoot of an owl to send me running—down a dip and then around a bend, past the leggy forsythia, up a hill, to the embrace of Carswold Drive, where I rode my tricycle, festooned with red, white, and blue streamers, in our neighborhood's annual Fourth of July parade.

Years ago, the state razed the forest to build a highway. For a long time, the nearby land lay vacant while developers tried to figure out what to do with it. They finally did—they built a swank hotel befitting a big city: the Ritz-Carlton.

On the afternoon of my tour, I stopped at the Ritz for the first time. From the outside, it was imposing, yet drab. It was a plain brick building about 200 feet back from one of the city's busiest streets. I counted 17 stories, but the hotel may have been taller. The entrance road led to a fountain of ballerinas.

Inside, oil paintings of hunting dogs, softly lit, hung on the walls. Guests murmured and sipped drinks while a man in a tuxedo played what sounded like Cole Porter on a grand piano. I took the elevator to the 15th floor, got off, then looked out a hallway window, searching below for something familiar.

The view offered me nothing. I couldn't see the pool, the deli, Amy's house, or the big bank clock. I couldn't see Dr. Wissmath's office. I couldn't see the blue-gray slate roof of my house on Oakley Drive. I couldn't see Clayton.

On my way out, I stopped in the hotel's shop. A clerk was folding T-shirts, each bearing a regal Ritz-Carlton logo.

"This was my school path," I told her.

"Really?" she said.

For a moment I stood there, watching her make perfect creases and stack the shirts, gently, into a neat high pile.

I thought she might ask what a school path was (or, better yet, if I missed it), but she didn't.

I fiddled with some pearl earrings on a rack, then left the Ritz, knowing there was no reason to return, ever.

Oncoming Winds
July 1992

In the sunroom of my grandmother's house there was a closet, where she stored old toys, a card table, and the Uncle Wiggly board game my four sisters, my brother, and I played with when we visited. "Yoo-hoo," she would shout from the bright room as the screen door in her kitchen slammed shut and we came tumbling in on hot afternoons, blowing down our cotton shirts to cool off.

After unloading our overnight bags, we would rush back outside and mount the creaky stairs of the rundown carriage house in her backyard, where we climbed over the piles of old Victorian furniture covered with cobwebs and dead flies. At night we returned to the sunroom, where my grandmother would bring my mother up to speed on family news while we kids rummaged through the closet.

It was during one of those searches that I found a bundle of letters, tied with a red ribbon. I can't recall if I asked my grandmother about them, but sooner or later I learned that the author was her husband, my grandfather, who had died in 1944, at the age of 44, long before I was born.

There were no secrets among the Rau kids, and although we never untied the ribbon, the word spread that they must be love letters.

Not long ago, when the letters came into my possession, I read them for the first time. They added a personality to the man who had been a mystery when I was a child.

His name was Jack, and he married my grandmother, Lorene, in 1928, after a whirlwind romance. They were divorced a decade later, when my mother was nine.

My early impressions of him came from an old black-and-white photograph that shows him standing on a street corner in front of his parents' big, white stucco house in the small Missouri town where he was born. His wrinkled cotton suit hangs loosely on his lanky frame. He has a high forehead and a strong chin. He is looking down at the pavement, smiling, just as the camera clicks.

My grandmother—we called her Mimi—was a beautiful young woman with deep-set dark eyes and a heart-shaped mouth. Although she had many suitors, she never remarried after her divorce. When I remember my grandmother, I think of the way she swept her wispy gray hair into a French bun, and the scratching noise her stockings made when she walked toward me. I remember asking my mother one night when I was a little girl what an intellectual was and she said, "Your grandmother."

I never asked my grandmother about her husband, and when she died, on December 28, 1980, it was too late.

And so I turned to the letters—seven in all.

As far as I can tell, they were written during the summer of 1928, when my grandmother was a new schoolteacher in a small town in Arkansas and my grandfather was working as an engineer, building state highways, dividing his time between "roads and thoughts of you."

I have no idea where they met, nor do I know if he was working a hundred miles or a thousand miles away from her. He wrote his first letter "one short week" after meeting her:

"Already it seems to me, I've known you months and months. We have much to learn of each other, and now that we know happiness is ours for the asking we should keep nothing from each other, should we?"

He often wrote at night, just before he went to bed, recounting the day—"goodnite letters," he called them. He told her about his moonlit "spin on the highway" in the Ford when the evening was "still as a mouse." He complained about the hot summer weather that left him feeling "emaciated," and about rainy days that made him "lonesome for you."

He always seemed to be "racing against terrible storms":

"There's a big storm brewing up here right now. Our foursome just got in from an airing in Jim's car, and after we made our predictions of the oncoming winds, I rushed to my room for this note to you."

Where was he, on a Tuesday night in 1928? Was he huddled over a small oak desk in a dimly lit room? Did the wind turn to rain? Were there flashes of lightning?

They visited on weekends, and he later recalled their dates "out on the river" and that he felt as though he were living in a "big sweet dream."

"I'm so happy," he wrote.

The letters stopped on September 17, 1928, three months after they had started, with his hope that, "even after the glamour of a new love wears off," the two of them would "never drift apart."

But they did.

My grandmother never spoke of my grandfather to me, and it never occurred to me that she ever thought much about him.

So why did Mimi keep these letters? She must have known that one day, someone else would untie the red ribbon and read them. I can only believe that she loved him—always—even with the heartache.

In most of the letters, my grandfather signed off by telling my grandmother how much he loved her—so much that he "ached clear through." But his send-off in one letter was a little different, and it keeps playing over and over in my mind. It might've touched my grandmother, too.

"Goodnite, sweetheart, goodnite. I'll never stop loving you. I'm missing you, missing you, missing you."

Hard News
May 1993

I lived on Jail Hill.

Officially my home was at the Warren Apartments, on Cedar Street in Norwich, Connecticut, a dying mill town on the Thames River. But as far as the old-timers were concerned, I lived on Jail Hill, named for the prison that used to sit there. I liked the way it sounded, and when I wrote letters to my friends, I'd say, "Come visit me up on Jail Hill."

Apartment 41C had a green shag rug and a nice view of the town, way down below. I slept on a lumpy mattress and used a beaten-up suitcase as a dresser. A wooden milk crate was my nightstand, and when it broke, I found an abandoned trunk. I rented the apartment for more than a year but never furnished it properly.

Truth is, I was rarely there.

Most of the time, I was banging out stories on a computer in the cramped newsroom of the *Norwich Bulletin*. I'd gotten a job there in the spring of 1985 as an editor, but failed miserably when I designed a special section with so many typefaces my boss said it left her dizzy. One afternoon I suggested a switch to reporting. She agreed. By the fall, I was covering Ledyard, a rural town outside Norwich.

I wanted to be a great reporter. I wasn't.

Although I dreamed of becoming a muckraker, I was loath to hurt anyone's feelings. And I was easily gulled—not exactly qualities that would make me the H.L. Mencken of southeastern Connecticut.

I'd rise early, rush to Ledyard in my rusty orange Rabbit, wander around Town Hall, then return to the newsroom with two or three story ideas in my pocket. I wrote about everything, even the creamy cheese Danishes at a local coffee shop.

Within a few months I knew almost everybody in town and went to great lengths never to offend anyone. When I wrote about the Native American tribe's secret plans to sell open space to developers, I begged the enraged chief to forgive me. When the school superintendent remarked during a telephone conversation about the school budget, "Gosh, you have a sexy voice," I said, "Thank you."

My first investigative story began when I got a call from Amos Banks. He was in a tizzy over "black stuff" bubbling up in his backyard. I sped to his house, thinking I was onto the biggest story of my fledgling career. Banks pointed to the ground. I got down on my hands and knees, scooped up some dirt, smelled it.

"Fuel oil," Banks said.

"Fuel oil," I said.

The only oil I had ever smelled was suntan oil, but I was sure Amos Banks knew what he was talking about. And by the end of my visit, I was convinced that leaky oil pipes were at fault.

I must've written a dozen stories, castigating the oil company so frequently that its owner once shouted to me on the phone, "I don't care what you put in your little paper." The real culprit was identified a few months later: a cracked fuel tank buried in Banks' backyard ages before he lived there.

I was mortified. Surprisingly, I still got good assignments, some even beyond Ledyard's stone fences.

One day I was sent to do a story on homeless people in Norwich. At a soup kitchen on Main Street, I met Adelmo, a 29-year-old native of Portugal who had lived on the streets of America for eight years. We talked for hours, and I was charmed by this man with two gold loops in his left ear.

"Dying is like losing a full glass of water," he told me, as he wrapped his skinny fingers around a half-filled glass of water.

I had no clue what he meant, but scribbled down every word.

"Fantasy can trick your mind and put you in misery," he said.

"Are you in misery?" I said.

He asked for my phone number, and I was tempted by this charming street philosopher, but said no.

Later in the day, I reconsidered. When a photographer went to the boarding house where Adelmo was staying, I cheerfully went along, hoping he would ask again.

"Adelmo, it's me," I shouted, standing in the dark hallway outside his room.

He was pulling down the sleeves of his sweater when he opened the door. He was courteous, as usual, but tense.

As the photographer took his picture, I glanced into his bathroom. A curled spoon—the kind used to cook heroin— lay on the sink, next to spent matches.

His life was more complicated than I had thought, and when I said goodbye in that dreary hallway, I meant it.

I was still in the newsroom when the Sunday paper with Adelmo's story on the front page rolled off the presses, just after midnight. There he was, standing by a dirt-streaked window, his arms crossed tightly, his glazed eyes fixed on the camera.

I tucked a paper under my arm and went back to my apartment, with the nice view, up on Jail Hill.

CHAPTER 2

....

Cat in the Closet
April 2007

My son, Henry, is learning how to read. He knows plenty of so-called sight words—dog, jump, funny, and so on—but he doesn't have the confidence yet to tackle a lengthy chapter book on his own. Books have a lot of type and pages, and chugging through all that alone can be daunting, not to mention frustrating, to a little boy who doesn't like to flub up.

Not long ago, Henry was on the playground and a friend told him a joke about Garfield, the lazy, self-indulgent, plump orange cat that has been gracing The Funny Pages of newspapers for nearly three decades. I don't remember the joke, but it made Henry laugh hard enough to ask if we had any *Garfield* at home.

By golly, we did.

My husband's uncle, Gordon Alf Lawrence Johnson, a descendant of robust seafaring men from Norway, was a big fan of the comics. On first impression, you wouldn't think so. A lifelong bachelor, Gordon was a taciturn and scholarly man, lanky and broad-shouldered like his forebears, who liked to wear his English bowler hat to dinner parties and scour the newspaper for grammatical errors, which he would underline in red ink, rip out, and send to friends with notes attached: "sp?" His birthday wish-list always included reference books.

On the rare occasions when he let his guard down his boyishness revealed itself, mostly through the twinkle in his pale blue eyes. He was really a grown-up kid.

He died a year ago at the age of 83 after a long bout with pneumonia. He was as sharp as a tack to the end. In his final days, we had conversations about his favorite book—Margery Allingham's *More Work for the Undertaker*—his beloved Red Sox, and Gloria, a retired schoolteacher from Ithaca, New York, who was the love of his life. I'd sit on the edge of his bed at Hallworth House in Providence, the nursing home where he lived in the weeks before his death, and read him the obituaries so he could find out if anyone he knew had, as he put it, "kicked the bucket." He couldn't sip water, much less eat, but still felt certain he would be going home soon. He was a dying man who wanted desperately to live.

When I emptied his apartment, I found collections of poetry by Wallace Stevens, novels by the American writer and sometimes Providence resident Elliott Paul (just months before he died, Gordon re-read *Linden on the Saugus Branch*, Paul's memoir of growing up in Malden, Massachusetts) and five dictionaries, including the grand 1902 edition of *Funk & Wagnalls A Standard Dictionary of the English Language*, which Gordon insisted was one of the best dictionaries ever published.

One literary genre stood out: collections of comic strips—fifty-eight, to be exact—that included a dozen musty smelling *Peanuts* half a century old and a stack of newer, glistening *Calvin and Hobbes, Dilbert, The Far Side,* and *Garfield.* I packed them away in a cardboard box and stuck them in a closet, where they remained until Henry and I retrieved them one evening after our playground visit. *Garfield Eats Crow* soon found its way onto Henry's lap.

In his first few minutes with the cat, it became clear that Henry had finally discovered reading material he could master without much help from his parents. He'd read a strip, rush downstairs, read it aloud to his dad, run upstairs, read another, descend, ascend. Panting, sweaty, cheeks flushed, he breathlessly reported to me on that evening that he could read six *Garfield* comics—all on his own. I taught him how to dog-ear pages that were especially funny, and scribble notes in the margins.

Garfield soon became preferred reading at bedtime. Henry chose episodes without a lot of words. In one, Garfield falls down a chimney, landing with a "Whump." Sitting in a fireplace covered with soot, the cat turns to his clumsy owner, Jon Q. Arbuckle, and utters: "Needs more lard."

"What's lard?" Henry asked.

"It's like butter," I said. "Slippery stuff."

"I get it," he said.

As his confidence grew, Henry selected strips with more complex sentences. "I'm pretty much sick of winter," Garfield mutters as a blizzard engulfs him. "Enough with the snow already!" Miraculously, the snow stops except for one stubborn flake; Garfield scowls, and the flake makes haste heavenward.

Under the sway of *Garfield*, Henry's vocabulary improved. He learned big words—soggy shorts, stomped flat, venomous fangs—but gems came his way as well. Whack. Smack. Poink. Harrumph. Aaugh. Slurp. Sheesh. Zip. Zap. Finally, words Henry could read—and write—with gusto.

My husband and I have been reading to Henry and his older brother Peder since they were born. I love the lyrical writing in the children's classics—*Goodnight Moon, Time for*

Bed, Harold and the Purple Crayon—and never tired of reading those books to my sons when they were toddlers. As they got older, books about construction workers, superheroes, knights, airplanes, motorcycles, and boats filled their backpacks. Gone was the rhythm of Harold and his walk in the moonlight. I thought I'd wilt if I had to read one more time that Bruce Wayne was one of the richest men in Gotham City. Later, Peder discovered the Magic Tree House books, stories about two siblings who travel through time to the Wild West and other places. The books were all the rage; I tolerated them. They seemed contrived and were too long.

My favorite children's book is *Amos & Boris*, by William Steig. Amos, a mouse, builds a boat and sets sail one day to see the world. He falls overboard and is rescued by Boris, a whale. They become the best of friends. Boris returns Amos to land, and they say their goodbyes. Years later, Boris is flung ashore by a hurricane on the very spot where little Amos lives. This time, Amos saves Boris' life by finding two whales to push him back into the waves. Their final parting is heartbreaking: they know they will never meet again. "Mom, don't cry," my sons would say as I lingered on the last page. I want all children's books to be like *Amos & Boris*—simple, funny, profound.

Garfield is rarely profound, but it is always simple and funny, and I'll take that over tedious and humorless. I'll take a wild "Whump" over a predictable "Zap!" any day. I wish Gordon had lived long enough to see the gifts he left Henry: his playful sense of humor and his fifty-eight comic books. I suppose it's fitting that Henry's middle name is his great-uncle's first. At night, after a laugh with the cat and just before lights out, I tuck my reader in and tip my hat to the man who loved the funnies: "Goodnight, Henry Gordon."

Mother of All Misses
May 2007

My husband and two sons took me to a Red Sox game in Boston for Mother's Day. Yep, that game, the amazing comeback game over the Baltimore Orioles. It was only the second Sox game I've been to in my life, and I'm pushing 50. If I'm lucky, maybe I'll get to one more before the twilight years.

My first game was a bust. It was cold—I wore my parka—I spent most of the time in line at a hot dog stand, and the Sox lost. At the start of Sunday's game, I was full of hope: It was sunny, and the Sox were on a roll.

We had fantastic seats: left field, second row grandstand, within spitball distance of the Green Monster. Manny was close enough that I could see him bite a nail on his left hand and curl his fingers to inspect his work. I could see Varitek's tidy goatee, Lugo's spindly legs.

I was so excited to be there, in seats with a clear view, it really didn't matter that the first 8 innings were duller than a bad soccer game. Hit—sometimes—throw to first, out. How many times can that happen before the mind starts to drift?

Bored but still charmed by the park, I kept myself busy people-watching: the red-head who tossed her Dice-K poster onto left field; the young man who concealed his beer in a Coke cup (Can anyone really drink six Cokes in one game?); the father who tucked his infant son's rotten banana peel under my seat, a violation of the park's 6th code of conduct: Respect other fans.

My young sons, Henry, 6, and Peder, 7, had a tougher time staying engaged. They made it through three ho-hum innings without a complaint, but by the top of the fourth they were asking for a tour of the Red Sox Team Store, known to parents as the money pit. That trip took 20 minutes, as well as $85 from my purse for a white Matsuzaka jersey and navy J.D. Drew T-shirt.

Back in their seats, my sons continued to fidget so we calmed them with Cracker Jacks, cotton candy, and ice cream. Henry ate a $4 hot dog. The undulating arms of the wave that swept through the stands kept them intrigued for another 10 minutes or so, but the silliness ceased when the Sox blew it, yet again.

"I want to go home, Dad," said Peder.

"I don't like what I got," said Henry. "Can we go back to the gift shop?"

The Sox were down, 4-0, in the bottom of the seventh when we stood up and said so long to seats 5, 6, 7, and 8 in sect 32, row 02, CVS Family Section: No Alcohol Permitted. I was discarding our ketchup-stained paper napkins and other trash—4th code of conduct: Help keep Fenway clean—when my husband heard what he later recalled as "the crack of a bat." He looked up at a television monitor under the stands; the score was now 5-0 heading into the bottom of the eighth.

I remember thinking as we walked past the turnstiles that no one else seemed to be doing what we were doing: leaving. Lansdowne Street was eerily quiet, except for a few vendors selling shriveled Polish sausages.

On the way to the car, a young man riding by on his bike noticed my boys' Sox hats.

"How'd they do?" he shouted.

"They lost," I said, and he frowned. I thought he might burst into tears.

For the heck of it, my husband turned on the radio just

before we got on the Southeast Expressway to drive back to Providence. The boys were asleep in the backseat. It was the bottom of the ninth. The sportscaster said something like, "The tying run is in the on-deck circle." Seconds later, I heard that the "winning run is in there." Where? I couldn't understand a thing.

"What's happening?" I asked my husband, frantically.

"Just listen," he snapped, and turned up the volume.

"Unbelievable!" the sportscaster shouted moments later, when the Sox won, 6-5. "Bedlam at Fenway!"

There were no yippees or yahoos in our car.

"We didn't have to leave," I said, through gritted teeth.

"You wanted to leave," my husband said.

"No, you wanted to leave," I said.

I pouted all the way home, like a schoolgirl who didn't get the iPod she wanted for her birthday. I thought of all the things I wouldn't be able to do: have a once-in-a-lifetime experience; brag to my sister Emily, a Sox fan who lives in D.C. and has to sit through Nationals' games; remind my boys in years to come that "you were by my side when...."

"I feel sick about this," I said, poking my peas at dinner.

My husband seemed nonchalant, projecting a kind of it's-only-a-game attitude, a strange position for a lifelong Sox fan, especially one who still has the team's official yearbooks from '64 through '67, all in pristine condition.

I see now that he was hurting.

At 1 o'clock in the morning, I found him standing in front of the television, tuned to NESN, watching the ninth, the inning when the Orioles' Chris Ray—bless his heart—drops the ball. My husband was in his pajamas, and he was wearing headphones with a long wire hooked to the television so only he could hear the call. He looked like Street Sense ready to burst through the gate at Churchill Downs, nose thrust forward, head bobbing with anticipation. My son sat next to him, in silence, on the ottoman.

"I'm tired, Dad," said Peder.

"Hold on," my husband said, never taking his eyes off the television. "This is the last play. I don't want to miss it."

My Hermit Crabs
May 12, 2007

I scooted the little stool next to my 7-year-old son and leaned in until our elbows touched. He pulled two wrinkled sheets of blue-lined paper from his folder and ironed out the creases with the palm of his hand. "Read it to me," I said. It was my first visit to his classroom as a volunteer writing coach, and I was eager to get started.

Peder's story was about our trip to Nantucket last summer. His ability to chronicle each step of our journey—the drive to Hyannis, then a ferry ride to the island—and his use of detail—"a kwik snak at the harbr"—were impressive. He mentioned hunting for shells on the beach with his 6-year-old brother Henry and he recalled how their dad cooked dinner one night. Finally, he crafted a solid ending sentence: "I Love Nantocit!"

But something was missing: me.

I didn't think much of it until my next visit when he showed me a story about our train trip—his first—to Boston. "We were going on a trane," he wrote. "I nuw it would be fun." The next sentence stopped me cold: "My mom yeld it's time to go." *Yelled?* I was tempted to cross out the word and write, in my best kid-script, the gentler *said.*

As a writing coach, my job was to encourage Peder to get his thoughts down on paper in a coherent way, without worrying too much about spelling and grammar. I suppose word choice fell into that category, too. I didn't touch a thing.

The following week he showed me a story called "My Famliey." I thought my star would shine this time. "My frst membr of my famliey," he wrote, "is Me." Me wrote that he liked football, computers, and cooking. Henry got second billing. Henry, he wrote, liked Batman and jumping. Dad was next. Dad liked sports. Dad liked eating. Dad liked cooking. I flipped over the paper. Blank.

"Missing someone?" I asked, peering over my reading glasses.

"Oh," said Peder.

He drew an asterisk between "Batman" and "My Dad" and wrote, on a new sheet of paper: "My thrd membr is my mom."

As the weeks passed, and Peder's stories progressed into novellas, my self-esteem plummeted. I was turning into an insecure mom wedded to what my 7-year-old thought of me at every moment. In a story about making a school project, Peder praised his dad—"He helped me with the hamering"— but left me out. In a story about a family excursion to a Red Sox game at Fenway Park, I received one mention: "Mom was gon most of the time geting food."

One rainy day, as my sons sat cross-legged on the floor playing with Legos, I took a deep breath and blurted out the question I had been thinking about for days: "Do you like hanging around with your dad more than me?"

"Yes," they responded, in unison and with a casualness I

found alarming.

"Why?" I said.

"Because Dad is funner," Peder said.

I agonized: Was I really second choice, the Saturday night backup?

Friends told me that it's normal for children, at varying stages in their development, to prefer one parent over the other. In my case, they said, the reason was obvious: They prefer the parent who is around less. I'm at home all day with my kids; my husband works full-time outside the house. Under that arrangement, most of the day-to-day parenting falls on my shoulders. I'm the bossy one: turn off the TV, cut your nails, brush your teeth. Please. When my husband comes home after work, he's the host of an all-night party—hoops in the backyard after dinner, German chocolate cake for dessert at 9, the Red Sox until 10—11 if it's close.

Still, the boys' favoritism bugged me. How could I woo them back? Maybe I needed to lighten up. I handed the boys the TV's remote. I lost the clipper. Toothbrushes collected dust. I lasted two weeks. I looked at days of nail growth and cringed. On the playground, I tossed the football around a few times, then retreated to a bench to read my morning newspaper.

I went back to my old ways. I have my style; my husband has his. Maybe my kids will thank me someday for bringing structure to their lives, for insisting that they do things that are tedious.

We all want our children to love us as much as we love them. My love for my boys is so strong that I admit, I can't bear to be away from them for long. When they climb into my car after school, I'm eager to connect—to pat their backs, tousle their hair.

When Peder left me out of his stories—or gave me a passing glance—I got lost in a maze of doubt: They love me; they love me not. Deep down, I know my boys love me. They show their love in so many ways, with hugs and kisses and hand-holding and flying leaps from the bed into my arms: "Don't drop me, Mom!" (I never have.) But I'm just as vulnerable as anyone when it comes to love, even—or especially—when it involves a 7-year-old.

By my next visit to Peder, my self-pitying phase was over. I vowed to accept, with grace, any misrepresentations of my character.

This time, Peder showed me a story he was working on called "My Hermit Crabs." He wrote about Orange Juice, the big, light-colored one that slept in a plastic palm tree, and Tiger, the smaller, dark-colored one that burrowed deep into the sand and rarely moved. They had two ponds, one for leisure, one for bathing. They ate hermit crab food. They needed lots of attention.

"Then they died," he wrote.

The story was unfinished. My son needed an ending. I knew it; he knew it. Here was my chance to go down nicely. After all, this was serious stuff, a collection of work destined for the keepsake box.

I reminded Peder that I buried Orange Juice and Tiger by the tulips in the backyard. He gave me a long, meditative look. I felt sure my compassion would be noted in "My Hermit Crabs."

He put pencil to paper and wrote: "I hope you learned sumthing from my story."

I did.

War

June 2007

I was eating breakfast with my 6-year-old son Henry the other morning and he brought up today's celebration at his school: Flag Day.

"What am I supposed to do?" he asked.

I looked at the flyer on the bulletin board: wear red, white, and blue.

"Wear red, white, and blue," I said.

"The colors of the flag," he said.

He shoved a spoonful of Rice Krispies into his mouth. I could tell he was about to say something important, something he had learned in school.

"Flag Day is to honor the flag," he said.

"Right," I said, pleased he got the point.

"And to honor the war," he said.

I wasn't quite sure what to make of that comment. I'm opposed to the war in Iraq but stand by our troops. Maybe my son was saying the same thing in his kid way. His next comment stunned me: "We want to win!" He turned his index finger and thumb into the shape of a gun and pointed to the wall: "Boom!"

It was time for a sit-down.

I've been talking to Henry and his 7-year-old brother Peder about the Iraq war for years. That's right, since they were toddlers. They would look over my shoulder as I watched the nightly news reports and pepper me with questions I tried to answer truthfully: *Why are buildings on fire?* We dropped bombs. *Who's driving the tanks?* American soldiers. *What's wrong with him?* He's dead.

Sometimes the boys, riveted to the screen, would make it through the entire report; other times they would lose interest, as kids do, and rush from the room to kick a soccer ball.

It never occurred to me to do what most parents do: Keep the war out of the house. I know a parent who rips out all the war photos in her *New York Times* (from the dead soldiers to the rolling tanks) so her daughters don't see them. Another parent never listens to National Public Radio because she's concerned her first-grader might hear the crack of an AK-47. Remember the *Newsweek* cover photo of an American soldier whose legs were blown off by a roadside bomb? A neighbor turned the magazine over when his son came over to our house to play.

I don't get parents who want to keep the war a secret, like a shameful family scandal. Are they afraid of nightmares and nail-biting? I bet a Scooby-Doo movie is scarier than an NBC report about Iraq. My guess is parents are worried about getting too many questions they can't answer. Their coddling wears me down and gets me down. It's the easy way out.

I'll never forget the newspaper photo I saw last month of Iraqi men pulling a body from the Euphrates River that was later identified as Pfc. Joseph J. Anzack Jr., only 20, one of three missing soldiers who had been the focus of a massive military manhunt. A boy not much taller than Henry was standing on the riverbank, hands on hips, watching. What were parents thinking when they tossed that photo in the trash? Iraqi boys can see this, but not their kids?

I try to be honest and open with my kids about Iraq and the rest of the world. I know they can handle it, as long as I'm there to listen and to answer questions whenever they come, even at bath time. If I kept the war a secret, my kids would eventually figure it out and question my deceptiveness. I want to be honest, even when the facts are unpleasant.

The downside of exposing kids to the war is that they can glorify it in a shoot-'em-up-cowboy way, as Henry did that morning at breakfast. That's the first time he has talked about the war in terms of "winning." It's also the first time he has played a gun-toting good—or bad?—guy. But those are the risks I take by leaving the TV on and the newspaper intact on the kitchen table.

After unloading his make-believe gun, I told Henry that killing people is bad, even imaginary people on the kitchen wall.

"Who started Iraq?" he asked.

"The United States," I said.

"How come?" he said.

"I'm not sure I know why," I said.

I told him I wanted the war to end and the American soldiers to come home. And then I said what I always say when I'm trying to get my kids to pay attention: "Look at me." He fixed his eyes on mine. "The people in Iraq are not bad," I said. "Boys like you live there."

"How big?" he said.

"Six," I said. "Just like you."

"If they put the white flag up, does that mean you can't fight anymore?" he said.

"Yeah," I said.

"So why don't we put the white flag up?" he said.

I didn't know what to tell him: Our president doesn't want to; people are afraid of losing; life isn't fair.

Henry made sense. Kids have a knack for thinking clearly.

"Maybe we'll put it up someday," I said.

He finished his cereal and wiped his mouth with the collar of his Red Sox T-shirt. "I don't want to talk about this anymore, Mom," he said.

That was fine; there would be other days. My son grabbed his backpack and rushed out the door to school.

Details
July 2007

I slid three large pepperoni pizzas onto metal racks, shut the door of my oven, and turned the dial to Broil. My guests were scheduled to arrive any moment, and I wanted to keep the pizzas hot. I did that, and more.

A few minutes later, while blithely talking about a newspaper story with my friend Jon, who had arrived early on that winter night, I saw flames fluttering against the greasy oven window.

"Fire!" I screamed.

Smoke engulfed my small apartment, as Jon and I raced around the three rooms, half hysterical, half laughing, opening windows and filling empty trash cans with tub water, which we foolishly threw at the closed oven door.

My blue jeans were soaked when discretion overtook valor and I finally telephoned for help. Moments later half a dozen firefighters with portable extinguishers strapped to their backs like scuba gear arrived and put out the blaze.

One fireman gingerly opened the blackened oven door and quickly deduced what had gone wrong.

"You got cardboard in there," he said.

He was right. I'd forgotten to take the pizzas out of their

boxes.

Later that evening, after I had scooped tiny piles of ash from inside my oven and scrubbed the soot off my kitchen floor, I called my family to tell them about my drama. No one seemed surprised.

"That figures," said my sister.

I have children now and would never dream of putting cardboard into an oven. Kids have a way of snapping you to attention and turning the lazy mind into a steel trap of to-dos. You either teach yourself to multi-task, or your kid doesn't get to his baseball game on time.

Thankfully, the years without children are self-indulgent, in both body and mind. You can space out; I certainly did.

A typical day in those careless years: I pay for my clothes at the cleaners and rush out the door empty-handed; I leave my purse on top of my car and drive off into the night; I lose one shoe.

"Dizzy Lizzie," my childhood friend and soccer partner, Abigail, would call me when I'd forget, for the hundredth time, whether my birthday was on the 24th or the 25th of September.

Sooner or later, I'd confer with my mother, who got so confused by my repeated inquiries that she started to doubt her own memory.

"Mom, is my birthday on the twenty-fourth or the twenty-fifth?"

"The twenty-fifth, honey."

"Are you sure?"

In the end, we'd retrieve my birth certificate from a big Manila envelope in the top drawer of her mahogany desk and settle the question, at least for that day.

Sometimes I'd misplace things. My sister still teases me about those frantic searches for my wallet, the one I had plunked in a drawer at night only to forget, the next day, where I had put it.

Mornings were a treasure hunt as I rummaged through dozens of drawers, shouting to my brother and sisters, who were devouring Lucky Charms at the kitchen table, "Have you guys seen my wallet?"

Other times I'd succumb to a kind of dreaminess. In Nancy, France, where I studied for three months during college, I gained a reputation for having my head in the clouds.

I never had answers for my tweedy French professor, probably because I never heard his questions. "Je ne sais pas," I'd reply, shrugging. I don't know. Conjugating French verbs was the last thing on my mind. I was daydreaming about smoking stocky Gauloises cigarettes in a cafe with deep booths at the Place Stanislas; about the steak de cheval on sale at the butcher shop; about the seedy section of town with the risqué posters pasted onto crumbling walls.

At the end of my three-month visit, the professor told my French professor back in the United States that I was doomed in the real world.

"She is a dreamer," he wrote in his evaluation; "not very keen in realistic details."

I was a dreamer and proud of it. And I was a fan of details, just not the ones he had in mind.

When I nearly burned down my apartment on that winter night long ago, I was probably thinking about a good book I'd just read or a movie I'd just watched. Maybe I was preoccupied with the one letter missing in the neon sign of the diner down the street: "INER." Maybe I was worried about the moldy feta in the fridge: Toss it.

I have two boys to take care of now, so my Dizzy Lizzie days are over. Every day I will myself to concentrate, to focus, to pack an apple for Peder, a granola bar for Henry.

Still, sometimes the fuzzy problem returns with a vengeance. The other day, I dialed a phone number and then couldn't remember the name of the person I had called. A man picked up on the other line.

"Hello," he said.

"Hello," I said, flustered. "Can I help you?"

"You called me," he said.

Too embarrassed to admit my mistake, I decided to put an end to it quickly.

"Sorry," I said. "You've got the wrong number."

And I hung up.

Waiting for Zak
November 2007

I was lying on the living room floor recovering from three hours of baseball practice when my 7-year-old son Peder walked down the steps and announced that he was heading to Brown University to get Zak DeOssie's autograph.

"Oh really," I said, turning my weary body in his direction. "And how do you plan to do that?"

"Dad," he said.

My husband always comes up with creative ways to keep Peder and his brother Henry engaged, but this was off the charts: Thrust a pen in Zak's hand as he and hundreds of other students graduating from Brown University walk into the First

Baptist Church of America for their baccalaureate ceremony. With any luck, my husband told the boys, they might get to see a Nobel Prize winner, too.

Zak's name has been mentioned so much in our house over the last few years, I know more about him than I do about some of my neighbors. Star linebacker for Brown's football team. Drafted by the New York Giants in the fourth round of the NFL draft. Works hard. Nice guy.

Peder met him through the "2005 Brown Football Outright Ivy League Championship Highlight Film," a rousing DVD, narrated by the gravelly voiced ESPN sportscaster and Brown alum Chris Berman, that chronicles games leading up to the Ivy Title the Bears won in 2008. Peder has watched it 22 times.

Zak is the movie's star, as far as my son is concerned. His performance impressed him so much he'd come downstairs after his fourth viewing of the day and talk until lights out about those "unbelievable tackles" by not just Zak or DeOssie but Zak DeOssie, as if anything less than a full-name reference was disrespectful.

In the winter, Peder was on tenterhooks waiting to see if Zak made the NFL draft, and when he did, Peder and his father talked about it over the morning paper and a bowl of Cheerios.

Zak is so talented, they concluded, he would sail through NFL training camp and make it on the field in the fall. After all, they reminded me, the NFL is in his blood; his father, Steve, also played for the Giants, as well as the Jets and the Cowboys, and our Patriots.

Getting Zak's autograph would be a real coup. We left our house an hour before the ceremony to prepare ourselves.

Peder carried three things: a pen, a photograph of Zak from Brownbears.com, and a clipboard to make signing a cinch.

Students would march from the Main Green on Brown's campus down College Hill to First Baptist on Benefit Street, so we found a spot on the grass in front of the church and waited.

"How will we know it's him?" Peder asked.

"He's tall," I said. "And he has a big neck."

"Will he write in cursive?" asked Henry.

The church bells finally rang out and we spotted the students in their long, billowy black robes, only their Birkenstocks, flip-flops, and pointy slingbacks hinting at who they are or want to be. Leading the pack was the baccalaureate speaker and 1982 Brown graduate Craig Mello, smiling radiantly.

I told Peder he was a famous scientist who had won something called the Nobel Prize and that his research could help people who are very sick. Peder waved to the brilliant man and asked, "Where's Zak DeOssie?" I'm afraid my kid wanted the beefy linebacker who led the Bears' defensive unit in 2006 with 110 tackles, not the lanky biologist whose discovery of RNA interference could lead to treatments for HIV and cancer.

For the next few minutes, we scrutinized the young men who passed by, eliminating the ones who seemed more comfortable in a library. As the line trickled to one or two students, and, still, no Zak, we wondered: Does DeOssie exist?

I saw him first. He looked just like his photo: thick neck; massive shoulders; cropped hair. A woman from Brown helping with the ceremony tapped his shoulder and explained why that blond-haired kid, over there, was holding a clipboard. The student smiled and looked at us but didn't stop.

"I'm sorry," the woman said. "He's Brian—another football

player. Zak isn't coming today."

I managed to hold back a sob. Peder was undeterred. "I'll write to him," he said. That night, he sat down and composed a one-page letter to his football hero: "Dear Zak DeOssie, Good luck with the New York Giants! Can I have your autograph? Please. A big fan, Peder." I delivered it to Brown's athletic department the next day and wrote on the outside: "Please deliver to Zak before he becomes a Giant."

Months have passed and we still haven't heard back. We finally spotted Zak, though—on television. Peder got to stay up late on a school night to watch the NFL opener that pitted Zak against the Dallas Cowboys. Once again, we waited for him to make an appearance, this time on a football field in front of millions of television viewers, including a wiry kid from Providence clutching a junior-size pigskin to calm his nerves.

"There he is," shouted Peder, as Zak, wearing a crisp jersey 51, transformed himself from a linebacker into a long snapper and hiked the ball to a punter. It was a good snap, a very good snap. Zak would remain in the NFL.

Peder agreed.

"That was pretty good snapping, Mom," he said, before nodding off.

Now if only I could get the Giant to snap his fingers to a pencil and write.

Norwegian Spruce
December 2007

When I was a little girl growing up in St. Louis, we bought

our Christmas tree every year from the Lions Club. A few days after Thanksgiving, hardy and civic-minded men in pea coats and steel-toed boots would set up a lot next to Commerce Bank and string up tiny outdoor lights that blinked through the night. Just before Christmas, my father would drive our wood-paneled station wagon to the lot and wander through the aisles looking for a tree, picking up, putting down, until he found one that could fit in our living room. He always chose a Douglas fir.

I'm embarrassed to admit that it took a move to New England for me to realize that Christmas trees grow on farms and that it's possible to cut and carry. I came across this knowledge one winter when I was working as a reporter for a newspaper in Connecticut, and my editor told me to grab my parka and head to a Christmas tree farm to write a Christmas story about Christmas trees.

The hills of God's country were dotted with newborn trees that looked like the green bristles on a new kitchen scrub brush. The farmer told me it would take years for the trees to mature, and I knew then that he was in it for the long haul. No chopping this season. Still, the saplings conjured Christmas merriment, and the photographer snapped a photo for the front page.

During my early years in Providence, I bought only one tree, a scrawny, wisp of a thing that I picked up at the Eastside Marketplace. Family and friends were joining me for the holidays, and I wanted to cheer up my apartment. Bad idea. The tree took up valuable sleeping space, was the target of cruel jokes, and came with needles that couldn't hang on through the plum pudding.

Children came along and Christmas took on more

significance. I could do better than my forlorn fir. I consulted my husband, who wasn't much help. During his boyhood, his mother refused to pay more than $2 for a tree and that frugality led her back year after year to a lot in East Providence. As the prices went up, my husband's trees got smaller and smaller until he, too, was celebrating with a sad sack.

It had never occurred to him to take the chop-your-own path; suddenly, it became the only option.

On a cold December day, we found ourselves roaming among the firs and pines at one of the most beloved tree farms in Rhode Island, Schartner Farms, in Exeter. Our boys, then ages 3 and 4, cut loose among the spruce while my husband and I sought perfection.

Anyone who has spent any time looking for a flawless teardrop of a tree on a tree farm knows there is no such thing. Trees have flaws—a limp branch, a crooked trunk, a patch of dried out needles, sharp to the touch. The imperfections are what make uncut trees endearing, but I didn't realize that at the time. I wanted a real, fake tree.

An hour into our search, my husband started to show signs of distress. "If you don't get something, I will," he said. Seconds later, I was standing beside a lovely tree that looked like a miniature version of a mature Norwegian spruce, mostly available in Oslo. The needles were thick and soft, and the deep green color of a lake up north. "This one," I shouted. The boys gathered around, as my husband picked up his hand saw and disappeared down under to commence cutting.

The saw did not move as swiftly as he had hoped. He blamed it on the sap. Sticky stuff, he said, that slows a saw's motion. Sweat poured forth and still he would not ask for assistance. A young man wielding a saw of his own asked if he could help. My husband said no and kept cutting. It took 45 minutes (and a few timeouts) before the tree fell into our hands. It was a beauty and worth the wait. We wrapped it in twine and tied it to the top of the minivan.

Back in Providence, we moved Orange Juice and the other hermit crab to the kitchen, put a festive tree skirt on the floor and loosened the bolts on the tree stand. The boys whooped it up when their father carried the tree through the door and placed it in its new home.

Their joy was short-lived.

The tree was too tall—by about two feet. My husband stuck it in the stand anyway. The top branch scratched the ceiling so fiercely it looked like the boys had been up there scribbling with a brown crayon. Eventually my husband hauled the tree outside and chopped off a chunk of the trunk and some bottom branches. But our conifer was never the same. It tipped to the right, and then to the left, and finally fell over one night, shattering the glass balls I had bought years earlier for my pathetic Charlie Brown tree.

This Christmas, we're keeping it simple. We're going to the grocery store.

Tunnels
January 2008

I'm not one for New Year's resolutions. Over the years I've muttered a few to-dos: cut down on the Excedrin; cook dinner at least once; wax the brows. But I never followed through and certainly never wrote anything down. This year is different. I have two problems that need to be addressed. One resolution concerns our hamster, the other our television.

Tunnels came to our house this summer at the urging of my son Peder after he reminded me nearly every day during the school year that he was the only kid in his first-grade class without a pet. Jake had a frog. Alex had a cat. Theo had a dog, no, Mom, make that two dogs.

I don't have anything against pets. Some of my best friends have pets, but I'm not ready for the big pet—the Golden, the Setter, the Lab. Like babies, they need attention and require caregivers who are selfless, especially during the house-training phase. "Your mother is selfish," I told Peder and his brother Henry. "No dogs this year."

We bought our hamster at Rumford Pet Center in East Providence. I've been taking the boys there since they were toddlers as a way to expose them to pets on a hit-and-run basis. They would sit in a pen and cuddle with a canine not much bigger than one of their Tonka trucks: the barks-a-lot Papillon, the plucky Cairn Terrier, and my personal favorite, the floppy-eared Cavalier King Charles Spaniel. From there, we would wander over to the hamsters, gerbils, and mice and then make a quick stop to see the birds, snakes, lizards, frogs, and hermit crabs before a candy bar and the door.

At the shop, Peder chose a dwarf hamster as opposed to the fuller, more robust Teddy Bear Hamster. We also bought a wire cage and household supplies—bedding, a bag of food, a water bottle, and, at the suggestion of a clerk, an exercise wheel. "Hamsters are on the go at night," the clerk said, and it suddenly occurred to me that I knew nothing about hamsters and that I had no idea how to care for them. When I got home, I Googled "hamster" and learned that we would have been better off with a fish. "Because of their nocturnal nature and tendency to nip," wrote the esteemed American Society for the Prevention of Cruelty to Animals, "hamsters of any species are not appropriate pets for families with small children."

The novelty of Tunnels lasted 24 hours. We assembled his cage and let him loose among the fluffy scraps of paper and timothy hay, and he seemed happy enough until Peder picked him up. The unexpected affection startled Tunnels, who retaliated with his teeth, just as the Society had said he would. Tunnels was not going to be a cuddly house pet. He spent the night in Peder's bedroom but made so much noise on his exercise wheel—imagine an emery board tumbling inside a squeaky dryer—we moved him downstairs the next day to a table in the living room, and there he sits today, largely ignored by all but me.

Tunnels has gone from being the family pet to my pet. I clean his cage, replace his bedding, refill his food cup, and wipe down his wheel. He is one of God's creatures, but he is also, as a friend reminded me with the kind of look reserved for those who have just eaten a bad SweeTart, a rodent. I am wracked with guilt when I put on my garden gloves to discourage physical contact and exclaim through clenched teeth before a cage cleaning, "Just let me get through this gracefully." Like the oxeye daisy picker, Tunnels must be wondering where he stands—she loves me, she loves me not. Poor guy.

One evening, I wandered over to his cage to say, Hello. He was nowhere in sight and I panicked, thinking he had escaped or, worse yet, gone to his glory. "Tunnels," I said softly, peering into his cage, "Are you in there?" Moments later, a whiskered nose emerged from the hay, and I felt enormous tenderness for the little fellow. I thought of all the children's books I had read to my sons over the years that featured rodents as lovable characters with families to support. I thought of the two-peas-in-a-pod mice, Chester and Wilson, best buds forever. I thought of Honey and Humphrey, those mischievous hamsters. I thought of Kipper's friend, Mouse, who persevered and taught himself how to count to ten.

And so, this year I turn my attention to Tunnels. I resolve to be kinder and gentler to him and discover his goodly soul.

My other resolution concerns the other creature in our house—the television.

I am not a television snob. I like to disassociate as much as anyone. One evening, I flipped on the television and couldn't turn it off when I stumbled upon *Psycho*, a movie that forever changed my comfort level in the shower. What a treat, I thought: 109 minutes of uninterrupted Hitchcock—for free.

My children, unfortunately, do not share my fondness for the classics. Their taste runs more to *SpongeBob SquarePants*. My limit is one episode at a time, two if I'm folding clothes. It's not the content I object to—SpongeBob is a sweet guy— it's the noise. I'd rather hear clanging water pipes, the drone of the dishwasher, a vacuum cleaner on top speed—anything but the incessant chatter of television characters.

Last year, the boys brought home a flyer from school urging parents to turn off the television for one week. We failed. I smelled defeat on day one when Peder climbed into the car after school and assured me that he knew how to read and watch television at the same time. Later that afternoon, I found him viewing *Tom and Jerry*, with the book, *The Jetsons*, sprawled across his lap.

Things got worse when my husband decided to toss our 20-year-old clunker and replace it with a flat-screen model, which led us to the next upgrade: High-Def. The picture won over my children and reignited a passion for *SpongeBob* that is now veering into the dangerous territory of compulsive viewing.

At the start of school this fall, I banned television after dinner, but then the Red Sox won the World Series, and sports reentered our lives with a bang. Why are all the games, from hockey to football, on at night? The phrase "Just let me turn on the television to check the score" has been uttered far too often in our house and usually minutes before bedtime.

And so, my second New Year's resolution calls for drastic, some would say cruel, measures to regulate television watching: Put a lock on the door to the TV room and hide the key under Tunnels' cage. Why not? No one in the house would ever think of looking there, except me.

Ruby Red
February 2008

Not long ago, my husband and I were invited to a party. Most people would welcome an evening of merrymaking, but I was immediately filled with dread. For the last eight years, I've been taking care of two spirited boys and my wardrobe reflects that effort: jeans and rumpled shirts. I gathered from the invitation that this would be a party for adults and that I'd be expected to look like one. My black fleece from The North Face would have to stay home. I would have to invest in a pot of rouge.

I'm a nature girl. The last dress I bought was for my wedding. I own one skirt. No heels, only the flattest flats. Back in '96, I purchased a tube of lipstick and, a year later, a wand of mascara, but threw them out when I read in a glossy that cosmetics more than six months old are a breeding ground for bacteria.

My unglamorous look has served me well. It requires no maintenance and it's easy on the pocketbook. No surprise then that the party invitation threw me off. I had two options. I could cancel or go on a shopping spree. I gave myself an early Valentine's Day present and took off for the Providence Place mall in search of a new outfit and face.

I'd rather drink hot oil than shop. I find the whole experience tedious and, besides, nothing ever fits. I worked as a newspaper reporter for many years and one of the best things about the job was that I could wear whatever I wanted: faded cords, an old blazer, scuffed clogs. I rarely ventured out to make a clothing purchase. No surprise then that I was feeling some trepidation when I left the house that day. If fatigue didn't crush me, frustration would.

My first stop was at Ann Taylor, a store that had been good to my sister when she worked in a law firm and wanted to look both stylish and imposing. I found the dress rack right away. I dislike trying on clothes. You have to take off your clothes and your shoes (in this case Sorel winter boots with pesky laces), and you have to take off your glasses if you're putting something on over your head. I hate taking off my glasses.

Fortunately, the dress I picked was what they call in the business a wraparound, which means it goes on like a coat, through the arms. It only took seconds to put on, and it fit. I bought it: Happy Valentine's Day.

When I was a kid, I played with a redhead named Jessica Dunn. Her white dresses embroidered with cherries were always clean and pressed, and her ponytails lacked the unruly wisps of a less tame child, like me. She had a teenage neighbor named Mary, a budding cosmetologist who liked to use us as guinea pigs. She'd brush our hair into tight ballerina buns and dust our cheeks with rose-colored powder, sometimes with such fury it seemed as if she had found the tip of a dinosaur bone and was in a rush to excavate the entire creature by sundown.

Thankfully, I grew up and out of those beauty sessions. Years later, I saw Mary in the park with friends and expected a greeting (Hey, your nose is shiny), but she didn't offer as much as a peep. Instead, she smirked and pointed my way: I used to put makeup on her. They had a good laugh at my expense.

I could link my distrust of makeup to Mary's mocking, but that would be a stretch. All I know is that I came of age without a compact. I never wore makeup in high school or in college or to my first job interview or on my wedding day.

As the years went by, the temptation to try the stuff grew. I'd read magazine ads about mascara that "brightens your eyes" or foundation that promises "new life to tired-looking skin," and wondered if the pitch was true or only for suckers. I became vaguely interested in makeup counters at department stores, seemingly staffed by clerks eager to do what Mary did, only better and without contempt.

I must have circled the cosmetics department at Nordstrom half a dozen times that day before I finally screwed up the courage to enter this foreign territory. I asked for advice about the only thing I was vaguely familiar with: lipstick. I soon discovered that the options were too numerous (100 varieties; I need limits) and that I wouldn't be able to make a decision. Paralysis set in. I could scoot or ask for help.

"I never wear makeup," I told a clerk. "I'm going to a party."

"I like parties," she said. "I never miss a party."

My face flushed. The clerk picked up on my discomfort. She asked me to sit down.

I had never been this close to getting a makeover and wasn't about to bail out now. I let her go ahead and do what she's trained to do: re-create a face. I took the cream, concealer, blush, mascara, and lipstick, but passed on the eye shadow. I'm not ready for eye shadow.

The mirror turned easily.

"Wow," I said. My lips popped and I had that dewy look. I've always wanted that dewy look.

I bought everything, no questions asked.

I still had on my makeup when we sat down for dinner that night. My 6-year-old son wanted to know what was up with my mouth.

"Lipstick," I said.

"Chopstick?" Henry said.

I took a paper napkin, planted a Monroe-style kiss on it, and held it up for all to see.

"Rose Aglow," I said, proudly.

Turns out I never got to show off my painted face outside the house. We couldn't find a babysitter for the party and had to send our regrets. The goods are still in a little gray bag that hangs on my doorknob as a reminder of the things I learned: grooming is good, concealer conceals, and there are alternatives to no-nonsense wool socks for Valentine's Day. I, for one, wouldn't mind a tube of what could be the most reckless offering in the house of beauty: Ruby Red.

Snow Day
March 2008

Bad weather kept my sons home from school the other day. We got only a few inches of snow, but it was enough to scare school officials, who feared a repeat of what happened earlier this winter when a blizzard brought the state to a standstill and created a giant traffic jam or, as they say in Italy, "un ingorgo grosso." Via Condotti in Rome has lots of "ingorghi grossi."

Snow days pose a challenge to parents. The ones who work outside the house scramble to find someone to take care of their children. The ones at home find ways to keep their kids busy to prevent the bickering that can occur when siblings are cooped up for a long stretch of time. I fall in the latter category and, as the parent of two boys only 13 months apart, I'm aware of the potential for great quarrels.

I had two options: I could anesthetize the boys with television and the computer, or I could persuade them to use their brains and bodies. I'm down on technology at the moment, so I decided to make a good-faith effort to fill our day with activities that did not include clubpenguin.com.

Most parents know it's important to give kids advance warning of your intentions if you want them to do something without a battle. The end of a trip to the park might be preceded by, Max, we're leaving in 15 minutes. Before entering a drugstore, a parent might utter, No gum, only Swedish Fish. When my sons got up that morning, I made it clear even before they brushed their teeth, that the day would be an adventure if they followed my lead.

My son Peder, who is 7, loves to cook. He learned how to cook from his dad, who prepares all the meals in our house.

Peder decided to show off his culinary skills on the snow day.

By 8 in the morning, he was sitting at the kitchen table reading the ingredients for "Fifi's French Toast" in his *Better Homes and Garden New Junior Cookbook*, and barking out orders to his brother Henry, who is 6. (Such is the fate of little brothers.)

"I want to cook," said Henry.

"You can get the utensils," Peder said.

After a few mishaps (yolk on the table, yolk on the floor, yolk under the burner), we settled down to eat and talk about our plans. Henry came up with the idea for a list. No. 1: "Ete." No. 2: "Brush Teeth." No. 3: "Bored Games." No. 4: "Arts and Crabs." No. 5: "Shovel Snow." No. 6: "Hot Chocolit." No. 7: "Pizza." I was thrilled. There were no references to Pokemon or aquatic birds. This was going to be a fruitful day.

The boys stuck to the schedule, until they got to No. 3. My boys are moving beyond the Lego phase, so I thought Christmas would be a good opportunity to push them further into the book and board game phase. I'm afraid I went too far. The books were a hit; the board games received a tepid response. Last count, we owned eleven board games, but only one really sees any action: Monopoly.

While Henry was rinsing the dishes (another little brother task), I went upstairs to tend to Marvin Gardens and look around for the old shoe. No sooner was The Bank in order when word came from downstairs that No. 3 and No. 5 were trading places. I wasn't surprised. Most boys I know love to shovel. There's something exhilarating about scooping up a pile of dirt and tossing it aside. Toy stores know that, too. That's why they stock kid shovels year-round. We own four.

Shoveling snow with kids is a humbling experience. They

are relentless in their pursuit of the perfect path. After one scoop, I need to come up for air. Kids can go at it a good hour without stopping. But the path is narrow and the elbows hard; there's always a bit of chaos on the front steps. A shovelful of snow aimed at the yew might end up on someone's face.

"Peder got snow in my eyes," Henry said.

"I did not."

"Did so."

The spat led to the inevitable snow-shovel fight that stopped only when I used another common parenting tactic: change of venue. We went next door to shovel our neighbors' steps and then walked across the street to tidy up another friend's house.

The boys were prepared to shovel the entire street, but Henry brought up the topic of food. Back home, they decided to pass on No. 6 (hot chocolate) and go directly to pizza. I put in the call—half-cheese, half-pepperoni—to satisfy both. "Thirty minutes," the man at the pizza parlor said.

Get-togethers are easy to arrange on snow days for obvious reasons—kids are home and ready to cut loose. Arlo came over in the early afternoon. He had eaten. We had not. Our pizza was late. Henry and Arlo passed the time playing Front Porch Classics Pinball Baseball Game, while Peder stood at the window waiting for lunch to pull up.

We should be forgiving on snow days. When the pizza delivery man finally knocked on the door two hours after my call, I accepted his apology. He said he had been swamped by requests.

"Something's going on out there," he said.

"Snow day," I said. "Tell your people."

The pizza was all cheese, and cold. Peder took one bite,

Henry two. "It tastes funny," Henry said. "I can't eat it." I couldn't either. We had more success with dessert, chocolate cookies. Then I asked for a show of hands: Monopoly or the backyard?

They raced out the door, leaving behind a trail of gloves without mates. Working as a team, the boys built a snow fort and filled it with snowballs.

"Come see what we did," Peder shouted into the kitchen, where I was scrubbing a pot.

I expected a tour of the fort, and instead I came under fire by little boys in puffy pants.

"Take this," said Henry, delivering a beauty.

"Cease and desist," I shouted and picked up a sled to shield myself from the onslaught. I stumbled back into the house and dusted off my coat. The boys played until dark, and when they came back inside, they checked off No. 6, hot chocolate. Lukewarm. No marshmallows.

"Can I have some whipped cream?" asked Henry.

You bet. It was a snow day.

Finding Zak
April 2008

I'm always grateful when someone is kind to my kids. I'm talking about genuine kindness, the sort that goes beyond a lollipop and a deck of cards. I'm talking about the kindness that gets me all choked up.

Let me tell you about Zak DeOssie.

Back in November, I wrote a story about my son Peder's fondness for Zak, the former football star for Brown University who made it as a pro with the New York Giants. For years, Peder has been following the linebacker's career on the field and in a riveting DVD about the games leading up to the Ivy Title the Bears won in 2008.

Last summer, Peder stood outside the First Baptist Church in America for two hours, hoping to get Zak's autograph as he marched by during his graduation ceremony. Zak was a no-show, but that didn't deter my son. Later that night, Peder wrote Zak a letter asking for his signature.

Months passed. Peder was about to give up when my husband, revealing a soft spot for his firstborn, dug up the Giants' address and mailed Zak my November column. A few days later (on Dec. 5, at 4:03 p.m., to be precise), we got an email that made us giddy:

"Dear Peder: I just received your article/letter you sent me, and I am touched. So sorry I missed you at my graduation ceremony. Keep an eye out in the mail for the next couple of weeks. I will send you my autograph as well as a little surprise for you because you were so patient. Go Giants!!! Sincerely, Zak DeOssie."

Peder was so excited he would rush up our front steps after school to see if a package from New York was leaning against the door.

Late December arrived, and still nothing. I told Peder that Zak was busy playing football and that he'd pull through eventually. Peder wrote another letter, and then crept upstairs to the computer one night and composed an email.

"Dear Zak, I think I've been waiting a couple of weeks for your package. Did you lose my address? Here it is again: Providence, Rhode Island. Sincerely, Peder."

The doorbell rang the morning of January 18. I looked out

the window. The postal truck was humming. Could this be it? I opened the door. "You got something from Zak DeOssie," the mailman said.

Rhode Islanders who follow pro football know Zak DeOssie. I told the mailman the story, and he said he wasn't surprised. He said Zak's father, Steve DeOssie, who played for the Patriots and other NFL teams, was a kind man, too.

I put the package on the kitchen table, and lured Peder there after school. He tried to keep cool but kept jumping around like a kid on a pogo stick. He called his father at work.

"Dad, I just got a Zak DeOssie thing-a-ma-bobber," he shouted into the phone.

The "thing-a-ma-bobber" was a Wilson Official NFL "The Duke" Football signed by Zak and other Giants: fellow linebackers Chase Blackburn, Kawika Mitchell, Antonio Pierce, Reggie Torbor, and Gerris Wilkinson, and the defensive end, Justin Tuck.

"I am not going to use this one bit," said Peder, quickly realizing that his precious pigskin was a keeper. "I am not going to get this dirty."

Zak also sent a signed football card—Peder, my #1 Fan, Zak DeOssie, 51, Go Gmen!—as well as a handwritten letter on a sheet of lined notebook paper:

"Peder, I am very sorry this package is getting to you so late. I have been busy with everything from football to the holidays. Hope you can forgive me. You better be watching the game this weekend vs. the Green Bay Packers. It is supposed to be -5 degrees outside. I can't wait. Take care Peder and keep watching. Sincerely, your friend, Zak, #51."

We watched the Green Bay game—the Giants won, of course—and the next day Peder wrote back.

"Dear Zak, Great game. It was a nail-biter. I'm glad you are going to the Super Bowl. I guess you were happy when Tynes made the kick. Did you know there has never been a kick over 40 yards at Lambeau Field? Tynes' kick was 47 yards. I want the Gmen to win the Super Bowl, not the Patriots. Thank you for the football, football card and your letter. I am going to show everything to my friends. My mom is going to buy me a glass case for the football and card and letter so I can keep them forever. I have a question for you: Who is your best friend on the team? Good luck in the Super Bowl. I will be looking for you on television and cheering you on. Your friend and fan. Peder."

XLII was the greatest Super Bowl ever, the game the Giants weren't supposed to win. With less than a minute left on the clock we worried whether Eli Manning—Yep, we're Giants' fans—would be able to complete the drive, but he came out of the pile and aired it to David Tyree, who made that incredible catch using his helmet, and our Zak won his first Super Bowl at the tender age of 23. The end was especially sweet when Zak nailed a Patriots running back after the final kickoff and the broadcaster, Joe Buck, introduced the former Brown Bear to millions of viewers: "That's the rookie, Zak DeOssie."

I stayed up late watching the post-game show and almost woke Peder up when a Channel 12 sportscaster interviewed Zak about the victory. He was just as I had imagined: a burly young man with a boyish face and a neck as thick as a redwood. "How do you feel?" asked the sportscaster, giving Zak a pat on the back. "Euphoric," Zak said.

Here was a young man who did something he didn't have to do. He paid attention to a kid who paid attention to him. With all the stories today about world-gone-wrong athletes—Clemens' steroid abuse, Vick's dog fighting, Pacman's fistfights—it's refreshing to find someone who understands that sports are really about making a kid's day.

Thank you, Zak DeOssie.

You're my hero, too.

CHAPTER 3

....

The Tulips and the Stone
May 2008

The day my husband found out that his mother's cancer had spread, he sat down with our boys, then ages 4 and 5, and told them the doctor couldn't help Grandma and that she was going to die. The boys knew she had been in the hospital and they had seen her at home feeling poorly, but it never occurred to them that she wouldn't get better. Peder, my oldest, started to cry. "I don't want Grandma to die," he said, sobbing. "Tell her not to die."

That night, as he was putting the boys to bed, my husband talked to our sons about what would happen afterward. We would keep Grandma's old house so they could still kick a ball in her backyard, slide down her bulkhead, and dodge cobwebs in her creepy basement. She would be buried nearby in Swan Point Cemetery, in Providence, where she liked to walk among the pin oaks. And she would have something called a gravestone, a big rock engraved with her name. Peder asked if he could design it.

Early in his life, Peder was drawn to the arts. When he was a toddler, I set up an easel in our living room and made sure the plastic cups were always full of fresh paint. He liked to paint rainbows—big arcs of blue and green with a dash of black, his dark clouds. I called the paintings his rainbow series and taped them over the windows at the top of the stairs, where the morning sun shines through.

His painting period ended around the age of 4 when he discovered the books of the architectural illustrator David Macaulay and learned that an intricate drawing of, say, a stapler was art, too. Over the years, he put his No. 2 pencil to paper and drew elaborate illustrations of whatever he was interested in at that moment: bridges, fire trucks, airplanes, sailboats, football fields, golf courses, ski trails, even an old apple press. Why not his grandmother's gravestone?

Henry, my younger son, didn't know much about gravestones, but Peder had seen his fair share during weekend tricycle rides at Swan Point. Still, he needed guidance: Would Grandma prefer a tall stone or a wide one? What color would she want: black, rose, or gray?

It was Peder who decided the stone should have an engraving of tulips or roses, which my mother-in-law loved equally and whose remnants remained on her lawn as a faded petal or curled leaf when she died just before her 80th birthday. He settled on tulips.

Grandchildren came late in my mother-in-law's life. Before the boys were born, she probably made peace with the possibility that she might not become a grandmother. She was thrilled when her only child—my husband—married and had not one, but two boys.

She lived close by, on Nisbet Street, so she saw them every day and let them run in her yard with its soft grass to cushion falls. She always had chocolate cookies on her kitchen counter and coffee milk in the clunky Hotpoint refrigerator she bought in 1949, the year she moved into the house. The boys loved going there. "Nisbet" was more popular than a trip to the park. It was heartbreaking for them to lose her.

After the talk with his dad, Peder sat down at our kitchen table and drew several illustrations of what he thought the gravestone should look like. He eventually chose a tall stone with a serpentine top. He wrote my mother-in-law's name in his best penmanship, Carol Johnson Schaefer, and the dates of her birth, Nov. 28, 1925, and her death, Nov. 1, 2005.

The tulips were the most challenging part of the design. How to express the simplicity of a tulip on a slab of stone? He found his answer one morning at The Providence Athenaeum after telling the children's librarian what he was doing. A few days later, Nancy appeared at our door with a book about the history of tulips in Holland, complete with illustrations, which Peder studied with an intensity usually reserved for his airplane books.

One Saturday, my husband took the boys and the sketch to Providence Monumental Works, the Branch Avenue landmark that my husband had passed many times as a boy during his weekly Sunday car rides to his grandmother's house in Smithfield, never once imagining that, one day, he would find himself inside the lot's chain-link fence selecting a stone for his mother.

John, the owner, gave everyone a tour and together they selected a stone of gray granite from Barre, Vermont. My husband told John he had specific requests for the engraving and handed him Peder's design.

A few weeks later, we received John's layout in the mail. The name and dates were correct, but Peder, the designer, complained that the flowers were all wrong. They looked more like cornstalks—without the corn. My husband asked for a new design. I chuckle when I think of John back at the drafting table, at the behest of a 5-year-old kid. My mother-in-law would have gotten a kick out of that, too.

The new design was perfect. My husband ordered the stone, and it was delivered to Swan Point just before the first anniversary of Grandma Schaefer's death. On a sunny afternoon, we made a special trip to the cemetery to see it. We drove slowly along North Way, peering out the windows, searching for Peder's work, and when we spotted it, the boys flew out of the car.

Peder inspected it to make sure it was up to his high standard of artistry. It was. And then the boys touched it. They ran their hands over the polished granite and two tulips. They hid behind the stone and popped their heads up over the arc. They climbed on the base—Henry on one side, Peder on the other—and talked about the top's rough, rock-pitch surface. They leaned against the stone; they hugged it.

We've been back many times to visit—and play. My boys own that gravestone. It is theirs.

Yard Sales
June 2008

A few summers ago, my husband took our sons on a Sunday morning walk through the neighborhood. Instead of returning home with a pocketful of rocks, the boys came back with an apple peeler. In my view, apple peelers are a luxury item and a frivolous expense. What's wrong with a simple paring knife?

I was pleased to find out that this particular apple peeler—still in its box—was a bargain: only 50 cents. It was gently used, but so what. For that price, I'll take a blunt blade. Besides, the peeler made the boys happy. Henry, the tinkerer, got something he could disassemble. Peder, the fruit lover, got to indulge.

What really amazed the boys, though, was where they closed the deal: at a yard sale.

If you've lived on the East Side for any length of time you've probably been to at least one yard sale. They are so common in the summer it's possible to spend an entire Saturday strolling from one block to another, picking through other people's stuff.

Last spring, we were driving home from baseball practice when we noticed a pile of plush toys in a driveway. The boys asked me to stop. I did, though I wondered, as I cut the engine, if dust mites had set up house in the fur. "Please Mom," said Henry, looking at me with superb tenderness. We bought a red-eye tree frog and a chipmunk.

I've been all over the state, and I can say with certainty that yard sales on the East Side are the best. The goods are in excellent condition and unique. We have gallery-quality paintings from art students at the Rhode Island School of Design. We have scholarly books from Brown University professors. We have steamer trunks lugged out of moldy basements by the next generation.

I'm not looking for socket wrenches or humidifiers when I go to a yard sale. I want a set of nesting bowls from Hungary ($2, Elmgrove Avenue, 2006) or a decorative pin made from Coke cans and wire ($1.50, John Street, 2002). I want something that satisfies (the saltwater blue Indian tapestry I bought for $4 on Morris Avenue in 2004) without the Tiffany's price.

My boys, of course, want toys. It's rare to find toys without defects. My sons always end up at the bin with toys so disfigured I wonder why the seller doesn't just offer them for FREE.

The boys don't seem to care. Afterward, they rush home, heavy hand the doorbell and shout, "Mom, look what I got," to which I might respond, "More plastic."

Playing cards are the boys' second favorite find. This might have something to do with their fondness for poker. My husband taught them how to play when they were toddlers, and turned their bedroom into a poker den after dinner. Four hands of five-card stud is a good way to wind down before bed.

Cards are popular at yard sales, and the boys scoop them up. The deck, however, is not always full. Some sellers are honest enough to warn us; the shady leave it up to us to find out. This lack of disclosure has created problems. Many of our decks are incomplete, which makes it impossible for Henry to draw his four-of-a-kind or, better yet, his straight flush.

East Side yard sales seem to specialize in high-brow kitchenware. They look good but won't turn a bad chef into a good one. My sons like collecting these objects and presenting them to my husband, the household cook. "Dad needs this," Henry said one day, as he raised something that looked like a shovel for a leprechaun. It was a corn zipper, and he bought it for a buck. Peder's treasure is the "yellow thing-a-ma-thing" that chops onions and keeps our kitchen free of food-related tears.

Our most intelligent purchase was a set of dinner dishes we bought on Humboldt Avenue for $15. Our old set had fallen into and from the hands of two rambunctious boys and dwindled to one or two plates. The boys have been reckless with the new set as well, but my husband turned to eBay for guidance and discovered that replacements cost a few dollars and that our blue-flowered, microwave-safe dishes have a regal name: The Churchill Finlandia Georgian Collection.

Most of our experiences at yard sales have been fun. The

sellers are laid-back and seem relieved to purge. Now and then, we run into a crank. Take the man on Taber Avenue in the summer of '02. The minute Peder and I entered his driveway, I sensed trouble. The man was wearing one of those mini carpenter aprons from Home Depot to collect his money. Peder, who had recently graduated from putt-putt to the driving range, asked if I'd buy him four used golf balls for a walloping $10. I reluctantly said, yes, and paid his assistant. I gave Peder the golf balls to carry, and as we walked down the driveway the man raised his brow and exclaimed in a booming voice loud enough for other shoppers to hear: "Did he pay for those?" "Of course," I replied. "Too much."

I like going to yard sales to find art by RISD students. Their creations are unique and affordable. My prized purchase is a portrait of a pigtailed young woman wearing a periwinkle muscle T-shirt. Two summers ago, I bought three framed photographs from a RISD student trying to raise money to move to New York. The frames were tree branches, and the photos—a pine tree, a telephone pole, a woman screaming—were suspended from the branches with wire and cord clamps. I was crazy about them and put them on a window ledge, out of reach of little hands. The other day, the photos disappeared, no doubt swiped by Henry, who probably took them apart and built a circuit board.

Our Land
July 2008

I wasn't much of a park person before I had kids. Back then, it never occurred to me to wander into a park, plop down on a city bench, and eat a tuna sandwich, while a pair of frenetic squirrels played at my feet. Parks were there for me to walk by on my way to the coffee shop.

It took one broken lamp for me to realize that my sons, Peder and Henry, needed a place to run and that our yard was inadequate. It was long and narrow, good for a trike ride, bad for tag. Worse yet, it didn't have any grass, only a patio with sharp pebbles. Two busted lips and a knee gash so deep I needed tweezers to remove the debris sent me on a quest for better grounds.

One Saturday morning, I buckled the boys into the double stroller and walked three blocks away to a park on Humboldt Avenue that everyone in the neighborhood called The Baby Park.

It was perfect—loaded with kids, flat and grassy, and enclosed by a tall, wrought-iron fence that belonged around the Munster mansion. The park had a sandbox filled with old Tonka trucks, swings with seatbelts, and a jungle gym with a tunnel where kids could escape from hovering parents for a precious two seconds. The boys mounted a stump and set up a fort among the withering hemlocks. We became regulars.

The parks on the East Side have been good to us; they're one reason we're here. I raise my juice box to the parks—my second backyard, a place where my kids can run free, shout as loud as they want, meet up with best buds, celebrate birthday parties, and smack a baseball without worrying about denting a car.

Our biggest adventure was in The Baby Park. Peder was 2; Henry, an infant. I was gabbing with another parent when Peder, stick thin, squeezed through the fence and landed in the backyard of a house on Orchard Avenue. I didn't know if I should panic or look at my son in happy wonderment. "Stop," I shouted.

He took off running toward the object of his affection—a swing set. The fence was too high for me to climb, so I raced around the block to fetch him. He was playing when I arrived and so was the black lab, which was big, but, to my relief, not ferocious. The homeowner spotted me through her window and seemed confused to see a woman standing at the bottom of a slide begging a boy to come down. I apologized as best I could through glass and left with a firm grip on Peder's hand. I went back to the park the next day and was delighted to discover that during the night the homeowner had covered the escape hole with chicken wire.

I'm sure the parks have official names, but I don't know what they are and don't intend to find out. I like the names we've given them: The Big Green Park, sprawling grounds at the end of Blackstone Boulevard with a canopy of trees and flat land for foot races; The JCC Park, a bustling place behind the Jewish Community Center that has a Little League field and a community garden; and Grandma's Park, a peaceful spot on the edge of a forest overlooking the Blackstone River. Most people call it Patterson Park. My sons named it after their grandmother, who lived two blocks away and would stop by on sunny days to watch her grandsons shoot baskets in the junior-size hoop, and buy them rainbow snow cones from the Palagi ice-cream truck.

I am not fibbing when I say I've visited every park on the East Side. One visit, however, did not always lead to another. Take The Red Park, a small lot in Fox Point with red monkey bars that look like ribbon candy. We had fun but no one showed any interest in returning. At the tiny park on Morris

Avenue, I felt like I was intruding in someone's private yard.

Some of our parks are really chunks of land that we use as playgrounds. They lack the trappings of a traditional park—jungle gyms, swings, slides—but are still good places to play if you're looking for privacy. We like a stretch of road along the Seekonk River that has an enormous flower box at the entrance to keep out cars. I sit on the curb and watch the boys ride their bikes and when they tire of figure eights, we wander to the road's end to hunt for river life—turtles and the occasional fish.

Our secret playground is on private land that we treat as public. The Big Green Field, known to most as the Aldrich Dexter Athletic Complex at Brown University, is where Peder learned how to pitch a three-fingered changeup, and Henry perfected his pop-up catching.

My favorite park is The Rope Park. Some people refer to it as India Point or The Spiderman Park. Besides having a fine view of the city's waterfront and a breeze that makes hot days seem cool, the park has a climbing structure that looks like a giant spider web. It's irresistible. The web is attached to a wobbly bridge, also made of rope, and a hammock sturdy enough to handle a six-kid pileup.

The Rope Park was the setting for our most memorable park experience—meeting Mika Seeger and Peter Geisser, the Rhode Island artists who made the playground's ceramic mosaic wall of India Point's maritime history. They were working there one afternoon when the boys showed up to play.

Peter and Peder hit it off. They are both friendly guys who like to talk. Peter, a stained-glass artist and former art director of the Rhode Island School for the Deaf, politely answered all of Peder's questions: "How hot is a kiln? What's a schooner?

How old are you?" Just before we left, he handed us a souvenir: a piece of the wall.

As we drove off, I told the boys that Mika is the daughter of Pete Seeger, a man who has been singing for decades about hammers and railroads and our land—all the things they love, too.

"Pete Seeger is the greatest folk singer in the United States of America, maybe the world," I said.

"What's a fork singer?" said Henry.

Peder couldn't get Peter off his mind. He wanted to go back, but it was late, and I was hungry. The ice-cream truck rarely makes it to India Point. We struck a compromise: Peder would bring his friend a cold drink. We bought two bottles of water at the drugstore and went back.

I sat in the car with Henry while Peder delivered the refreshment to the grateful artists. The tears started as he ran back to the car, and by the time he opened the door he was sobbing. He knew he had had one of the best play dates of his life, and it was over.

Your Irises are My Irises
August 2008

The most beautiful yew I've ever seen sits in front of a stately house on Freeman Parkway, in Providence. It looks like the plume on a giant's hat, green and fluffy and full of itself. I've driven by it so many times over the last several months my children are fed up. "Mom," they grumble from the back seat, "not the yew again." I'm amazed by the evergreen's height (one giraffe) and girth (two baby elephants), and I'm grateful that someone had the good sense a century ago to plant it in a place with plenty of open space where it could thrive and become what it is: magnificent. Someday I'd like to knock on the homeowner's door and ask: Who prunes this yew? What's her name?

Dawn, on a summer day in Providence, and I'm in the backyard of my house, watering my sweet woodruff. I should be sleeping, but my plants are thirsty, and I want to feed them before the clouds part and the sun beats down. I wonder if my neighbors think I'm nuts. I know my husband does, and my children are beginning to show signs of distress now that my dalliance with gardening has turned into a full-fledged affair that threatens to slow my response to queries such as, Where's the bike pump?

I never imagined I'd be interested in tilling the soil. I lived in apartments without backyards until I was 40, and when I finally moved into a house with land, I was so busy running after two toddlers I was lucky if I had enough time to brush my teeth. When a woman once told me that her passion was "working the earth," I shuddered. But this spring I gazed at our grounds from the living room window and turned a deep crimson. Our yard was a mess. The weeds were so healthy they were flowering. The boxwoods were entangled in tree branches. The ivy was limp and brown and leggy.

I'm reluctant to describe my early days on the land as gardening; it was more like renovation work. I pulled up the ugly stuff, cut off dead branches, clipped bushes, and removed intruders the earth-friendly way—with my hands. Anyone who believes that gardening involves nothing more than sticking a pansy in the ground and going about your business is reading too many glossies. Gardening is hard work. Over two weeks, I filled fourteen leaf bags and tied up two bundles of sticks. I turned over the soil and sweetened it with all sorts of healthy stuff, like cow manure. I got so close to the ground I could see worms squirm like mad snakes.

At the end of the day, I was exhausted, but it was a good fatigue, the kind that didn't pull me down. I reveled in my filth. Stringy hair. Fingers swelled up like pork sausages. Dirt on my face, under my nails, between my toes. "See these grubby hands," I said proudly to my boys. "Beat that." I pushed forward with a single-mindedness I reserve for cleaning the tub, and when it was over, I stood in my tidy yard and knew that I would never again tolerate the depressing stillness of backyard decay.

The East Side is a good place for beginning gardeners. We are a rarity, but instead of feeling odd we can rejoice in the opportunity to learn from others whose yards are a testament to their gardening skills. I have the *Reader's Digest Illustrated Guide to Gardening* and *The Rhode Island Gardener's Companion* and, my favorite, *Gardening for Dummies*, but I want to see a limelight hydrangea in the rough, not in a book.

The gardens around here are beautiful. Flowers, bushes, trees, ground cover—they are all there in various stages of growth over the spring and summer months to provide guidance and inspiration and remind us that goodness still springs from the earth.

I spend a lot of time in my car taking my kids to where they want to go: the baseball field, friends' houses, the drug store for a squirt gun. These trips give me a chance to gawk at my neighbors' gardens so I can decide if I want a particular flower or shrub on my land. I use my Reader's Digest book to identify plants I like, and if the book disappoints, I leave notes.

One evening, I was driving to the market when I came upon a hedge in front of a house on Lloyd Avenue. It was stunning—ten bushes with arching branches covered with tiny white flowers that looked like snowflakes.

I left a note, and my email address, in the mailbox: "I love your bushes. Could you let me know what they are?" A few days later, I got my answer: bridal wreath spirea.

As a novice gardener, I have nagging insecurities about plants. The more I plant, the more I learn, but along the way I've made plenty of mistakes. The fern I dug up at my mother-in-law's house belonged in the shade; I planted it in full-sun, and it died. Jane's bush wilted and left us when I neglected to water it on a brutally hot day.

Fortunately, my nursery of choice is sympathetic to the anxieties of new gardeners. This spring, I was looking for shrubs to hide my neighbor's cable lines. I bought two red-vein enkianthus, an upright bush with bell-shaped flowers. Moments after I planted them, I knew I had flubbed up; they were too skinny. The nursery has a return policy, and I took advantage of it in the worst way. I brought the shrubs back and came home, this time, with four doublefile viburnums, hardy shrubs that bloom white flowers. I dug two more holes and, once again, felt regret. The leaves were big and droopy. I took them back.

I considered buying four mountain laurels—a brainy bush with petals that look like fossils tinted pink—but talked myself out of it. I was too nervous; a third mistake, I feared, would require intervention. I kept the four holes until my son Henry asked what could only be obvious to a kid: "Are those booby traps?"

Gardeners like to share their plants, and this generosity

leads to new friendships and strengthens old ones. What better way to express kindness than to offer the better half of a divided hosta (thank you, Kathy) or four healthy hens and chicks (thank you, Holly) or a fistful of sedum (thank you, Francesca). These exchanges, however, can get out of hand. Before you know it, you find yourself with a truckload of day-lilies (a common giveaway) and not enough space to plant them.

Sometimes, the give-and-take is comical. One day, I left a dozen iris rhizomes on Francesca's porch, thinking she might want to replant them in her garden. I came home a few hours later and found a surprise on my steps—a bush of peonies, along with the same irises. I called Francesca with the intention of laughing about the mix-up, but, in the end, I didn't have the heart to reveal the truth—that her irises were my irises. I planted the peonies and took the irises to yet another neighbor's house, and for all I know, by now, they could be in a garden somewhere in the South of France.

Fisherboys
September 2008

A hot summer day, and I'm driving down the highway with a bucket of minnows in my passenger seat. I'm observing the bittersweet, worrying about how this ropey vine is sucking the life out of every tree and bush in the state, when a minnow leaps out and lands at my feet, plop.

It's a lot for me to process all at once: a flying fish, the speedometer edging toward 60, and my two boys in the backseat accusing me of bad deeds: You killed it. You killed the fish.

I get off at the nearest exit, scoop up the minnow with my bare hands and return it to its habitat. It is lifeless, but I dare not relay that information to the boys, just yet.

All I can think about is the man in the bait shop. He must have known that my bucket wasn't deep enough for his minnows and that attempts would be made to break free. I imagine him crushing the stub of his Camel and flicking it across the curb and looking at his watch and saying: Now, just about now, those fish should be airborne and, anyway, what kind of a lady wears a skirt to go fishing.

These are the things I carry in my car: two fishing poles from Target; 8-pound test; snelled fishhooks; split-shot sinkers; snap swivels; needle nose pliers; red-and-white bobbers; a purple plastic bucket, a Swiss Army knife and two tackle boxes equipped with green twine, hooks of various shapes and sizes, Day-Glo rubber worms, and shiny metal sinkers so refined they should be dangling from a charm bracelet. The car smells like rotten something; I suspect it is pond scum.

This is the year we learned how to fish. Actually, this is the year I learned how to fish so I could take my boys, Peder and Henry, fishing. They are 8 and 7, old enough to cast a line, too young, I'm afraid, to untangle it from a barberry bush. In time they will learn, but for now they need my nimble fingers to make sure they hook fish, not their right femur.

Zack got us started on fishing. Most kids celebrate their birthdays at the Bowling Academy or Regal Reptiles or Monster Golf; Zack had a fishing party. On a sweltering day in July, we gathered in Slater Park, in Pawtucket, for hot dogs, cake, a surprisingly civilized game involving water balloons, and fishing at a pond near our picnic site.

Only one adult at the party seemed to know anything

about fishing and that was Charles, who prepped the kids' poles, a process that involved a hook and a line and lots of wrapping and then two good tugs, and, bingo, you are ready for your first cast. Charles is modest about his fishing skills, which he acquired only six weeks before the party.

He taught us how to attach hooks and bobbers and gave free demonstrations on the proper way to remove a hook from a fish's mouth (gently)—all the while tending to the needs of his son, Alden, who, not surprisingly, was the best of the bunch and who, according to my sons, achieved a personal best at the party with 23 strikes.

The fest included two fishing expeditions, one before hot dogs, the other after cake and goodbyes. The pre-food expedition yielded mostly weeds and crushed Coke cans, although a freckle-faced boy called Finn, named after that Huck, caught a smallish fish with a $7.99 rod from Benny's.

After the party ended, a few kids, including mine, begged for more and off they marched into the bramble and found a shady fishing hole on the water's edge that my sons now call The Secret Spot.

The place was teeming with sunfish, and just when I thought it couldn't get any better, the birthday boy snagged a catfish the size of a large man's foot. Zack's face lit up, and the honors of removing the hook from the whiskered fish fell to Charles, who winced when he gripped the slimy black bottom feeder—"Gross"—but managed to toss it back intact.

We've been fishing nearly every day since the party, and when we are not fishing, we are thinking about fishing. One day, I ran a quick errand and left my cell phone in the car. There were three messages from Peder when I got back: Mom, can we go fishing? Mom, I want to go fishing? Mom, I really want to go fishing and that's the bottom line.

Unfortunately, the East Side does not have a good fishing hole. The pond by the Seekonk River looks like a cesspool and although I've seen people fishing in the river, I'm reluctant to take my kids to a place that has speeding cars on their backside and a slippery bank that could lead to a reckless cast. Henry, I remind myself, was voted Most Likely to Hook Someone, at Zack's party. The dock at India Point is more suitable for serious fishermen, the sort who bring jumbo-size coolers to chill their Bud and know how to slice open the belly of a striper and peel off its skin. We catch and release.

We've returned to The Secret Spot at least a dozen times, and one afternoon we ventured into Riverside, in East Providence, and checked out Willett Pond, which was unfit for even a trailed finger through the water.

On a trip to Roger Williams Park Zoo in Providence, we spotted some teenagers carrying rods, and they directed us to a fishing hole with the send-off, "Don't tell anyone." This experience was more successful, with two strikes each. Peder was certain he caught a small-mouthed bass, and though I have my doubts, I'll give it to him since harmless embellishment is part of our rich fishing culture.

My only disappointment with this new hobby is that my boys refuse to touch the bait. When Henry was a toddler, he dug up worms in the backyard after a gully wash and kept the invertebrates as pets for a walloping 15 minutes. Now, he won't come near a night crawler, and neither will Peder. Minnows are off limits, too.

I admit that the first time I impaled a worm I felt a lot of revulsion and some guilt, and then I got over it. No bait, no strikes. I was, however, surprised to discover that night crawlers, as well as fish, bleed red, a fact that is hard for Henry to absorb.

During a recent outing at The Secret Spot, he caught a sunfish. I struggled to get the hook out with my nose pliers but couldn't and dug deeper. Henry watched in horror as the fish's blood trickled down my hand. He knew his hook had wounded the fish and that it was dead, or dying. I finally completed the ghastly task, but the damage was done in the form of a gaping hole.

"I don't want to fish anymore," Henry said, and he put down his rod.

His brother refused to leave, and I soon realized I had a crisis on my hands: a pacifist and a hunter in the same fishing spot.

"Sorry about the fish," I said to Henry.

"I don't want to talk about it," he said. "Can we go home?"

Rising Star
October 2008

I walked down the street the other day to visit my friend Annabeth Gish. Annabeth and I met in 1987 at an old church in Connecticut, where she was filming scenes from *Mystic Pizza*, a romantic comedy about three young women who navigate life and love while working in a pizzeria. I was an extra in the movie and wrote about my experience for *The Providence Journal*, my former employer. Annabeth played one of the women, the guileless one, as I recall.

My editors told me Annabeth was a rising star and that I should try to interview her, not her co-star, Julia Roberts, who, at that time in her career, was not even vaguely alluring to the public. This is what I remember: Annabeth was warm and talkative and accompanied by her mother, who gently clarified that, no, the family was not related to the silent film star, Lillian Gish. I followed my editor's advice and ignored Julia, who giggled a lot on the set and flirted with one of the male leads, Vincent D'Onofrio, better known today as Detective Goren on *Law & Order: Criminal Intent*, a long-running television series about criminals and the detectives who chase them.

Annabeth never made it into my story and I never made it into the movie, but we both managed to carry on and lead fulfilling lives. When I found out that *Brotherhood*, the Showtime series starring Annabeth, was filming on the East Side, only two blocks from my house, I decided to track her down again, even though two decades had passed.

Hollywood likes Rhode Island. Production crews always seem to be filming a movie or television show here or talking about filming one. *Brotherhood* has been filming in the state for years. To be honest, I've never watched the show. I'm usually asleep by 8. From the little I know about it though, it seems like a good fit for Rhode Island, which is dogged by a culture of mob violence and political scandals. The show is about two brothers on opposite sides of the law—one brother a gangster, the other a politician. Annabeth plays the politician's long-suffering wife, Eileen, who abuses drugs and booze and has an affair with the mailman. Not the Annabeth I knew.

Reporting is a good profession for meeting famous people. I've mingled with the best: sausage king Jimmy Dean on his yacht in Newport; a pig-tailed Willie Nelson in his concert trailer in Warwick; Woody Harrelson, of *Cheers* fame, on a basketball court at a YMCA; and, at an event for an alarm company, a still-dashing Robert Vaughn, whom I knew as a kid as special agent Napolean Solo of the United Network Command for Law Enforcement, or U.N.C.L.E., as in, Man from.

Though their celebrity status often left me tongue-tied, most of my encounters with Hollywood types were pleasant. Some were not.

My *Mystic Pizza* job comes to mind. An editor from the *Journal* calls up and offers to put me in the movies. The next thing I know I'm sitting in a rock-hard pew at St. Peter and Paul's Church in New London, Connecticut, watching Jojo (Lily Taylor) and Bill (Vincent) walk down the aisle, as Daisy (Julia) stands by as a bridesmaid. Lovely wedding dress, I think, and then JoJo faints. I endure 12 more hours of JoJo fainting, and when it's finally over the director tells me that 2 minutes and 34 seconds of the day's filming will be used in the movie.

I'm tired of gasping on cue, and I'm feeling giddy, so during a break I corner Vincent in a nice way and muster the courage to tell this budding star that he was "really good" as the dangerously unstable private in *Full Metal Jacket*.

"Thank you," he says, with no twinkle in his eyes. "Now I'm going to eat my dinner."

Movie stars are different from you and me.

My time with the crew and cast of *Providence*, the soapy television series that aired from 1999 to 2002 and starred a house on Taber Avenue on the East Side, wasn't much better. I hung out on the set during a week of filming and filed stories daily. It was a tough assignment, and I had to dig deep.

In one story, I wrote about actor Seth Peterson's obsession with his eyebrows, how they had to be perfect arches before he exited his trailer to play Robbie, the sweet but directionless brother. Seth's makeup artist gave me the scoop and I ran with it. I almost got kicked off the set the day the article appeared. No one was happy with my disclosure. I now realize it was a mistake (and mean-spirited) to publicize the actor's idiosyncrasies. I offer a belated apology.

The *Brotherhood* trucks pulled into the neighborhood just as my son Peder was finishing his Corn Flakes. I asked if he wanted to come along.

"I don't want to be in a movie," he said.

"Hollywood doesn't pluck people off sidewalks," I said, lying. "Suit yourself."

I fluffed up my hair and hoofed it up to Wayland Avenue to gawk. The grand silver trucks looked like they had been wrapped in aluminum foil. A zeppelin of a camera brushed up against a mature Pieris Japonica and survived. The film crew rushed in and out of the Community Church of Providence, and I thought I might witness yet another fake wedding. But the action was across the street in a house occupied by Jeff Pine, of Rhode Island Attorney General fame. How did the state's former chief law enforcer land a part—however bit—in the show? Lucky duck.

A guy in a New York Giants T-shirt told me that the scene was an Irish wake and that Jeff and his family were extras. Jeff's dark suit made sense on this steamy hot day. I saw other extras—fire marshals in their crisp dress uniforms and women in black—enter Jeff's parlor, but I did not see her.

I did not see Annabeth.

I was about to give up and go home when I spotted a woman walking down the street with the pep and confidence of a working actor. Annabeth, I thought. Long brown hair.

Tall. Dark eyes. A closer look revealed that she was Annabeth's lookalike, Leslie Sweeney, who lives across the street from Pine and owns a handbag and jewelry shop on Elmgrove Avenue called In the Bag.

Rhode Island is so small we all know each other or know of each other. I wasn't surprised to find out that Annabeth and Leslie had exchanged pleasantries—and a few dollars. One day during a pause in filming, Annabeth stopped in Sweeney's shop and was delighted to find Me&Ro jewelry.

Annabeth bought a piece, but I didn't ask Leslie what it was. Bad reporting, good manners. I learned my lesson with Seth's brows. Some things are better kept private. A woman's jewels are her own business.

You Don't Say
November 2008

My son told me he wanted to get "pacific." I was just about to reach for the Atlas when he launched into a long explanation of why he should be allowed to stay up way past his bedtime on a school night. "You go to bed late," he said. "Why can't I? I'm indistinguished from you." Good try. I told him to brush his teeth, but, I admit, I had a smile on my face when I barked out those orders. How could I not be impressed with his eagerness to take his argument to a higher plane with his use, however flawed, of the Big Word?

Raising children is hard work. Anyone who says otherwise is lying. But the other indisputable truth is that parenting is also a blast. Ask any mom or dad to describe one of those it's-all-worth-it moments and they'll probably come up with a list as long as a city block. One of my personal favorites is when my sons used a Swiffer and a dash of Fred Astaire-style dancing to clean the kitchen floor.

Lately, my good times involve the boys' rhetorical skills.

I'm not a wordsmith, so I have no idea why my kids are trying to sound like William F. Buckley, the conservative commentator who liked to toss out a florid word or two to impress his viewers—and himself. As a kid, I was painfully shy and rarely spoke, even when spoken to. Besides, as one of six children, I could barely get a word in edgewise. I was a lousy speller in elementary school and even mixed up my sister's name, writing "Umily" instead of "Emily."

Peder, who, at 8, is my oldest, has always been a talker. He babbled and cooed nonstop as a baby, and I thought that was normal until my mother-in-law told me that once Peder learned how to speak, he wouldn't stop. She was right. Our house is quiet—too quiet—when Peder is gone.

Television gets a bad rap, but, in this case, I honestly believe it might help with expanding my sons' vocabulary. Sure, they get an earful of stupid stuff, but they also hear meaty words on channels that deal with politics, science, and history. They enjoy listening to the cable shouters, and Peder has grown fond of the military channel, which is probably where he picked up the word "mayham."

I sensed changes in Peder's word use last year when he came home from school one day bursting with so much energy, he hopped up on the kitchen chair and exclaimed, "I have so much to tell you, you will automatically be recombusted."

He proceeded to talk in an influential manner about a project in his technology education class that involved building a house on a $100 budget.

"We're learning how to be econominal," he said.

"Great," I said. "It's a good time to pinch pennies. The economy is tanking."

Henry jumped into the conversation with news about a classmate who got upset when challenged on his claim that the soles of his sneakers were made of gold.

"He's an over-reacted," Henry said, throwing his empty chip bag in the "crash can."

My neighborhood provides plenty of opportunities for the boys to show off their intellectual chops. A recent trip downtown, for example, sparked a family discussion about the boards and poles on the historic First Baptist Church of America as it undergoes a paint job.

"Look at that scapholding," said Peder.

"What's scapholding?" said Henry.

"Whatever," said Peder.

Peder believes the graffiti in the neighborhood is scribbled by people who are "wrongdoing," and that the creep who smashed a window at an art gallery near our house is a juvenile "delicate." Henry refuses to sleep on the "tufon" in our guest bedroom.

Sometimes, the boys come up with phrases that are completely off the mark but sound good. The other day, I asked Peder for lunchbox advice. He requested no-frill snacks.

"Keep it low pitch," he said.

"No problem," I said.

He came up with a doozy one afternoon when he tried to wiggle his way out of responsibility for teasing his brother.

"I lit the teeny flame in the oven," he said, "but didn't cause the fire."

I'm not sure if a late-night infomercial or a peek at my

women's health book prompted the most eye-popping remark from Peder so far.

"You are anti-sexual," he bellowed one evening.

"You don't say," I replied.

I suppose hard-driving parents with dreams of a perfect 800 might suggest I correct my sons before it's too late and they end up roaming the world as adults muttering, "Where's your Arts and Crabs section?" But I'm not about to intervene.

Really, how can I resist Peder's explanation of a world gone wrong?

"Today was a horrid monster."

Lincoln Logs
December 2008

I once read that it's best to live without regret. You don't want to be gazing out your window at the age of 80, feeling remorse for neglecting to plant that Kousa in your front yard decades ago. Oh, to enjoy those creamy white petals today. For the most part, I've made peace with my decisions—until now.

I never took my children to see Santa.

My sons are 7 and 8, too old to believe. I'd have about as much success coaxing them onto Santa's lap as I would persuading them to give me a hug in front of their friends on the playground. It's not going to happen.

I know what you're thinking. I had a lousy experience with Santa when I was a girl, and I'm protecting my kids from similar trauma. That's not the case.

A Christmas memory: I'm standing in line at Famous-Barr, a department store on the edge of our suburb in St.

Louis, and even though I'm inside, I'm wearing my rose-colored wool coat with brass buttons. My older sisters are with me and so is my mother, who is holding my hand because I'm the youngest. We're moving slowly, and I can't take my eyes off the fat-cheeked man on a platform two steps high. Finally, it's our turn and my mother places me on his lap. He asks the question, so I tap my white lace-ups together nervously and whisper: "Lincoln Logs."

A visit with Santa was the highlight of the holiday season for me when I was a kid. My memories of Santa are so vivid I can tell you the color of his eyes (blue), what he sat in (a nubby brown wingback probably borrowed from the store's furniture department), and where he sat (between the toys and a café whose specialty was hot chocolate with a dollop of whipped cream).

Looking back on the early years with my sons, I don't see how I managed to avoid a Santa sit-down. He is in malls and mom-and-pop stores and even hangs out on street corners waving to motorists. It's possible to see Santa at dawn ringing a bell in front of the market and then standing outside a gas station at high noon holding a sign that says: "Happy Holidays, Free Coffee."

It's too much.

When I was a kid, only one Santa came to town and he always set up shop in the same place, Famous-Barr. When my boys were toddlers, I was turned off by all the Christmas hype and ran from it.

A trip to the Warwick Mall years ago comes to mind. On that day, Santa was holding court in a gold-trimmed chair, not far from a water fountain, fully operational and accepting your money. A man was playing "Jingle Bells" on a baby grand, while a chorus sang "oh what fun" and hummed and swayed. We bolted.

A visit to the Providence Place mall the following year was worse. Santa appeared in a sleigh the size of three Buicks and the cost of a keepsake photo was something like $1,000. I could not bring myself to participate. I thought another opportunity to visit with the North Pole celebrity would arise.

It did and I failed to take advantage of it.

One winter we were browsing in a toy store at Wayland Square and I spotted a Santa sitting upright in a La-Z-Boy and ready to hear your confession.

"Is that Santa?" my sons asked.

"No," I replied. "He's just dressing up like Santa."

Here was a chance for my kids to meet the man in a modest setting, and I blew it.

An opportunity like that never presented itself again.

I tried to compensate in other ways.

I wrote letters postmarked from the North Pole and taped them to the fireplace on Christmas Eve. I even burned the missives' edges to give them a sooty, down-the-chimney authenticity.

2004: "Thank you for the cookies and milk. Sweet of you. Rudolph thanks you for the carrots. Love, Santa."

2005: "You are good boys. Read. Love, Santa."

One of my favorite childhood photos is of me sitting on Santa's lap. I guess I was 1, maybe 2. I'm squeezed between my sisters, and Santa's hand is wrapped tightly around my waist to keep me from falling forward. I have a round face and rosy cheeks.

On the wall behind us hangs a curio shelf with toys: a tiny gray pony, a curly-haired doll in a blue dress, a soldier riding a wooden horse with a flaxen mane. Two glass jars are filled with red-and-white ribbon candy.

I'd be lying if I told you how I felt back then. It was too long ago. This much I do know: It was frigid outside—St. Louis winters are always bitterly cold—but inside, in this make-believe corner, it was warm, and I felt safe in Santa's arms.

I wish I had at least tried to give my boys that experience. I goofed. Sorry guys. Here's hoping your Christmas memories are still merry. Love, Mom.

The Good Slope
January 2009

We walked to the steep hill at Moses Brown School and watched the boys and girls race down so fast their unzipped jackets opened like parachutes. Shoes flew off. Maybe the laces were loose, but I doubt it.

Peder stood on the sidewalk and tried not to act like what he was: a spectator. He knew the hill was too high—he was only 4—and I knew it, too. He had to face that fact by himself, and it wasn't easy. At the bottom, after a harrowing ride, the big kids whooped it up. What could be more fun than that?

He stuck his hands deep into his coat pockets, and stared at the others, as though in a mild trance. I suggested we hunt for another hill, one with an easy slope that wasn't so menacing. But where would we go?

As far as I knew, this was the only sledding hill within a few miles. The neighborhood parks had modest mounds, but

Peder had outgrown them. He was looking for a challenge, a hill taller than, say, the silver slide at Lippitt Park, shorter than the Moses Brown hill. We found Golf Hill.

When I was a kid, my hill was Art Hill, a perilous descent that started outside the Saint Louis Art Museum in Forest Park, the sprawling city park, and ended in the Grand Basin at a frozen lake. My sisters and brother and I would pile on top of rusty Lightning Guiders and tip forward. What were we thinking? We always managed to coast to a halt at the lake's edge.

After we tired of that run, we'd scramble over to another hill, this one covered with oaks and weeping willows and Missouri red granite that we had to dodge to reach the bottom without a wipe-out. I hadn't yet read *Ethan Frome*, Edith Wharton's tale of doomed passion that ends with a tragic sledding accident, so I raced with abandon.

My sons don't share my youthful recklessness. They're cautious boys. Sometimes I want to push them out the door and say: Go down to the forest and don't come back before dark.

Still, I respect their restraint. Sledding can be dangerous. Miss Wharton knew that; I know it, too. Years ago, a high school classmate and his girlfriend were sledding on my weeping-willow hill and struck a tree. He never walked again.

When the boys were babies, I'd drag them across our snow-covered patio on a saucer sled. Then one winter day, I took the boys to a park on Humboldt Avenue that everyone in the neighborhood called The Baby Park. The park is flat, except for a small hill (really a bump) behind the swings.

My younger son Henry, only 2 at the time, took one look at the course and refused to even sit on the saucer. Peder is my fearless one. His first run was a success; his second was not.

The saucer hit a tree root and Peder tumbled onto the slushy snow, and chunks slid down the inside of his red rubber boots and soaked his socks. That marked the end of our sledding adventures—temporarily.

The cold makes me shiver, curl my shoulders. As a girl, my fingers turned pink and stiff under wet wool mittens, and the sledding was good for a thrill, but I couldn't wait to sit on our hissing radiator at home to thaw out. What I really lived for was the dense heat of a St. Louis summer so I could wear my sleeveless cotton shirt with the blue flowers or dive for pennies in the warm water of the Clayton Shaw Park Pool. My aversion to the cold has rubbed off on my kids. They are not winter people.

I was surprised when Peder agreed on that January day years ago to look beyond the Moses Brown hill and try something else. A friend suggested a hill in East Providence on Pawtucket Avenue across from the Boys and Girls Club.

We arrived just before noon. The parking lot was jammed. Henry stepped outside the car, and the wind stung his cheeks. His eyes teared up. I was afraid we might have to end it there. From the front seat Peder could see that the slope was gentle and ended in a wide and flat clearing.

"I'm good," said Peder, and we left Henry behind in warmth and peace with his dad.

The toboggan was orange, a present from Peder's great-uncle, Gordon Johnson, who believed all boys should have three things: a pocketknife, a pocket watch, and a sled. Gordon was a man of the slopes. One of his fondest childhood memories was zipping down Log Road, a twisty country lane in Smithfield, where he grew up. Back then, chipmunks ruled the road, not cars. It was always a terrifying and lonely ride, and Gordon loved it.

The hill in East Providence was packed with kids, laughing, joking, rolling in the snow like puppies. Tubes, saucers, plastic sleds, wooden sleds, foam sleds, snowboards—they were all crisscrossing the slope with ease.

Then I spotted a sign in the parking lot: "Spring Hill. Semi-Private." We were on a six-hole golf course and probably trespassing. Would we all get kicked out? I was imagining our mass exit when I looked to my side. Peder was gone. He and his sled had run off, together.

He was on top of the hill, a scrap of bones even in his puffy blue parka. He was surveying the land below, considering his options, waiting for a path to open. The snow fell. The wind tore at his hat. He climbed on his toboggan, and it swallowed him up; he was so small.

He seesawed back and forth and gave one last push. Down he went, over one hill and then another, working up speed until he was going faster than he had ever gone before. Ramrod straight, focused, he was beside himself with what he had done. He would reach the clearing soon.

He was far away, and he was happy.

Cuts
February 2009

My son cut his finger. I was upstairs, pecking away on my computer, when his friend, Oren, rushed into my room full of urgency and bad news. My first thought was that Henry had a paper cut. Kids can be dramatic; mine certainly are. Any time they see blood, even a tiny amount, they run for help.

I found Henry halfway up the stairs with a paper towel wrapped around the index finger of his right hand. He was calm, almost indifferent. I thought this was a minor cut. We walked into the bathroom, and I removed the bandage. As tap water washed away the blood, the enormity of what had happened came into view: The tip of his finger was gone.

I told myself not to panic. To try to stop the bleeding, Henry shook his finger, as if he were flicking off a bug, and red drops splattered on the white tile. It was either my rapid-fire instructions or high-pitched voice; Henry could tell something was terribly wrong.

"Don't worry, Mom," he said. "I'm going to be fine."

The first fall is always the hardest. Flashback to the fall of 2001: Henry's older brother Peder is in the living room scooting along on his Thomas the Train ride-on. He's traveling at a good pace—molasses-slow—but I think he'll have more fun if he speeds up. I give the rear bumper a kick with my foot, the toy flips over and down goes Peder, chin first onto the hardwood floor.

Before then, my boys' skin had been marred only by scrapes and bruises that healed quickly. I could tell right away that this cut was different—the skin parted easily, like the top of an envelope sliced open with a letter opener—and that the wound was deep. Six stitches in the ER.

Peder was fine that night. I felt awful. *It's my fault*, I thought. *What was I thinking?* The next day I bought some cheap rugs—ugly brown and gray threads that looked like hastily crafted potholders—and unrolled them on the floor.

I didn't stop there. I looked around the house and saw danger at every turn: the sharp edge on the window seat; the hot-to-the-touch radiator; the eleven stairs to the second floor; the banister on the landing with the 10-foot drop.

I went on a shopping spree at Home Depot. I bought gates for the top and the bottom of the stairs. I bought safety locks for the windows on the second and third floors. I bought rubber padding so thick my sons used leftover pieces for baseball bats.

I am certain people walked into my exquisitely baby-proofed house and murmured, "She's nuts," but I didn't hear them. I was too busy locking the gate. My husband's uncle, the frugal octogenarian, considered my purchases frivolous and suggested the unspeakable: a playpen.

Despite my defensive efforts, the accidents continued: 1.) Peder climbed over the gate at the top of the stairs and tumbled down, nose over foot, in a series of descending cartwheels. (He laughed it off; I mixed a stiff drink.) 2.) Henry fell against a door jam and split open his head. (Three staples and a scar only the barber sees.) 3.) Peder lunged at three floor pillows propped against the dining room wall and crashed into the baseboard. (Seven stitches and a fossil scar below his left eyebrow.)

There were more, too numerous to count. We became best buds with the receptionist in the emergency room at Hasbro Children's Hospital, which, barring an ice storm, is 9 minutes and 42 seconds from our house and, yes, they finally got valet parking.

All these mishaps led to the realization that I have little control over my sons' lives. I can guide (don't climb too high, wear your seatbelt, eat apples), but I am not all-powerful. Stuff happens. The branch breaks. The truck runs a stop sign. The virus finds a home and thrives. My fatalism allowed me to relax a bit—and then Henry cut his finger.

A part of him was gone, just like that. My first thought was to find what was missing. Maybe they could stitch it back on. I got down on my hands and knees and gently teased the rug, as if I were looking for a lost contact lens, and when I found what I wanted, I put it in a baggie—with ice.

On the way to the hospital, Henry asked if he would need stitches. "I don't know," I said, hold the towel tightly. I asked him, once again, how it had happened. Henry and Oren were playing. Henry was taking apart a toy (always the tinkerer) and he needed to pry off a piece of plastic; he looked for—and found—the camping knife we had bought days earlier, mostly for the tiny flashlight included in the package. It was on a top shelf in the kitchen, but Henry found a chair.

As we sat in the waiting room at Hasbro, I scolded myself for leaving out a knife and then, for buying it in the first place. I told the nurse about my baggie. She either thought I was overwrought or understood the force of a mother's love.

"Hmm," the doctor said, inspecting the cut. "This isn't so bad." It would hurt for a few days and, in a few weeks, the skin that he lost would grow back. Henry would have a perfect finger again.

I rejoiced. Henry wept, not for the joy of regeneration, but because the clock on the hospital wall was edging closer to the start time of his Cub Scout meeting. The Bears were scheduled to gather at 6:30 in the basement of the Central Congregational Church, and Henry wanted to be there. The kind doctor worked swiftly.

We were only 30 minutes late. Everyone knew about the mishap, thanks to Peder, who is also in the den and cannot resist telling a good tale. Henry, his eyes pink from the tears, did not want to talk about it. He only wanted to be a Cub: To do my best.

He kept his hand with the bad finger in the pocket of his sweatshirt to hide the injury, and by the end of the meeting he was laughing. He was with his fellow Bears. They were playing hide-and-seek. He was not the counter—his brother was.

That night I put Henry to sleep, and after he nodded off, I threw the knife in the trash. The finger healed in a few weeks, just as the doctor had said it would. Henry continued to wear a Band-Aid for the next month, long after it was necessary, as a reminder, I suppose, of his great adventure.

CHAPTER 4

....

I Love Cheese
March 2009

I'm looking for a job. I've been talking about looking for work for years, but this time I'm really searching. I put together a fancy-schmancy resume and copied my clips (I used to be a newspaper reporter), and I wrote several cover letters that exude confidence. Unfortunately, I started my quest just before the economy tanked. I haven't gotten a bite, much less a nibble. I'm lucky if I even get a rejection letter. Let me rephrase that: I'm happy when I get a rejection letter. At least someone read my application.

The last time I looked for full-time work was in 1984, when I was young and full of beans and newspapers were thriving. After a short but intense search all over New England, I found a job as a reporter at *The Providence Journal*, where I stayed until my first son was born. I have not held a steady job since, unless you call raising two boys a steady job.

Despite the grim unemployment news, I'm forging ahead. I have spent far too much time at Kinko's, watching a temperamental copy machine spit out my life's work, to give up now. Besides, I have $10 riding on a bet with my sons that I'll have a job before the first pitch of Little League this spring.

My inclination is to go back to what I know: newspaper reporting. I told that to a friend who is still in the business, and he told me that I might as well open a factory that makes buggy whips. Newspapers are firing, not hiring.

Still, I couldn't help but feel nostalgic. I imagined my favorite depressive, Joni Mitchell, wagging her finger and singing from her big yellow taxi: "Don't it always seem to go that you don't know what you've got 'til it's gone." I never thought I would say this, but I miss writing 5,000-word stories about the state's formula for school aid. I miss zoning board meetings. I miss the police log. I miss house fires.

I broadened my search, though it quickly became apparent that I can't do much of anything but string two sentences together—and that's open to debate. Before my job at the *Journal*, I worked for a small newspaper in Connecticut and, before that, I worked as an assistant editor at a skiing magazine and, before that, I worked for the National Kidney Foundation in St. Louis, giving speeches to the Lions Clubs and elementary schools about the "bean-shaped organs that filter your blood" and "Guess what, boys and girls? You can live with one kidney."

With so little experience in any field but journalism, the pressure to draft persuasive cover letters is intense. In one sweet sentence, I have to explain why I'm qualified to work as, say, a "special events coordinator" at a local hospital, even though the only event I've ever organized was my son's 6th birthday at Monster Golf. I have to explain why I can raise money for a university, even though I've never solicited one penny from anyone in my life.

On second read, I realize now that some letters were unintentionally comical: "Please do not be discouraged by my lack of experience with HTML, PowerPoint, Excel, Adobe Acrobat, FileMaker Pro, and Flash," I wrote when I applied for a secretarial job. "I'm a quick study."

Other letters were overwritten—and perhaps a tad overwrought. In one missive to a college, "good writing," "burning desire," and "wet and stormy weather" appeared in the same sentence. Sometimes I think my letters should just get to the point: "I won't bore you with platitudes. I'm desperate for work."

One problem I've encountered in my search is trying to understand the job descriptions, which are written in prose so impenetrable I need a linguist to translate: "Responsible for high-level correspondence in a fast-paced environment." "Calendar management a must." "Ability to engage in a conversation about current growth trends." And this zinger: "Standard operational reporting documentation, i.e., picture taking, recap completion and submittal."

My best chance for a job might be at Whole Foods, the cozy market on Pitman Street, across the street from the house with the yellow coreopsis.

Everybody needs a hideaway, and for the last few years mine has been the store's parking lot. That's me, sitting in the front seat of my silver minivan eating an egg salad sandwich and Kettle barbecue chips and taking swigs from a bottle of bubbly water, saving the best for last: a chocolate truffle from Lake Champlain. It's my 15 minutes of peace.

If I got a job at Whole Foods, or WF, as we call it in our house, I'd like to work in the cheese department. I love cheese. One summer, back in high school, I was wandering around my neighborhood looking for work and came across a soon-to-open cheese shop. The owners were two recent law school graduates who had no intention of practicing law. The future, they said, was in cheese.

At the interview, I confessed that my knowledge of cheese was limited to cellophane-wrapped American, but that I would learn more once I got behind the counter. Instead of offering me employment, they handed me *Quick Guide to Cheese*, a chatty, 100-page book that is still in my possession.

"Go home and study this," said Phil, the more erudite of the two. "Come back tomorrow and tell us what you know."

I memorized as much of the book as I could in one night. The next day, I knew that Gorgonzola is a creamy blue Italian cheese with a taste that ranges from mild to sharp, depending on the age. I knew that Gjetost is a Norwegian cheese that no one likes except Norwegians. I knew that Brillat-Savarin is a deliciously sinful French cheese that should be eaten at room temperature to fully enjoy its taste, and that Manchego is a semi-firm Spanish cheese that pairs nicely with a glass of sherry.

The guys were impressed. I got the job. The shop eventually went belly-up, but I came away with a passion for cheese that has led me to the sample table at WF many times. I should make a "submittal" to my resume: "High School to Present, Cheese Lover."

Fred the Barber
April 2009

The day Fred closed his barbershop I felt a pang of grief, not just for the loss of yet another small business within walking distance of my front steps, but for what I knew I'd soon confront as the mother of two boys: long hair.

Fred knew how to cut hair, and how! He'd start with the

clippers, gently plowing up the nape in three side-by-side paths, and then move to his silvery shears, sharp as a paring knife, and the rest was a sight to behold: A snip here, a snip there, he'd orbit around my son's head with the grace of a maestro, all the while talking, talking about the price of gas or the shenanigans on Smith Street or the long-ago days when you went to the barber to get not only a cut, but a shave.

The end product was always perfect: even sideburns, subtle layering, and, for the boys, a tasteful up-do in front—if they wanted one.

I liked Fred's simplicity. Three wonderfully distressed barber chairs, a thirsty fern in the corner, a stack of yellowed *National Geographics*, and a kid's drawing taped to the wall— wherever. Each boy got a lollipop and then hopped off the Koken to the black-and-white checkered floor littered with wisps and curls—tiny piles of half-moons and springy coils the color of burnt orange, hayseed yellow, slingshot brown.

On the rare occasion when Fred wasn't cutting, he was leaning outside his front door chewing the fat with anyone lucky enough to walk by: the lady in the blush-pink cashmere swinging a shopping bag; the woman who owned the sweet shop down the street; the mailman; the window washer; Judge what's-his-name; me.

I don't know why Fred left. Maybe his rent went up. Maybe his feet hurt. I do know that his departure on that gone-fishing day a few years ago left me with an anxious feeling that waxed and waned amid the distractions of tending to family: What was I thinking about? Oh. Fred's gone. I need to find a new barber.

I approached the task with a determination to find just that, not a stylist, never a stylist. I shuddered to think of placing my sons in the hands of a fetching Felice, who would dab and fluff and then draw from her hip pocket the salon version of a leaf blower: the hair dryer.

I looked for other Candy Land poles in the neighborhood, but never felt fully satisfied with the results. I was looking for a bespectacled man of medium build and sturdy frame with a shock of salt-and-pepper hair and an earnest face that could have landed him a bit part on *The Andy Griffith Show*. I was looking for Fred.

Against my better judgment, I took the boys to Kidz Adventure Cuts, a salon that subscribes to the theory that the only way to keep kids still during a haircut is to anesthetize them with television. A television, usually blasting a Disney movie, is in the waiting area, and if that's not enough, each workstation has a television for a movie or video game. I learned to tolerate the place and always asked for the buzz cut, a kind of self-imposed baldness.

And then the unexpected roared into our lives. H.P. Snow, also known as Harry, decided to let his hair grow. Henry, my 7-year-old, took note of his friend's cascading locks.

"I want hair like Harry," said Henry.

"Short is good," I said. "I can see your face."

"It's my hair," he said. "I can do what I want with my hair."

How could I argue with that? Henry made perfect sense. It was his hair. I was being selfish, but all I could think about was the high maintenance that long hair requires. I thought of tangles, knots, bangs obstructing vision.

Weeks passed. The hair grew, as did Henry's fascination with it. It felt good to have a mop—finally. With a cock of his head, Henry would flick back his bangs or shake his head, like a swimmer fresh from the lake, eager to impress the girl on shore. He was getting his first whiff of vanity and enjoying it.

This transformation into a teenager was charming until I looked in his classroom early one morning and recoiled in horror at the sight of my ragamuffin. He looked disheveled, like a farm boy on a dusty road with a three-legged mutt.

Eventually he warmed to the idea of a cut but always came up with excuses at the last minute: I need pipe cleaners for my science class. My foot hurts, and so does my big toe. One afternoon, I parked the car in front of Super Cuts and urged him to go inside.

"It's my hair," he said, glaring at me through wayward strands.

In time though, even H.P., the arbiter of cool, conceded that Henry needed a cut. I enlisted him to draw up a document. During a sleepover one night, he taped two pieces of blank paper together and wrote up the terms:

Haircut Contract

I, Henry, solemnly swear to get my hair trimmed and styled.

I, Mom, solemnly swear that I will pay H.P. Snow $10 if he encourages this behavior toward Henry.

I, H.P. Snow, solemnly swear to guide Henry in the process of trimming and styling his hair. I will encourage this behavior toward Henry.

Henry
Mom
H.P. Snow

On a Saturday afternoon—183 days after his last cut—Henry crossed the threshold of Super Cuts and instructed the woman on what should stay and go. He lost the mane on his neck but kept the sideburns. His beloved bangs were lifted no higher than his brow.

"I look like a warthog," he said. "I hate it. I'm not taking another cut."

The truth is his super cut was not. It was choppy, incomplete, and hastily executed; it reflected no grand plan. It was not the work of an artist. It was not the work of Fred.

The Bears
May 2009

The graphite smudges were everywhere—on walls, tables, jeans, shirts, fingers, cheeks, noses, lips. A stranger walking into the basement of Central Congregational Church probably thought a priest had missed his mark or a chimney sweep had run amok. Doug, our Master of Ceremonies, had so much gray powder on his face he looked like the Tin Man, with a heart, of course—and a big one at that.

No one bothered to wash off the stuff and, anyway, why would they want to? If you're a Scout, you wear your Hob-E-Lube with pride. It means you did your homework and dabbed the dry lubricant on your axle to make your race car go faster and maybe even finish first on a silvery mountainous track fueled by grit and luck.

"Three, two, one," shouted Doug, and our pinewood derby began with a whoosh.

In these uncertain times I take solace in our Scout

gatherings, where boys of various ages and talents come together to learn how to tie a bowline or lead a game of Simon Says or build a car from a block of wood—all while hanging out with their best buds.

My sons, Peder and Henry, are Bears. Their official designation is Pack 88, Den 3, Netop District, Narragansett Council, Boy Scouts of America. A Bear is what you become after you've been a Wolf and before you become a Webelos, as in We'll Be Loyal Scouts.

There are six boys in our den. I'm den mother. Brian, another parent, is den father. My job is to send out emails alerting parents of our meetings. Brian runs the meetings. He's good at that; he's a third-grade teacher and knows how to captivate a roomful of energetic boys wearing yellow neckerchiefs.

When I raised my delicate hand a few months ago to volunteer, I was a tad nervous. I'm a Brownie and will always be one. And there was the obvious: They're boys and I'm not. Would I be in over my head? And then I remembered I was a tomboy as a kid and that I'm raising two boys and that just last weekend I had six boys in my house on a Sunday afternoon and the worst thing that happened was that someone spit their partially chewed Skittle into the tub.

Our first meeting was good; our second was even better. By the end of our third meeting, I was laughing so hard my jaw hurt.

Me: "Today we're having a presentation on knots."

Cub: "Can we tie each other up?"

"Not today, honey. You're going to learn the half hitch."

"Can I tie my sister up when I get home?"

Cubs need space. The church basement is vast and sparsely decorated with indestructible objects, including a long table that looks like it belongs in the banquet hall of a medieval castle. There's a walk-in fireplace, blocked up, of course, and the bottom half of the Dutch door to the kitchen is locked as a safety measure.

Our pack of 25 boys meets once a month; our den meets twice a month. It's usually a challenge to get my kids to activities. With Scouts, they are out the door before me.

At the beginning sessions we practiced the Cub Scout promise, handshake, motto, salute, and sign: the V-shaped peace sign with arms straight up.

You'd have to be a sad sack not to be moved by the sight of boys bedecked in their crisp blue shirts, neckerchiefs with gold sliders, and baseball-style Cub caps, reciting the Pledge of Allegiance to an American flag.

So far, we've covered a lot of topics in our den, thanks to our parents. We learned about Nikola Tesla, an inventor who made groundbreaking contributions to electricity. We drew superheroes. My husband gave a knot-tying lesson, and Brian brought in bars of Ivory soap that the boys carved into bears.

We toured the Rhode Island Community Food Bank and donated eight bags of groceries which the boys weighed on a massive scale, along with themselves. In the winter, we went ice fishing on a pond at Lincoln Woods and, although no one caught anything, it was fun to skate in sneakers.

Badges are big in Scouts. You could go crazy buying them; our den tries to keep it simple. Our Cubs got a patch for donating food, and Brian handed out palm-size certificates in recognition of soap-carving skills. Earlier this year, we had a ceremony to award red beads to the boys for completing three achievements in the Cub Scout Handbook, my bedtime reading.

"Well done," I said to Peder, Henry, Henry B., Owen, Will and Zack, after a round of handshakes.

One of the highlights of Scouts is the pinewood derby. It's what Thin Mints are to Girl Scouts. It's a festive event that takes months of preparation and a few trips to the hardware store. We cleared all the clutter off our dining room table and then the boys set about carving a car from a block of wood. Cut, sand, paint—each task required skill and patience.

On the night of the event the Cubs were Nervous Nellies. We crowded into the church hall, where the track stood off in a corner protected by a string of black-and-white checkered racing flags. The Cubs weighed their cars and then turned to the tubes of Hob-E-Lube, which they applied with careless pleasure.

Folding chairs were available for seating, but the Cubs chose to kneel by the flags to be near their creations. The cars raced three at a time. The results of each heat flashed on an overhead screen: 219 mph. A new track record! The crowd roared and quieted and then roared again.

I watched my son Henry. His face grew serious as M.C. Doug gently placed Car #21, painted blue with a Cub patch on top, at the starting gate. Henry glanced at me glancing at him and he stuck his hand deep inside his pocket, where I imagine two fingers were crossed hard.

He came in dead last in all his heats. And then the unexpected during the awards ceremony: "Best Cub Scout Theme, Henry Schaefer," Doug announced. He was beaming when he rushed to pick up his ribbon.

Peder's car, an ice cream sandwich, scooped up Most Likely To Be Eaten. Zack's fire truck earned Most Unusual Theme. Owen won first place for speed and got a photo op with the Cubmaster.

No one wanted to go home—and why would they? I never knew the unutterable joy of racing a 5-ounce block of wood with greased axles. It felt wonderful to be alive.

Party Favors
June 2009

I did not go into the darkness. Another parent went into the darkness and he emerged unscathed and, what's better, spiritually reborn—or at least I'd like to think so since he had a smile on his face.

The pitch-black rooms at Lazer Gate are not for fraidy-cats. They are for fearless souls, like the 14 boys at my son Henry's 8th birthday party who assembled in an old mill in Fall River, Massachusetts, to shoot red beams of light at each other amid fog and chaos.

What could be more fun than that?

Even when the economy is in the pits, one activity is recession-proof: the blowout birthday party. It thrives, even in bad times.

True, I could simplify. I could throw a home fest with a no-nonsense sheet cake and a game of marbles. But I've had a pack of boys with sugar highs running around my living room shouting, "Get him," or, worse yet, "Pass the ball." Parents will dole out big bucks to let someone else clean up the mess and save the Delph.

When did this madness begin? When I was a kid, birthday parties were modest affairs that never deteriorated into free-for-alls. We'd trot around our backyard for a while and then my parents would move the sofa against the wall, and we'd sit cross-legged on the rug and watch *Johnny Appleseed*, a 10-minute motion picture on a reel-to-reel borrowed from the Clayton Public Library.

I always wore a party dress, white with cherries embroidered on the front, which never endured a chocolate stain or rip. The boys wore collared shirts. Goodie bags didn't exist. If you were lucky, you got a lollipop with a string handle shaped like a teardrop. Parents did not hang around; it was strictly drop-off, and only for an hour.

Enter the kid birthday party of the 21st century: extravagant, over-the-top events so complicated that some people even hire party planners to organize it, down to the finger bowls filled with Smarties. I have not traveled that road, but I'm ashamed to admit I browsed party-planning websites to come up with ideas for my sons' parties.

After every fest I vow to simplify the next year, but the D.O.B. nears and I always relent because 1.) I like it when my kids run my life; and 2.) I cannot pass up an opportunity to try my luck at arcade games.

The upside of the blowout is that the kids have a blast. Some parents might object to the lavishness, the gambling, the deafening noise, the use of laser tag guns, but the kids enjoy themselves, and so I say: So what?

The birthday parties my husband and I went to and had for our sons when they were toddlers usually evolved into child-safety drills with the occasional embarrassing moment: the bald-headed clown who teased the bald-headed parent not once, but twice. (We're twins. We're twins.) The magician who flubbed the simple card trick. The empty piñata.

All that partying has exposed me to a side of life I never

thought I'd experience. At Regal Reptiles we watched a croc eat a rat—a frozen one, but, really, a rat is a rat. A bullfrog jumped into my lap during a party at the Audubon Society in Bristol. At Battleship Cove in Fall River, Massachusetts, we walked the decks of WWII Navy warships and ate hot dogs in the mess hall.

The yoga party stands out. We did back bends and splits and then all held hands and hummed Om Shanti, Shanti, Shanti. Our treat was whole wheat bread smothered in cashew butter.

At a gymnastic party my boys jumped into a pit of squishy foam balls. They tumbled in a good way at a pee-wee sports fest at the Jewish Community Center. At the archery party in West Warwick they progressed from boys to bowboys in less time than it takes to say flu-flu arrow.

My favorite party place is the Bowling Academy, in East Providence. Henry and my older son Peder have both celebrated there. If I had my way, the Academy would be my only choice. The charming, competent, infectiously peppy teenagers do everything.

You sit in a folding chair on the upper deck while the teens scurry around like doting aunts tending to the guests' every whim. They slice the pizza, pour the pink lemonade, and cut the Academy cake, always light and fluffy, and generously frosted. They even bag the presents to take home.

I tried to persuade Henry to bowl for his 8th, but he refused. He wanted a fresh venue. I suggested taking the kids on a long hike up Cupcake Mountain. He would have none of it. What to do?

My friend Denise beat me to motherhood by a decade. For years, I heard stories about Joey and his birthday parties, including one with laser tag. I remember thinking I'd sooner eat fried liver than throw such a fest for my sons.

Fast forward six years, three months, and 14 days: I am watching Henry's friends enter Lazer Gate's debriefing room to learn the rules of engagement. A sense of panic overcomes me when I see who else is in the room: teenagers, two dozen. I had assumed my son and his friends would have the space to themselves.

My tact and decorum start to fail when the manager informs me that the laser room is open to the public, even during parties: Read the fine print. My heart quickens. One parent from our group joins to chaperone (and play), but, still, I worry. I wonder if it's too late to bolt. The door shuts.

I imagine all the apologies I'll have to make to parents. What was I thinking? Second graders alone in the dark with gun-toting teens twice their size—and dressed in black. I could cry.

Twenty minutes later, the door swings open.

I see them emerge, with sweaty foreheads (exercise!) and smiles.

"That was awesome," says one guest. "Can I go again?"

That night, I call Denise and report the news: Laser tag was a success. She suggests a paintball party next year.

"I'm not doing paintball," I say.

Denise says, "Wanna bet?"

On the Mound
July 2009

He was a kid who just wanted to play ball.

One Saturday afternoon, the Reds were practicing at Tockwotten Field, in Fox Point, and Alex rode up on his bike and asked if could join them. He knew one of the players—they were third-grade classmates at Vartan Gregorian School—so the coaches said sure, and Alex was on the field.

He was spunky, but was he too late? The rosters for the Reds and the four other AAA teams in the Fox Point East Side Little League were full and, anyway, Alex would have to officially register just to get on a waiting list. When he left that day, most people thought they'd never see him again.

But he showed up a week later at the next pre-season practice, this time with a well-oiled glove. Again, he rushed onto the field.

After practice, he stuck around. He followed the Reds a few blocks away to Engineer's Field off Gano Street for the league's opening day ceremonies and posed with his new friends—including my two sons, both Reds—during a team photo with the mayor.

When I heard about Alex from my husband, a coach for the Reds, I pounced. Why not give this 9-year-old a turn at bat?

No one was sure of his last name or where he lived, so our head coach did some detective work and discovered that home was just a few blocks from the field. The weekend before opening day I drove to Alex's apartment building and rang all four doorbells, hoping he would answer.

He didn't. Instead, an older woman poked her head out of a third-floor window, and I cupped my hands around my mouth and shouted up, "I'm here to sign Alex up for Little League."

"Come back in two hours when his mother is home," she

said, and gave me the thumbs-up sign before disappearing inside.

I don't know much about the rules of baseball, and I don't do stats and I only follow the Sox when they're on a winning streak, but I do know this: of all my sons' sports—soccer, hockey, football, tennis—baseball is my favorite.

We started with T-ball on a weedy field next to the Jewish Community Center, progressed to AA with parents pitching, and then graduated to AAA, where the kids pitch from a mound, just like the pros.

If my boys told me they wanted to give up baseball, I'd ask them to take a walk around the block and reconsider, and if that didn't work, I'd beg. Baseball is graceful and brainy, a sport to showcase the talents of one or many. It's a game for plucky kids who thrive on challenge; a visit to the plate offers so many possibilities. Give up soccer, but baseball, never.

I went back to Alex's apartment that afternoon and this time his mother was home, as well as Alex. We talked in the parking lot. She filled out the registration form on the hood of my car while Alex stood by. No guarantees, I told him. He would only get to play if someone dropped out.

Still, he turned to his mother and said, "Mommy, I'm going to play baseball." He was right.

A spot opened up in the division and Alex landed on our team, Lynch and Greenfield Reds.

At our first games Alex struck out a lot and was no cat in the field. It quickly became clear that he was a novice and had never played AA ball, which prepares players for AAA. He didn't know the basics: overrun first; run back on a fly out; if you miss a throw to first and the ball ends up in the dandelions, go fetch it.

What he lacked in experience he made up for in enthusiasm. He came to all the practices, even the ones in the rain. He didn't saunter onto the field, he galloped. Out there he was focused and alert, knees bent, back hunched, a tad jumpy. "Where do you want me to go now, coach?" he'd say after a drill, socking his glove with his balled fist.

One day during practice, the coaches let him pitch. His pitches were strong, but he couldn't control them. He would have to work on that.

What could be more stirring than seeing a child succeed in something he wanted to do but wasn't sure he could: The shy kid who delivers a flawless speech in front of his classmates; the reticent boy who swims the length of the pool and then turns around and does it again; the girl who blocks the puck not once, but twice, to win the championship.

The Reds were behind by two runs (and that's not much in AAA) when the coaches decided to let Alex pitch in Game 3 against The Law. Alex tucked in his #15 jersey and straightened his cap. From the dugout he curled his fingers around the metal gate and said through the wire to his father in the stands, "Daddy, I'm going to pitch."

I stuck my hands in my pockets and crossed my fingers until they ached.

Strike. It was a beauty, fast and on target. Most AAA pitchers just try to get it over the plate. Alex had bigger plans. He wasn't pitching; he was firing the ball from a canon. He was a powerhouse: full body turn; high arm stretch; crossover on follow through. I thought I was seeing the beginning of greatness—or at least I could only hope so.

We won.

Back in the dugout the boys gave Alex high-fives, and I

gave him a hug which he was gracious enough to take, even though, as the mother of boys, I know that embraces in public are prohibited. I asked him later why he chose baseball and his reply revealed what could only be uttered by someone who plays for love: "It's fun."

Years from now, I'll probably get a call from some hot shot reporter for *Sports Illustrated* and she'll pump me for details about Alex and wonder how we found a kid with so much talent: Did you have a scout? Did he get lessons at a pitching school?

No, I'll say. You got it all wrong. Alex found us. We gave him a ball and put him on the pitcher's mound, but Alex moved the mountain.

Alex Morales. Remember that name.

Dr. Ed
August 2009

His name is Edward Iannuccilli, but I have a hunch most people call him Ed, or if they're feeling playful, Dr. Ed. His last name is hard to pronounce, unless you're the kind of person who flings open your shutters on a warm spring day and proclaims in your best sing-song voice, "Che bella giornata," and then takes a sip of espresso from that dollhouse cup you bought in Roma back in '82.

I first exchanged pleasantries with Ed online. He heard an essay I wrote for WRNI's radio series, "This I Believe— Rhode Island," and sent me an email saying he liked the piece: Let's meet for coffee? His name sounded familiar from my newspaper reporting days, and after a session with Google

I discovered he was a former chairman of the board at both Rhode Island Hospital and United Healthcare. Still, I knew I had seen his name elsewhere, beyond the headlines.

Down the street from my house sits one of my favorite hideaways, Books on the Square, a bookshop that manages to be both cozy and airy and is staffed by courteous bibliophiles, including Chris, the dog-dodging mailman in the locally produced movie *Underdog*. Rain, sleet, snow, Chris always says hello when I walk into the shop. Grazie, Chris.

I like to follow our local writers and enjoy fossicking through the stacks of homegrown books when I visit. One day, I came across a memoir by a Rhode Islander and thumbed through the pages.

If you are flummoxed and allow yourself time alone with the willow on the upland ridge, the puzzle will fall into place, and this is what happened with Ed. After that email, I realized that Ed was also Edward the Memoirist, the author of *Growing Up Italian: Grandfather's Fig Tree and Other Stories*, the book I had flipped through weeks before. I wrote back to Ed and told him I would like to meet and that I had seen his book and would now buy his book. We set a date.

My WRNI essay was about homesickness, an ailment I've suffered from since I moved to Rhode Island more than two decades ago. I wrote about my affection for the state, how I'm charmed by its sea glass at Goosewing and buried little necks at Fogland and rope swings on the Pawcatuck River, but also how I'm never quite at home, here, in Rhode Island.

My real home is a leafy suburb of St. Louis, and my memories are of Virginia creeper crawling up our red brick house, sunbaked sidewalks that warmed my bare feet, and the elementary-school monkey bars I climbed across with ease.

Providence is where I live, I wrote, but it's not my home; I'll always be a visitor.

Ed happened to turn on the radio just as my essay began. He had found a kindred spirit. Ed, too, understood that we are among the lucky ones, the ones whose childhood days were filled with great adventures that are sorely missed. If only I could cup my hands around a firefly one more time.

Ed suggested meeting at Starbucks on Wayland Square. "I have white hair," he wrote in his email. "I'll be the one drinking espresso."

The weather did not cooperate. A blizzard made driving treacherous and we decided to reschedule. Then we rescheduled again. I was grateful. It gave me more time to read his book.

Most doctors cannot write. That's a harsh statement, but true. We don't expect them to craft gems; we just want them to keep us alive. As I hunkered down with Ed's book, I discovered that he is the exception. He can decipher a complicated pathology report to gently offer notice—and I want notice, thank you—and he can write sentences that linger after the book is closed, and I have always thought that skill is the mark of a gifted writer.

Consider Ed's description in his book of a man who cleaned rags for a living:

"Joe the Ragman was an unshaven, musty-smelling, gnome-like character who wore a long, gray tattered coat buttoned at the top, and a small-visored, matching hat. His horse-drawn cart was laden with stacks of rags that smelled of the dampness of a cellar. Squeaky wheels carried it down the street. His nasal twang, 'Rrraggs, rrraggs,' gurgled in a voice almost too low to be heard. "Up here, up here," residents responded from their windows. And up the stairs he went, plodding on worn, dirty boots, empty satchel over his shoulder, gathering rags along the way."

So far, Ed has sold 5,000 copies, many more than he expected. He knew he was on to something when 400 people showed up at Caserta Pizzeria, on Federal Hill, for his book release party.

I won't give away details, but I will entice you. The book is a collection of 58 essays about growing up in Providence's Mount Pleasant neighborhood, where Ed and his extended Italian family lived in the 1940s and 1950s. It was a time when kids played sandlot baseball, rode their Rocket Royals all summer long, and put on their bathing suits to run in the rain.

Ed wrote about his three-decker on Wealth Avenue, with his family on the third floor, his grandparents and great-grandfather on the second, and his aunt and her family on the first. He wrote about the well-swept back staircase that he raced up at "top speed," the creaky cellar, where he made a clubhouse out of old coal bins, and the massive cast iron stove with its simmering pot of "gravy," red pasta sauce.

Our meeting took place two months after our exchange of emails. I was nervous. I didn't know what to expect. Doctors can be intimidating. Writers can be aloof. Who would I get? I got a friendly and funny person who knew half the people at Starbucks on Angell Street, even though he lives in Bristol. I got a man with a zest for life, a man on his second wind.

Ed's journey to writing has been remarkable. Eight years ago, he submitted an essay about his grandfather to *The Providence Journal*, which published the piece on the op-ed page. That success gave him the confidence to write the essays that now appear in his book.

Ed and I talked for hours about his family (his wife, Diane, is his editor), his career (he is a gastroenterologist and was the first appointed clinical professor at Brown University's medical school), the presentations he gives about the state's Italian community, and his plans to write a sequel, focusing this time on his high school and college years.

I told Ed that my favorite essay is about his grandfather's ritual of burying his fig tree every fall to preserve it for spring. Vincenzo Troiano would dig a ditch beside the tree, wrap cloth around the trunk, pull the tree into the earth and then cover the grave with dirt, leaves, and, finally, wooden boards.

"Winter came, and daily, as I sat at the window, I looked down into the snow-covered garden, imagining that the hump was a sleeping elephant," Ed wrote. "But it was grandfather's treasure."

Now our state has another treasure. *Grandfather's Fig Tree* is 137 pages long. Read it slowly. You will miss it when it's over.

The Shrine

September 2009

We live up the street from the Humboldt Fire Station, so I'm used to hearing sirens at all hours of the day and night, and this familiarity has lulled me into a shameful indifference that, I suppose, comes with city living. When we moved into our house eight years ago, I'd rush to the window to investigate the wailing; now I barely lift my head.

One night in June, I heard the sirens and figured that the trucks were responding to something harmless, like a burning pot on a stove. I don't know why I settled on a kitchen fire, but

I did, and I was wrong. The awful news was in the morning paper.

There had been a motorcycle accident at the corner of Irving and Arlington Avenues and a man had died. The paper withheld the man's name—that would come later—but the story did say that he was speeding and not wearing a helmet.

I had two thoughts: death can be swift, and newspapers can be harsh. Why pass judgment on his last day? We all do reckless things. I dare anyone to come forward who has not allowed the current to carry him beyond the jetty to the still and steel-gray part of the ocean where there are no whitecaps.

I finished the article and didn't think about the man until later in the day when I drove up the street to the spot and saw a woman holding something in her arms the way I'd hold a baby—close to the chest.

She was tall and thin, and her brown hair hung down her back, loose and untangled. She was standing on the curb, and I slowed to let her pass, but she tilted her head and smiled as if to say, you go first. Now I wish that I had stopped. She was the one who probably got the call and had been up all night, picturing him as he was, the last time. What did he say? Love you, and then a walk down the gravel driveway.

As I drove off, I looked in my rearview mirror and watched as she studied the orange words the police had sprayed on the black asphalt: "BRUSH," "JACKET," "LSHOE." I saw her bend down by the stone wall around the playing fields at Brown University and turn the corner for home.

We live mostly quiet lives on the East Side. Our streets are clean, our lawns free of cheatgrass. We have graffiti, fender benders, and break-ins, but nothing too serious. The break-ins usually occur when no one is home, which is the way I like it.

Sometimes I think I should just tape a note to the door when I leave: Take the television; I'm sick of it.

It felt strange to know a man had died two blocks away and that I was trying to get my kids to brush their teeth while he was dying on the street.

The next day, I drove by the spot again and, this time, I parked and got out and looked at the ground. I realized that the woman I had seen the previous day had been carrying flowers, and now they were in a bouquet on the grass: pink and yellow sweetheart roses. Fresh wildflowers exploded hat-trick style from a canning jar filled with water.

Amid nature's bounty were hints of the man's life: an airplane-size bottle of Jack Daniels, empty; a blue 2010 Ford Mustang GT matchbox car; a shiny chrome axle nut that said Harley Davidson; and a medal with the inscription: Harley Davidson Festival, The Celebration, 1903-2003, Kansas City. A man who rides from Rhode Island to the Heartland on his Harley, I thought, loves his bike—and country.

Driving down the highway we glimpse other people's lives and those of us who like to daydream tend to re-create without much regard for the truth: a man named Rego tends to the grape arbor on the hilltop; that ice-cream shack will close, for good, by summer's end; the tall fence hides a tire swing.

And then there are the memorials, those simple wooden crosses, painted white, festooned with beads and plastic carnations, blue, always blue. What do people say, I wonder, as they pound the cross into the lousy dirt? You are somebody.

After my inspection that day, I left town for a week and expected someone to remove the site while I was gone. To my surprise, the memorial was not only there when I got back, it was bigger. A foot-high Celtic cross initialed with "JC" and cut from what looked like the fender of a motorcycle was bolted to the stone wall. A cigar and Irish flag poked out from behind the cross like souvenirs on a cluttered curio shelf.

There were three framed photos of the man, and he had a name or, at least, a nickname: Big Jon. He had pale reddish hair and his long beard, the same color as his hair, cascaded over his belly like a roll of cotton candy. He wore his bandana as a pirate would, above the ears and knotted in back. His eyes were blue.

"Brother, we will miss you," a note said. A banner twisted through the flowers like a vine on a spring-rain run. It said in gold letters: BROTHER.

The follow-up article in the paper gave Big Jon a name—Jonathan M. Conway, of Riverside, in East Providence—but provided no intimate details, apart from his age: a very young 31.

The story did, however, return to the speeding issue, saying the police believe he might have been traveling more than 60 miles per hour on Arlington when he was thrown from his motorcycle and his body crashed into a car driving on the road. There were witnesses and he left evidence: a 168-foot skid mark.

When I read this, I did not judge. I thought, *How long does it take to skid 168 feet? How many seconds? What was he thinking in those final terrifying moments?* No. Oh my God. Our Father who....

Months have passed and the memorial is still there, rained on, but still there. Thieves must know stealing from the dead brings consequences outside the law. Once I saw a man let his dog sniff at the flowers, now wilted and brittle, and felt certain he would pay for this indiscretion, maybe with a mysterious rash.

My boys have driven by the memorial many times, and once they asked to see it up close, and I took them. My son Henry, who is 8, asked if Big Jon was buried in the stone wall, behind the silver cross. I said no, that he's probably buried somewhere else. "Then why are all these things here?" he asked.

I told him the truth.

This is Jonathan Conway's resting place, and his friends want to make sure we know.

Junk
October 2009

Halloween is here, and this is a good time to reveal all those skeletons rattling around in our closets. I have a few secrets, but one in particular makes me so uncomfortable I am tempted to write under a pen name.

I shall not. We have all sinned with a Milky Way or three, especially during this sweetest of holidays.

My scary story begins long ago in my kitchen.

A friend stopped by and made the mistake of opening a kitchen cabinet that is off limits to everyone in our house except my husband. Without looking up, she closed it quickly, averting her eyes from mine, as if she had spotted a mouse.

For a moment, I considered consoling her about the discovery, only to keep her from exposing me to the neighbors, but the look of shock and disapproval on her face was enough to kill a talk.

And anyway, this was a parent who had scolded her child in public for eating an AirHead that flew out of a busted piñata during my son's 4th birthday party. She would not understand my husband's affection for Little Debbie cupcakes.

He wasn't always that way. When we were dating, he wooed me with the gourmet meals he had refined during his years as a bachelor: grilled pork chops with capers, chicken cutlets meunière, chicken curry in a hurry with sour cream.

He knew where to buy the best fruit, vegetables, fish, and bread. He enjoyed wandering the aisles of Eastside Marketplace looking for condiments with un accent aigu, and he could cook for twelve people and, at the same time, carry on a decent conversation about whether it's easier to reduce sail on a cutter or a sloop. He owned a slotted spoon.

I, on the other hand, stunned him with my ineptness in the kitchen. My culinary repertoire included a limp Caesar salad and spaghetti, no sauce, just butter and a sprinkle of bottled Parmesan. Single until 40, I never took to cooking the way my husband did when he also was unmarried and without children.

I would eat a box of kumquats for dinner. My refrigerator held only milk, a wedge of cheese, a carton of orange juice, and a box of All-Bran. Why did I need more? I was single, a newswoman, a workaholic.

Although my diet was colorless, a chip never crossed my lips. I didn't feel any righteous opposition to junk food; I simply had no taste for it. A Pringle was about as appealing to me as a mayonnaise sandwich on Wonder Bread.

In the beginning, my husband shared my indifference to junk food, which I appreciated since he not only cooked our meals but also did the grocery shopping. Vanilla ice cream was as junky as he got. Grateful for his high nutritional standards and culinary skills, I happily ceded the kitchen to him.

It became his domain, the only room in the house in which he wielded absolute power.

It started with Fritos. I distinctly remember watching him unpack the groceries on a crisp fall day—one of those Miracle-Whip days when the sky is a vast blue with the occasional dollop of white—and place the non-perishables in a patch of sun on the kitchen table.

"What's this?" I said, holding up a slick yellow bag.

He put the bag on top of the refrigerator, out of reach but not out of sight, of our two boys, then ages 6 and 7, who spotted it and a step ladder and were soon eating the bag's contents.

Horrified, I spoke of how junk food ravages the teeth and asked my husband not to bring it home. A week later, he showed up with Cheetos. What's worse, he served them in our French mise en place bowls as an appetizer before dinner.

"Look at their lips," I said, frightened by the electric-orange powder that coated the boys' mouths and lingered even after a vigorous face-washing.

I used another tactic: compassion. Is there any medical reason behind your craving for Chex Mix? Nope, my husband said. He wanted something to munch on at night while he watched the game. I knew then that I had about as good a chance of banning junk food as I did at getting my boys to swear off dustups.

I had to think of another way to get rid of the stuff.

A spring day. The scene unfolds as it always does—in his kitchen. My husband comes home from the market with the good and the bad. He unpacks everything: the milk, the cheese, the butter, the Ruffles. I am delighted we are having his celebrated chili for dinner. I thank him for cooking.

"Now go play catch with the boys," I say, flashing a Little Debbie-like, sweet, dimpled smile.

Alone, I hide the junk food on the top shelf behind the ho-hum boxes of wagon wheels, bow ties, and ziti. My boys do not ask for what they cannot see. But at night my husband finds the stash and indulges.

Morning comes, and I check the hiding spot for bags with his imprimatur—opened, wrinkled, rolled up. Far too much is left.

Good riddance, I say.

The sticky cotton balls of Fiddle Faddle, the corrugated metal roofs of Sun Chips, the arthritic finger bones of Cheetos—all dumped in the trash by me, except for a few pitiful strays at the bottom of each bag to conceal my deceit.

That night, my husband says, "Where did all the Cheetos go?"

I say, "I ate them."

Letting Go
November 2009

Two blocks. That's how far it is from our house to the convenience store on Lloyd Avenue. I know this because my son, who is 9, asked me if he could ride his bike there to get a Del's lemonade, and I said, "No, not yet," and then I went outside my house to the corner a few steps away and counted.

Elmgrove to University. University to Lloyd. Only three streets to cross. For my son that's like biking to California, a freedom ride that tests his independence and ability to travel over cracks and bumps alone, unsupervised, far away from a hovering parent.

Why can't I just say, Yes.

When I was a girl, I roamed. I roamed up and down the sidewalks of my neighborhood for hours, wandering barefoot through fenceless backyards to find friends or climb a tree, maybe that one at the Tallys' with the low branches that stretched out like the withered arms of an old woman. I'd stop at Peggy's to play with her frizzy-haired trolls and then walk a few steps to Gibby's house to build castles in his giant sand box.

It might sound as though I spent my childhood in the country, but I did not. I lived in a suburb of St. Louis like the East Side, with sidewalks and ancient trees and small shops where I could buy penny candy or a root beer float or a tortoise shell barrette for my hair. The difference was that I grew up when children were expected to explore the world by themselves and stay out until the sun went down—and what joys and mysteries we encountered.

The woodland near our house on Oakley Drive was really a tangle of trees, but for a tomboy unruffled by bloody knees it was a wonderfully menacing Sherwood, where I could get lost amid the curvy vines and towering maples that blocked the sun and made the forest as dark as a cellar. What was in the middle? I never found out. I didn't have the courage to go that far.

I remember sitting in the V of a tree branch somewhere on our block, spying on my friends like a sailor on watch, hidden by a canopy of leaves that I'd pluck off and let spin to the ground. My favorite solitary endeavor involved the black metal pole in our backyard that stood eight feet high next to a wooden fence low enough for me to mount without help.

I'd climb atop the fence and cup my hands around the upper part of the pole—hollow and curved at the top—and whisper secrets into the opening: *Susie Ouellette is my best friend. I love barbecue potato chips. My favorite color is green.* The pole was an old clothesline; to me, it was a gatherer of secrets.

The East Side is relatively safe. In some ways we live in a bubble, and the ills that plague many communities, violent crime, poverty, urban decay, can sometimes seem distant. I remind myself daily that I am lucky to live here. Still, I worry about a child's short trip to a neighborhood market, and from what I can tell, I'm not alone. Other parents feel anxious as well.

I think hard about two things: cars and the unspeakable.

What parent has not been tempted to hurl a rotten egg at a driver racing through our streets, oblivious to stop signs and crosswalks and the routinely violated speed limit? I have never seen a police officer give out a speeding ticket on the East Side. Speeders speed because they know they can get away with it.

We have no lack of reckless drivers on our street, Irving Avenue. Our stretch begins on Arlington at the stone wall, passes over Taber by the lemon-colored Victorian, and then cascades down a gentle hill before intersecting Elmgrove. Pitch a fastball from Elmgrove and you will hit our house. Our street is wide, designed that way a century ago, I am told, to allow the horse-drawn milk trucks to turn around with ease.

You try to learn as much as you can about a house before you buy it and lug all your stuff there, but it's impossible to know everything. When we moved in years ago, I did not know that wide streets appeal to truck drivers who see open space and heavy foot the pedal. I did not know that Irving is a cut-through to Blackstone Boulevard. I did not know that teenagers like to speed down Elmgrove, take a sharp left onto Irving and accelerate to the riverbank.

A few years ago, I asked the city for a four-way stop at the corner of Irving and Elmgrove. I circulated a petition among neighbors and submitted it, with signatures, to the City Council's public safety committee. I attended a committee hearing to pitch my case. The committee approved my request and a few weeks later the full council gave its blessing.

Time passed and nothing happened. I called the city traffic engineer. An assistant answered. The request had been struck down by the traffic department. Stop signs, the assistant exclaimed, do not slow cars. Really? I felt both angry and frustrated, which might explain that very naughty word I blurted out. It soon became clear that the city was not on my side in trying to make the roads safer for kids playing—and so I worry.

My other concern is the hardest to shake: abduction of children. There is virtually no chance of that happening here. But there is also little chance of my plane going down, and I still get the jitters. The reality is that the number of abductions in the United States is no more than it was 20 years ago. What's different is that the horrific details of these gruesome acts are broadcast day and night by the media until parents are paralyzed with fear.

All this coddling is bound to influence children—and not in a good way. Imagination can't blossom and thrive when parents are always directing the show, intervening so much there is no room left for spontaneity or creativity or mistakes that can be self-corrected. I doubt I would have felt uninhibited enough to talk to a pole if my mother had been on the fence with me, eavesdropping.

This fall, my son and I went biking in Swan Point Cemetery. We had the place to ourselves. The sky was blue, the sun was strong, and the cool breeze felt good against my arms. Peder led the way, biking past the pines and faded headstones with old-fashioned names like Phinney and Ida, and I felt connected to him and nature in a way that made me happy. And then my heart half-broke. "I feel so free," he shouted. He's been on this Earth for nine years and that was the first time I had ever heard him rejoice in liberty and risk.

I thought to myself that if he races ahead and disappears, I'll be tempted to call him back, but I won't. I'll let him go.

Keep Throwin', Boys
December 2009

The holiday season is here, and at the top of my 8-year-old son's list is a yo-yo or, more specifically, the Legacy. If you know anything about yo-yos, you know that the Legacy—the latest sensation among the yo-yo crowd—is great for grinds and long spins, dead smooth, and way better than the Crucial Cream, which, to be honest, is far too advanced for any regular use.

I'm happy to put the Legacy under the tree for Henry.

I love my kids, and I love yo-yos.

If you're searching for a toy that exudes goodness, look to a yo-yo. It is simple, small enough to fit in the front pocket of a pair of jeans. It is humble—a spool connected to a string. And it is smart. In the right hands, a yo-yo can perform as well as a high-wire acrobat in Cirque du Soleil or a Westie chasing a rat.

When my son is yo-yoing, doing, say, the Jamaican Flag, I feel completely at peace with my decision to become a parent. There he is in his baggy jeans and baseball cap tilted slightly to the right, twirling and talking, looking boyish and wonderous, the freckle-faced kid on his way to the pond to skip rocks.

Henry: "Mom, do you want to see my new trick?"

Me: "Sure."

"It's the Trapeze Replay."

Flip. Mount. Bounce.

"Where did you learn that?"

"I invented it."

It all started with the Duncan Butterfly. Henry's friend, Zack, spotted the yo-yo at Shades Plus on Thayer Street and persuaded his mother Gayle to buy it. Zack discovered that he not only enjoyed yo-yoing but was also good at it. The Butterfly accompanied Zack on a visit to our house and, in less time than it takes to do the Dizzy Baby, Henry was hooked as well.

The yo-yo is simple-looking, but far from simple-minded. Early versions of yo-yos appeared in China, the Philippines, and ancient Greece. Yo-yos arrived in France in the 18th century and took off in the United States in the 1920s when Donald F. Duncan created a slip-string that enabled the toy to sleep—a necessity for advanced tricks.

If you think the yo-yo is easy to master, you are mistaken. Try doing the Brain Twister 16 times in a row while chatting away about the words you got wrong on your spelling test and whether footballs are made of pigskin or calfskin.

We had some histrionics in the beginning, but eventually Henry figured it out. Yo-yos are for kids who climb to the second branch. I applaud my son for his persistence, a crucial character trait of any yo-yo enthusiast.

Yo-yoing also requires a skill that is underrated in our technology-driven culture: the ability to take things apart and put them back together. Yo-yo fans are tinkerers from way back.

Henry has been disassembling toys since he was a toddler. Our house is cluttered with the detritus of his life—wires from old toys, the battery box of a pencil sharpener, the chassis of a Tonka truck, and, of course, the components of yo-yos. Halved spools, o-rings, axles, ball bearings, and enough string for a mop are scattered throughout the house and picked up when the urge hits to reassemble a better, faster yo-yo.

Zack is especially adept at untying knots in yo-yo strings. He is also good at untangling a fishing line. I suspect he'll be a neurosurgeon when he grows up. Henry's strength is fiddling with some tiny thing in the middle of the yo-yo to make it sleep longer. I'm thinking theoretical physicist.

People with a passion for yo-yos are called "yo-yoists." We always have a bunch of yo-yoists in our house. Usually the boys will retire to the television room upstairs and pop in an instructional video starring Outch, a fabulous yo-yoist whose real name is Brett Outchcunis. I'm crazy about Outch. He doesn't have tattoos and he seems kind and well-mannered, the sort of fellow who would say, "Thank you, Mrs. Rau, for these delicious peas."

I once asked Henry, "Why yo-yos?"

"If you had a hobby chewing bubble gum, would you stop? No," he replied. "It's the same thing with yo-yos."

If your child wants to get started on yo-yoing, scrap the rule about no computers and check out Yomega.com. Better yet, go to the factory in Fall River, Massachusetts. Call Zack's mom if you want directions. She's been to the factory so many times she keeps the route on her BlackBerry. Concerns about liability prohibit tours, but you can call ahead and have your pick of, say, the state yo-yo, Rhody-O, ready for you at the front desk.

At the factory, Zack bought a black shoulder bag that holds 24 yo-yos and still has room in a zipper pocket for homework and a pizza strip. This summer, Henry bought the Maverick at the factory and got a quick tour of the corporate office; he even shook hands with the owner, Mr. Amaral, a gregarious man who practiced law before getting into the yo-yo business.

Just to warn you, yo-yos are addictive and often become another appendage of the true yo-yoist. Those two boys you saw doing two-handed loops in the movie theater at the Providence Place mall were Zack and Henry. The yo-yo that broke apart mid-air and went soaring over the allo mutter at Whole Foods had Henry's name all over it. And that kid in the navy shorts on YouTube standing in front of the Eiffel Tower doing the Eiffel Tower was Zack.

The holidays are still with us, and Henry is already thinking about his birthday in March. He's been browsing the internet to narrow down his choices.

"I'm thinking I either want the XConvict or the Mini Motu or the Mighty Three."

"Mighty Three?" I said.

"Flea. Flea," he said.

"Why do they call it that?" I said.

"It's small, small," he said. "Get it. Big as a quarter."

Got it. Keep throwin', boys.

CHAPTER 5

....

Cry for the Trees
February 2010

I was trying to read a book the other day but couldn't. It was too noisy—outside my house, not inside. That awful grinding sound was back again. Another tree was coming down, this one a lush pine that rose above the rooftops and made my view from the bedroom window more pleasant.

The racket was impossible to ignore, so I left the house and stayed out until the execution was over. On my way home, I tried not to look because I knew if I did, it would put me in a foul mood, and I have two sons to raise. Of course, I did look, just as I pulled into the driveway, and I saw what I always see after the fall: a strange vacant space.

Tree-removal trucks are all over the East Side, all the time, except during a blizzard—maybe. We keep Bartlett and North Eastern and American and all the other arborists in business. Just on my street alone, in the last few months we've lost five trees, ones that appeared to be healthy. Their leaves were green—that should count for something.

I love trees. I'd much rather plant a tree in my yard than a tulip. Trees improve the air, moderate the climate, conserve water, and shelter wildlife. They are beautiful, even the scraggly ones, and they give us privacy. We live on top of each other on the East Side. The good tree can block your neighbor's bathroom light.

City living is hard enough for humans, never mind a tree, forced daily to contend with telephone wires and fussy home-owners and heartless trash trucks, which carelessly snap off branches and then disappear without administering First Aid.

Trees do their best to live with us and our modern-day neuroses—and you've got to admire them for that. They hang in there like the old man limping down the aisle at the market searching for a jar of hot mustard.

One of my favorite trees is a withered-looking something-or-other a few steps from my house. I lie on the sofa in my living room and stare at the tree for a moment of peace. If the Hindu goddess Durga, protector of the universe, were a tree, she would be this tree, with her curvy limbs waving us closer.

I thought the tree was an eyesore, until my neighbor Tom revealed his fondness for it and said he would be sorry to see it go.

Let her rest.

I did.

Remember that goofy question Barbara Walters asked Katharine Hepburn during an interview years ago: "If you were a tree, what kind of tree would you be?" Walters was widely lampooned, but I thought it was a good question. Are you a sturdy pin oak or a dolled-up Kousa? A tender Mimosa or a scrappy swamp maple? For the record, Hepburn said she'd like to be an oak. No surprise there. She seemed oakish: strong-limbed, enduring, and tough.

I grew up on a street named Oakley Drive (for the oaks) in a neighborhood called Wydown Forest (for the forest). Trees ran the show, not the homeowners. Our house was built between two mighty oaks whose leafy branches cooled us in sticky St. Louis summers.

I remember lying on the grass in the backyard, looking up at the leaves shimmering in the sun, tracing the meandering branches, first in our yard and then to the Ellstons' and finally over to the Fords' next door. You could get lost in those leaves, and I did. After summer passed, they shook free, and we made big piles and jumped.

If a tree is dead, it should come down, but even then, it's painful. During a visit to St. Louis last summer, it was obvious that the oak in front would have to go. The branches were bare in July. Before leaving I took a long look at the massive trunk, so close to the house I could swing open our casement window and touch the bark.

It was late afternoon, and the soft light made the trunk look gray, like a sullen sky hastily sketched by a kid with a charcoal pencil. The oak was as familiar to me as the house's black shutters or flagstone steps. I knew I would miss it. How could I not?

You don't want a tree busting through your roof during a nor'easter. But if a tree is alive, it should be allowed to run its course. Some people don't feel that way. It seems at every turn on the East Side there's a stump—headless, limbless, just enough of the trunk left to stir regret. Is there such a thing as cutter's remorse?

What about tree rights? Where are the lawyers?

I've never asked anyone why they are cutting. It's their property after all, and Rhode Island is the state of the Independent Man. Usually I keep my mouth shut and stew about it and imagine that I'm living on a farm in Maine surrounded by woody specimens that topple only when they can't hold on any longer.

This winter, I looked out my window and discovered arborists cutting branches off pines to install a new roof on a house. I figured only wisps would disappear. The trees were butchered, cut to the trunk. The delightful mess of branches is gone; now I see floodlights two blocks away. Maybe I should wave: Can I borrow some ketchup?

I still miss the hemlocks. I don't remember how many there were in front of Carol's house on the corner, but I do remember that they were tall and feathery, limber enough to shift with the wind.

The woolly adelgid, an aphid-like insect that gets its name from its white appearance, is killing hemlocks throughout the eastern United States. Scientists are trying to save the trees, without much success. The insect sucks sap from the young twigs and the needles dry out and drop, and eventually the tree dies. To find a stand of healthy hemlocks is an occasion to rejoice.

Carol doted on her trees, spraying them yearly to keep the bugs at bay. I once walked through her house, and it was clear that that she had spent decades creating a sanctuary. Every window had a shade of green foliage. A few years ago, she sold her house, and the new owners cut down the hemlocks, every last one.

On a fall day not long ago, I saw Carol pull up in her car to look at her new, old house, and I wondered if she missed her trees. She sat there for a while and then drove off, and I thought to myself that she'll probably avoid this road from now on. She'll find another way to get home.

My Box
March 2010

When I came back to the old house the porch was gone. The carpenter had pulled it up with a crowbar and the busted-up lattice and floorboards sat in a pile next to the lilac.

A century of living, and now it was over. To get one last look, I got down on my knees and sifted through the porch's underbelly of bad dirt and soggy leaves.

I found an old glass medicine bottle, a clothespin, a hand-carved statue of the Virgin Mary, and a 1910 penny cut the way they used to make coins—thick and heavy.

I found a wingless wooden airplane with a red cross painted on its side, a blue metal car missing its front wheels, a rusty pop gun, and a yellow marble—toys that a kid in knickers probably dropped through a hole, for the heck of it.

The haul was better than I'd expected, treasures uncovered during renovations at my mother-in-law's house on the East Side. I dusted off the booty and took it home to add to my collection.

My things are small. They fit in a straw box. I keep the box in the bottom drawer of my dresser. The only other person who knows this is my son Henry, who is 8. He likes it when I bring the box out and explain what the items are and where they came from and why I have them.

"You can have everything in here when you grow up," I say.

"Can I have the box, too?" he says.

I once read a story about a woman who said her books were a map of her life and that she would never get rid of them. Richard Wright's *Black Boy* in high school. Ayn Rand's *The Fountainhead* in college. Raymond Carver's short stories in the struggling years. Elizabeth Strout's *Olive Kitteridge* in mid-life, and, near the end, anything by William Maxwell.

I, too, cherish my books, but they are not essential. If they went up in smoke, I would survive. And anyway, isn't a book-shelf just a vanity or, as the poet Billy Collins says, "an elaborate announcement of one's literary credentials." Does the world really need to know you read *One Man's Meat*?

When the fire alarm rings in my house, I'm rushing to my bottom drawer. The things in my box tell my history; without them, my memories would be cloudy and, in some cases, simply lost. My things remind me of where I was, back then.

I've always liked small things.

When I was a kid growing up in St. Louis, I decorated my shelf with knickknacks I bought with babysitting money.

A buck in my pocket, and I was ready for a trip, alone and on foot, to Famous-Barr, where down the escalator I went to the bargain basement searching for something cheap, like the finger-high glass bottle shaped like a goldfish or the yellow lamb pulling an ox cart, which I still have—in my box.

My hobby continued in college—I still own the tattered brown leather gloves from a semester abroad in Florence—and got serious when I started working as a newspaper reporter, a job that paid so poorly I could barely afford new shoes.

I still bought things, but they cost pennies—the bird whistle from Chinatown, the flip card of Alice's cat from a bookstore on North Main Street, the crescent-shaped moon molded from melted crayons, the set of Jacks, whose red rub-ber ball and six-pointed jacks reminded me of the bounce-and-pick-up game I played with my girlhood neighbor and babysitter, Mary Mabrey.

Eventually, I discovered found objects—castoffs on a street

corner or a sandy beach or a rickety dock. I went through an especially productive period when I worked as a reporter on a series called "Water's Edge," for which I roamed Rhode Island's beaches looking for stories. I left each interview with at least one memento.

For years, I displayed my stuff on a wooden spice rack in my kitchen; then I moved to a new place, with a new beginning, and everything went into the straw box. Each item has a story that only I know. If I were to leave this Earth today, my stuff would become a meaningless pile of junk.

A catalog is in order.

The tiny pitcher. When I arrived in Providence, I lived in a studio apartment on Gano Street. My neighbor across the hall was Angela, a vivacious woman in her 80s who liked cats. We became good friends. She had a stroke, and when I cleaned her apartment, I found the tiny pitcher I had given her as a present. My name was on the bottom. "Liz" she wrote in her sinewy scrawl. I knew Angela would never make it back home, and so I carried it away with me.

The dog. I was walking to the Gano Street apartment one day and spotted a piece of paper on the sidewalk. It was a pen drawing of a dog, a mix between a dachshund and an Australian shepherd. Masterful is an understatement. On the back was the artist's name, Alan Tuan. I framed it.

Sea glass. Emerald green, pale blue, fire-licking amber—all gems with uneven edges polished by the water and sand. I was walking on the shoreline at Goosewing Beach, in Little Compton, picking up sea glass by the handful. I had never seen so much at once. I put them in my beach hat and took them home.

The pillow.

"What's this?" says Henry, rummaging through my box. "Did I sleep on this when I was a baby?"

I could tell the truth—*No, this is a pin cushion a friend made for me years ago*—but I don't.

I wouldn't dream of it.

The Block
April 2010

It was a Saturday night ritual: climb into the minivan and head down to the corner Blockbuster for a movie. After some debate, usually around a pinball machine that spit out gumballs, the boys would make their selection.

The Pacific, Mall Cop, Spy Kids, Space Monkeys—they all made it home and into the DVD player, supplying an evening of mindless pleasure sorely needed after a school week packed with long division.

Now that weekly trip is a memory.

My Blockbuster has closed its doors.

I know it was a chain, but this Blockbuster had a mom-and-pop quality that made it one of my favorite hangouts on the East Side. I loved searching through the stacks, reading the case covers of films I wanted to see but knew I never would. Cliff Notes for the movie-deprived.

My boys visited the place when they were toddlers, little guys with big appetites for any movie that involved fire engines, talking trains, or Macks with fat wheels that dug big holes.

How many times did we rent *Monster Trucks*?

Matt might know. He was the soft-spoken guy with the

spiked black hair who worked behind the counter and was always helpful, a kind of roving, in-house movie critic who could tell you whether a kid flick was good, bad, or ugly. My boys trusted his judgment completely.

The scene:

Saturday night, and the Norwegian meatballs are gone. "M-O-V-I-E," my son Henry says. "Block, guys?" I ask, and off we go. Matt is by the door checking in movies, when my boys stroll in and march through that beeper arch as if they don't have a care in the world, and they don't. It's movie night. Henry takes out his yo-yo.

"What's new on the horizon?" asks Peder, and Matt takes the boys back to the new stuff and pulls *Alvin and the Chipmunks* off the stacks. Peder reads the summary and says this will do and then Henry, still yo-yoing, disagrees and says he wants to keep looking because he's already seen Alvin three times—two times with Oren, one time with Yaseen. Matt offers another, then another, a Steady Eddie to Crazy Jacks.

Change is not good. If everything stayed the same, always, I would be content and calm. I'm the kind of person who misses the creaky screen doors that slapped shut at markets (never grocery stores), where you knew the blue-haired lady at the cash register and the butcher; his name was Carl. I mourn the loss of beauty salons, where the beauticians (never stylists) wore crisp white uniforms and sensible shoes, and you had two options, short or long.

In my two decades on the East Side, I've seen so many places and people come and go, I'm fairly dizzy with loss.

Let me sit down.

Cheeseburger, fries, an Awful Awful and, to distract them until the meal arrived, a package of oyster crackers; nary a day passes without wistfully remembering my Newport Creamery on Angell Street, the restaurant of choice for those of us with kids whose table manners were worse than food-fighting chimps.

The food was good and cheap, and you could see the cook (never chef) customize your burger to the happy side of medium.

Who can forget the maze of books at the College Hill Bookstore, messy and cramped the way bookshops should be, but with enough space to hide in a corner—that spot near the rear door that led to an office, up or down: I can't remember, it was so long ago. The patrons of College Hill devoured their books and appreciated them and, I suspect, a latte never passed their lips, only coffee, black, please.

An upscale clothing store just opened at Wayland Square. The clothes are chic, but let me be frank: I don't understand them. Call me plain-Jane, but I still miss the Gap on Thayer. I could buy jeans, a scoop-neck shirt, a belt, a pair of socks—all in one glorious 30-minute trip. The clothes were accessible, devoid of the artifice you might find in more upscale shops. A lace cuff is pretty, but you can't roll up your sleeve.

I panic when I think of all the small businesses on the East Side that could close if we stopped visiting them—Books on the Square, Wayland Square Bakery, Hope Street Pizza, Eastside Mart, the convenience store on Lloyd where Lily, the owner's toddler daughter, greets you at the door with her dad's cell phone, and the cleaners on Elmgrove Avenue, Green and Cleaner, where David, an employee, exhibits his paintings of lush fruit.

The Block, I suspect, fell prey to Netflix, the online company that allows you to rent a movie without leaving the house.

I'm a homebody and appreciate sofa service, but it's important to get out now and then, and therein lies my reason for missing the Block, besides, of course, the conviviality of the staff, which also included the manager, Michael, whose low-pitched, patrician voice reminded me of the droll theater critic Addison DeWitt in *All About Eve*.

The placard said, "Everything Must Go," and I thought many times about stopping by to say so long, but I couldn't bring myself to do it. I heard from friends that the inventory was weak, and all I could think about were people descending on the place for a deal (*The Sandlot*—a buck), lacking any remembrance of nights past spent searching for a two-hour diversion from life's improbabilities.

The Block is gone.

Long live The Block.

Yousef and Me
May 2010

Writing is a solitary pursuit. It's just you and the computer screen, often blank or sparsely populated, which makes the experience even lonelier. When you get something going it can be exhilarating, but the road there can be long.

With the exception of the reclusive writer J.D. Salinger, who reputedly wrote only for his own pleasure in the last fifty years of his life, most writers write to an audience. These people are called readers, a diverse bunch that could include everyone from the barber to the retired judge who orders the same breakfast every morning at the diner: eggs, over-easy, and dry toast.

Every now and then, I hear from my readers, usually by email. I'd like to thank them—all three. My sincerest thanks, however, go to my friend Yousef.

The other day, I was lying on the grass at a playground—trying to get some shut eye—when Yousef, who had just crawled off the monkey bars, strolled over and asked what I had planned for my next column.

"I have no idea," I said. "Why?"

The sun was beaming down on Yousef's back, casting the perfect light for his finger shadow puppets. As he talked, a butterfly—of his creation—fluttered across the stubby grass. He explained that he had read a recent column, the one about my treasure box, and enjoyed it. He said he, too, has a treasure box.

"That *East Side Monthly* article ran in March," he said, sounding very grown up.

No," I said. "It ran in February."

"No," he said. "March."

I sat up. I've written so many columns over the last two years they're all a blur. Also, my memory isn't as good as it used to be. I thought back a few months. I took my time. A rabbit hopped by.

By gum, Yousef was right. The column did, in fact, run in March. I was impressed. Here before me in the flesh was a loyal reader, maybe the most loyal I'd ever met. I perked up. I had had a rough day and needed to connect with my fan base.

"Did you read my other columns?" I asked.

"Yes," he said. He had read three columns, including the one about the joys of yo-yoing. "They all just made me feel happy," he said. "Somewhere in the yo-yo one, it tickled my funny bone."

I met Yousef—nicknamed Youyou—a few years ago through his brother, Yaseen, who is one of my son Henry's best friends. Yousef is 7 ¾ years old, 50 inches tall and weighs 51 pounds. He has lost five teeth, including his two front ones. His lower left cuspid is "wiggly" and might fall out any day. He has jet-black hair and a button nose, but he is best known for his eyelashes, long enough to ski off. He is often the youngest among a gaggle of older boys, which might explain his gentle, reserved way. But make no mistake: he is listening.

One day he showed up at his brother's basketball game at Moses Brown School with a manila envelope. He asked me to look inside, and I pulled out his newspaper, *Yay, My Name is NEWS!*

In between jump shots and rebounds, he explained how it came to be: "Well, I just thought about how fun it would be making a newspaper and passing them out on people's front porches and they would pay me if they wanted to—one quarter—and after I finished thinking about it, I got to work the next day because it was bedtime when I told my mom."

The following day, as planned, he sat down at his dining room table, pencil in hand. He created a cover, essentially a table of contents of "very silly" comics; "extreme and super funny" comics; news stories, and, finally, "much more fun" stuff.

The page one article was about something most can relate to, young and old: "Getting Hert at Recess": "Once upon a time Yousef Nagib whent to school. At school in the morning we whent to recess. Someone named Sally sat on my arm and almost broke my arm. Me and Rose whent to the nurse and got an ice pack."

To assure readers of his swift recovery, Yousef ran a photo of himself smiling, his injured arm now resting purposefully—and peacefully—by his side.

A comic strip about Carl the Alien, who hates his toys and longs for a simple ball, ran on page 2. The funnies also dominated pages 2 and 3, and a dizzyingly complicated word search appeared on page 4. The last page featured Vegas-style jokes. "How does a farmer count a herd of cows? With a cow-culator."

I dug into my pocket for 25 cents.

Yousef told me that the next edition of *NEWS!* is scheduled to roll off the press this summer. He plans once again to offer comics (Carl will return, but, sadly, it will be his last appearance in print), and Yousef's in-depth piece will be about Egypt, where his father was born. I asked what he intended to cover in his reportage. He said he would write about the water god Sebek, irrigation projects near the Nile, and Egyptologists.

"This would be a nonfiction article," Yousef said.

I didn't think much about Yousef's journalistic skills until we met up on the playground that day. After our talk, it soon became clear that he was not only deft in the craft of expression, but that he was also a discerning editor. He pressed on with queries about my next column. I'm a procrastinator, so I appreciated his guidance.

Given that my column about the treasure box ran in March and my column about the closing of our neighborhood Blockbuster video store ran in April, he concluded that my deadline was looming and that I needed to come up with a topic for May. I told him I was drawing a blank.

"Any ideas, my friend?" I said.

He thought for a second.

"Me."

Flip

June 2010

His name was Philip Slier, but everyone called him Flip. He had skinny legs with knobby knees and wore big owl-frame glasses. He played the mandolin and liked to take photographs, mostly of his friends. He seemed thoughtful and kind, loathe to hurt people's feelings or to impose his worries on others. If he had lived, he might have grown into the sort of man who shared his hot chicken soup with the neighbors.

I met this Dutch-Jewish teenager through the eighty-six letters he wrote to his parents from a forced labor camp in Nazi-occupied Holland. His letters were published in a 200-page book, *Hidden Letters*, which I've read three times and will probably read again. I can't shake Flip, and I'm certain I don't want to.

Hidden Letters was written by Flip's cousin, Deborah Slier, who is 78 and a children's book publisher, and her husband, Dr. Ian Shine. Deborah's father and Flip's father were brothers, but Deborah's father moved to South Africa to work in 1922, long before the war started. Deborah never met Flip. She grew up in South Africa and later settled in New York.

How the book came to be is astonishing.

Thirteen years ago, a Dutch carpenter was demolishing an old tenement at 128 Vrolik Street in Amsterdam. Flip, who was an only child, and his parents had lived on the third floor. When the carpenter lifted the attic floor, two bundles of letters fell to his feet. He took the letters to the Dutch National Institute of War Documentation, which tracked down one of Flip's distant Dutch relatives, who, in turn, contacted Deborah.

A few months ago, a friend told me that Deborah and Ian

were coming to Temple Emanu-El in Providence to talk about their book for a Holocaust remembrance service. I bought a copy and couldn't put it down.

Deborah and Ian spent eight years researching the book, traveling to Holland five times, talking to Flip's childhood friends, and reading other accounts of the war, all aimed at recreating what life was like for Flip during the German occupation. No detail is spared.

Flip's letters, written nearly every day from April 1942 through September 1942, are not what you would expect from a teenager separated from his parents by the Nazis and sent to a labor camp to dig ditches from dawn to dusk. He was courageous and upbeat. And, in a role reversal that most parents cannot relate to, he worried more about his beloved "Eliazar and Seline" than he did about himself: "Ma, be strong," he wrote July 24. "Then everything will be all right again."

He had no idea that his labor camp, outside of Amsterdam, was a holding pen for death factories. But in time, as other inmates in the camp disappeared mysteriously, he realized his life was in danger. Even then, he showed courage. "Chin up," he wrote to his parents. "Be brave."

We all bring our personal experiences to the books we read, and I did with *Hidden Letters*. I have two boys who, one day, will be teenagers, like Flip. As I read, I wondered what it would be like to have your child ripped from your arms, without any hope of ever getting him back. I wondered how my sons would feel to be alone suddenly, living in a shack with other frightened youngsters, away from the safety of home: Are they getting enough to eat? Are they sick? Are they sad? It is almost unbearable to ponder.

All the letters are poignant, but for me, as a mother, one

stands out. It is a love letter to his parents. "Dear Pa and Ma," he wrote August 23. "Today I'm allowed to write a letter to you again and therefore begin by asking how you are doing." He was "still OK." But the food was "so terribly little for us young people."

Then he wrote of an ache that, I am sure, consumed him: "Isn't it a long time since we saw each other? It is already 18 weeks since I left. Do you remember on the platform that Saturday morning? And when will we see each other again?"

Terrified that he might be shipped off to Auschwitz, Flip eventually escaped from the camp and hid out in Amsterdam in a secret apartment that was not at 128 Vrolik Street. Did he ever see his parents again? I can only hope.

His life underground ended on March 3, 1943, when he was arrested at Amsterdam Central Station, waiting for a train to freedom in Switzerland. His offense was "Ohne Stern"—not wearing a Jewish star. He was sent to the concentration camp in Sobibor in Poland, where he died in a gas chamber. He was 18 years old.

I was so moved by Flip's letters I decided to attend the Holocaust service at Temple Emanu-El.

In the sanctuary, as I listened to Cantor Brian Mayer sing haunting prayers to the dead, I thought of Flip and the tender way he ended his letters: "A big kiss, Flip." Deborah was seated in front, along with her husband. She was soft-spoken, with dark eyes. Her white hair was cropped short.

Afterward, I asked about Flip. She told me that his honesty touched her. He wasn't writing for fame or posterity, she said. Flip was simply writing to the two people he loved most: his parents.

Hidden Letters is packed with black-and-white snapshots

of Flip, taken in his carefree days, long before his exile to the labor camp. His smile is radiant. He's a young man excited about what lies ahead: life. It's disturbing to look at the photos knowing that when the camera clicked, Flip had no inkling of the horror that awaited him. "No one can envisage his own death," said Deborah.

Deborah told me Flip's close friend, Karel, who survived the war and is still living, gave her the photos. All these years, Karel had kept the pictures in a box at his house in Holland. Now they are in a book for the world to see, along with Flip's eighty-six letters to a place he desperately wanted to return but never did: home.

Snowflakes
July 2010

The other day, I read in the paper that Cate Blanchett, the movie star and mother of three boys, vacuums. That's what she told a celebrity reporter, who went on to applaud the Australian actress for "staying real" under the bright lights.

"I enjoy vacuuming," she said, sounding peppy. "It's a very satisfying noise when you hear all that grit sucked up from the floor and into the machine."

Really?

I'd bet the family homestead that Cate is fibbing.

I hate to clean and so do most of my friends. I hate sucking up all those tiny Lego pieces and kernels of dried rice. I hate the way the stuff crackles through the hose of my lousy vacuum cleaner and lands in a bag bloated with dirt and dust. I hate cleaning so much that I throw out dirty pots to avoid scrubbing them.

Let's be frank, Cate. Nobody wants to clean unless they have to.

It's summer, and the glossies at the checkout counter tell me I should pick up a mop. I suppose that means I should launch a spectacular scrub-down at our house, a dusty, drafty relic built in the age of horse carts.

Well, tough. I'm not going to do it.

I enjoy being a parent, but one of the things I wasn't prepared for is the mess. It's like falling snow: despite your best efforts to shovel the driveway, the flakes keep coming back. Make them stop.

No chance of that happening. Better to make peace with the disorder than fight it in a war that cannot be won.

I once wrote a story about a man named Sam, who was so absorbed in cleaning his cabin cruiser he spent his summer days scrubbing and vacuuming instead of motoring on Narragansett Bay.

He kept a collection of cleaning products and supplies on board, including the Singer 3-in-1, an electric broom that sucked up everything in its path—dog hair, grains of sand, my reporter's notebook.

I loved the guy and so did everyone else on the spotless dock at the Newport Yachting Center. Sam knew he was quirky but didn't seem to care what anyone thought. He reveled in his fastidiousness.

"I like to wash my boat," Sam told me after he did just that three times one day. "That's the thing I do. It's my therapy. Some people drink, take drugs. I run the vacuum."

If I had my way, I'd be like Sam only when I've got household tasks ahead of me and can't muster the strength to get off the sofa, much less buy a sponge and can of Comet.

Take the tub. Go ahead, take it. I'm sick of cleaning it. If you have kids, you know how quickly scum builds up in a tub, especially during the summer when shoes are cast aside to go barefoot. That black footprint next to our drain is my son Henry's after a hike in the woods at Patterson Park.

I've trained my eye to ignore the grime until a Sam-like feeling overwhelms me and I get to work. I am Sam, Sam I am for the 15 minutes it takes to make my tub acceptable to my family and the occasional visitor. Job complete, I revert to my sloppy self until I am seized, once again, by the urge to clean.

As I write, I see sticky fingerprints all over my computer screen. I could reach for the Windex that sits on my bookshelf for a moment such as this, but I'm resisting because my sons' DNA will be there again tomorrow and the day after that, so what's the point. "Rise above it," as my mother-in-law used to say about accepting what we cannot control. Those dust bunnies under the bed are pretty blow-away dandelions.

A quick search on the internet revealed what I already suspected about all this housecleaning business: Women clock more hours pushing the Hoover than their spouses. Married women with three children do about 28 hours of housework a week, while men do 10 hours a week, according to a study by the Institute for Social Research at the University of Michigan.

No surprise there. Sam was truly the exception. When was the last time you saw a man scrub a toilet?

My situation is unique. My husband cooks (for which I am truly grateful), so in our division of labor the laundry, vacuuming, mopping, dusting, pot scrubbing, and other chores fall to me.

I could enlist Henry and my other son, Peder, and I'm

going to do that once I sweep up all those crushed Cheerios on the kitchen floor and wipe the toothpaste off the bathroom mirror that arrived there via Henry, who was aiming for the sink, but missed.

By doing the work myself, I know I'm feeding the beast and furthering gender inequality in housecleaning for the next generation of women, but, to be honest, I want the kid mess cleaned up quickly and without the "one-sec, Mom" refrain sung fortissimo in our house far too often.

There is an upside to life behind the broom. What the Michigan study failed to mention are the cardiovascular benefits of housework. If you've ever lugged a 50-pound vacuum cleaner up three flights of stairs, you know what I'm talking about. Washing the sheets on five beds in one day probably burns up more calories than 20 minutes on a stationary bike. And scrubbing hardened maple syrup off the kitchen table really gets the heart pumping.

During an annual checkup a few years ago, a doctor asked how my family was doing and I said fine and then the doctor looked up from my chart and asked if I was getting any exercise.

"Are you kidding?" I said. "I've got two little boys."

"Oh," the doctor replied, blushing from embarrassment.

Hmm. I wonder who keeps his house tidy.

Michael's Watch
August 2010

We talked for a few hours and then went upstairs to her son's bedroom so she could show me his things. The walls had a fresh coat of paint. She was getting ready to sell her house and wanted everything to look clean.

Back in his childhood days, the room showed signs of a busy life—history books strewn across the floor next to a half-finished paper on the Bosnian conflict. Now the space was tidy, nearly empty. Michael Bhatia had been dead for two years, and, over time, his mother, Linda, had been packing up his possessions or giving them away.

It's not easy to let go of the things left behind. In an instant, a simple object takes on great importance—the cheap Bic pen becomes a treasure; the tattered wallet, a keepsake; the hairpin, a jewel. Linda knows this is the way, although she wishes she didn't. A parent is not supposed to outlive her son.

"It's not the right order," she says. "It's not natural."

The former Brown University honors student was killed on May 7, 2008, in Afghanistan when the Humvee he was riding in hit a roadside bomb. Thousands have been killed in the war. What made his death different is that Michael was a scholar, not a soldier. He was working with the military under a program called the Human Terrain System.

Launched in 2006, the project embeds civilian academics, like Michael, with combat units to advise soldiers on the local culture, with the aim of using diplomacy instead of guns. A Brown professor and two Providence filmmakers made a documentary about the program that was shown at the Avon Cinema this summer.

The film features Michael, as well as academics and soldiers offering opinions about the project. Opponents argued that scholars are nothing more than information gatherers for the military. Supporters insisted that knowing more about the culture cuts down on fatalities.

The most compelling person in the film is Michael, who was only 31 when he died on a dirt road in Khost Province. Why did this robust, brilliant young man go to one of the most dangerous countries in the world? I turned to his mother for answers.

Linda still lives in the sprawling colonial in Medway, Massachusetts, where Michael grew up. The house sits at the end of a cul-de-sac in front of a forest bordered by a thriving garden of hostas, ferns, and mountain laurels. We sat down in the living room. Michael's books were on a table—*War and Intervention; Afghanistan, Arms and Conflict; Terrorism and the Politics of Naming.*

She told me that dozens of articles have been written about Michael since his death, and she didn't know what she could add. "Plenty," I said. "You were his mother." The more she talked, the more she opened up. It was obvious that she adored him and misses him.

As a boy, he liked to read and play with Legos. He was a Scout, progressing all the way to the rank of Eagle. In middle school his passion shifted to politics, and by eighth grade he knew he wanted to study international relations in college.

In 1995, on his first day at Brown, he hung a United Nations flag across his dorm room, along with a quotation by T.E. Lawrence, also known as Lawrence of Arabia: "All men dream: but not equally. Those who dream by night in the dusty recesses of their minds wake up in the day to find it was vanity, but the dreamers of the day are dangerous men, for they may act their dreams with open eyes to make it possible."

If anyone lived his dreams, it was Michael. At Brown, Michael "exploded" intellectually and socially, Linda said. A gabber with a disarming smile, he attracted friends throughout the world. His brain went into overdrive. Once a professor asked him to write a 20-page report; he wrote 180 pages.

His future was in academia, but he wasn't comfortable cooped up in an ivory tower. He needed to be in the field talking to people. After Brown, he traveled to the newly independent East Timor as a U.N. observer and to Kosovo to supervise elections.

He ended up at Oxford University to pursue his doctoral degree. As part of his studies, he visited Afghanistan five times to conduct research, always roaming freely, often drinking tea with villagers.

In 2006, he returned to Brown as a visiting fellow at the Watson Institute for International Studies. Out of curiosity, he attended a military conference on the Human Terrain program. A few months later, he signed up to work in Afghanistan.

"He knew about the country and thought he could help," said Linda. "He had a big heart and mind."

His mother wept the day he left. He sent emails and called when he could. He was content. He was learning more about the Afghan people and, at the same time, serving his country, which Linda said he always wanted to do. She urged him to be careful. "Don't worry, Mom," he told her. "This is safe."

When she opened her door on that Wednesday in May and saw men in military dress, she knew immediately. She ran to her living room to get away; she wasn't ready yet to hear the word.

The box from Afghanistan arrived a few weeks later. It contained the things he had in his last days. They were wrapped in paper or enclosed in baggies. She removed the items, held them in her hands: This was Michael's. His fingerprints are still there.

She put everything out on his bed: his compass, his wallet, the dimes in his pocket, two cigars in tin cases that said Enduring Freedom, a ring of keys, military badges, the nametag from his camouflage shirt: BHATIA.

And then there was his watch, still ticking on Afghan time. She kept it in his dresser drawer. Not long ago, it stopped, at exactly 2:54. What do you do with your dead son's watch? You keep it. But do you wear it?

Linda is small-boned, and this is a man's field watch, large with a black nylon strap, frayed at the edges. That doesn't matter. She doesn't care about the way it looks. She could get a new battery, maybe repair the strap.

"He was probably wearing this when it happened," Linda said.

After Michael died, Linda wondered for many months if she should have begged him not to go. In time, she came to the conclusion that a parent doesn't have the right to keep her child from living the life he wants to lead.

"A mother's love is strong," Linda said. "But I couldn't keep him back because I was afraid. He wouldn't have become who he wanted to be. Do you know what I'm trying to say? Do you know what I mean?"

Moon Ball
September 2010

This time, we stayed.

We stayed for the fly outs, pop-ups, errors, and lousy turns at bat, but it was worth it: there was a breeze and we got to see our first moon ball.

Sure, we could've left when the Orioles were way ahead during that July 4th game at Fenway Park in Boston this summer, but we learned the hard way a few years ago that it's not a good idea to make an early exit at a Red Sox game.

Flashback to the summer of '07:

I'm sitting at Fenway with my husband and two sons, Peder and Henry, then 7 and 6. The boys are starting to fidget and for good reason: the game is duller than a curling match. Pitch, grounder, throw to first, out. The Sox can't get on base.

We try hot dogs, cotton candy, ice cream. Even a quick trip to the The Red Sox Team Store does not satisfy. And then I hear the dreaded words: "I want to go home, Mom," says Peder.

The Sox are down, 5-0, heading into the bottom of the eighth when we say so long to our precious seats—left field, second row, grandstand—and make that lonely trek back to the car. Just before we get on the Southeast Expressway to Providence, my husband turns on the radio.

"Unbelievable!" shouts the sportscaster, as the Sox make an amazing comeback, winning the game 6-5. "Bedlam at Fenway!"

You might remember that game as the Mother's Day Miracle. I think of it as the Mother of All Misses Day. I still get a knot in my stomach thinking how, in our haste, we missed that once-in-a-lifetime opportunity.

On this trip, we vowed to remain, no matter the score.

It was a sweltering 90 degrees, but our seats were in the shade. Only one problem: there was a pole, not the pesky "Pesky's Pole," but a towering steel beam obstructing our view. Let me rephrase that: obstructing my view. Being the sacrificial mother and all, I took the seat where it was impossible to see home plate and the pitcher's mound at the same time.

Turned out that the other fans in section 11, right field, grandstand were a generous bunch. They took pity on us. A father and his young son moved to two vacant seats, allowing us to sit in their seats, which were pretty good. We could see Kevin Youkilis' shiny bald head. We could see the big hurler, John Lackey. We could see Brian Hall's rose-tinted sunglasses.

Everyone seemed in high spirits, chatty.

"Hot day isn't it?" the kid sitting next to me asked.

"Nice breeze," I said.

"Plus, we got some shade in this spot," he said. "Peanut?"

The game was going our way, with the O's striking out or hitting ho-hum grounders easily scooped up by Sox infielders, who fired off beauties to Youk on first. But then Big Papi struck out and, in a huff, stomped his very big foot in the dirt.

"Hang in there, David," I shouted.

His next turn at bat, he struck out again. This was not a good sign.

I was sipping my son's warm lemonade when latecomers arrived, and we had to go back to our old seats. I was disappointed, but not crestfallen.

I was thrilled to be at a Sox game. Baseball rules in our house. My sons play in the Fox Point East Side Little League, and I'm happy to report that their teams won the championships in their divisions this year—Hot Club for Peder, the mighty Nitros for Henry. I can think of no greater pleasure as a parent than watching Peder steal a base or Henry pitch.

If you passed by our house on Irving Avenue earlier this summer, you might have heard a loud thud against our backyard fence and a gaggle of boys arguing about whether the side-arm pitch by Henry "The Closer" Schaefer was a strike or outside. You might have seen that beaten-up baseball bag on our porch or that tattered baseball under the yew.

A ballpark beam was not going to spoil my day at Fenway.

The Sox started to collapse in the third (maybe the fourth), and before you know it the score was something like 4 (maybe 5) to zip. The Sox couldn't get a hit against the O's pitcher, Brian Somebody.

My mind started to drift. I'm a people-watcher, an acceptable pastime at a Sox game. It's encouraged. What else to do while Big Papi adjusts the Velcro straps on his batting gloves for the third time?

I took an interest in the four guys and two young women sitting in front of us. It was obvious they weren't from around here. They snapped a lot of photos of each other, with the field as a backdrop, and dressed differently, as if they were on their way to a polo match instead of a grubby ballpark. I figured New York.

As the game progressed, not in our favor, they left their seats often for hotdogs and beer. They were tipsy, maybe drunk. Glassy-eyed and goofy, they belted out Neil Diamond's "Sweet Caroline," the Sox's unofficial anthem, as it blared on the loud-speaker. How did they know the lyrics? Of course: Diamond is from Brooklyn.

Henry asked me if it was the top or bottom of the fifth. He was rooting for the sixth. He wanted to go home, I could tell. The beam was bugging him, but he decided to tough it out, like the time he pitched in the bottom of the sixth (Little League ninth), with the bases loaded and two outs. (The outcome was sweet: A victory pile-up on Henry as bedlam breaks out at McKenna-Frutchey Field on Gano Street!)

I looked at the filthy cement floor. It was covered with

peanut shells and the empty beer cups from our New York friends. I wondered why Theo Epstein didn't put out trash cans. I felt sorry for the poor guys responsible for cleaning up this mess.

My boys yawned.

"My head hurts," said Peder.

The breeze ceased. Everyone seemed to be getting cranky. A fan a few seats down nodded off. Others veered into other topics besides baseball. "Corn is a vegetable," said a man behind us. The grumps started to leave after J.D. Drew made a horrible error in right field, losing an easy fly in the sun. "Can't take it anymore," a fellow mumbled, and off he went with his friend.

We took their seats, the best in the house. Now we could see the entire field.

And then Youkilis swaggered to the plate and raised his bat. He looked like a human corkscrew, with his arms held high and legs turned at funny angles.

The pitch was fast and hard, and Youkilis took a swing. The ball disappeared into the summer sky. In the end the Sox lost 6-1, but it was a beautiful day; we got to see what everyone hopes for. Thanks, Youk. Thanks for hitting it out of the ballpark.

Spaghetti Cowboy
November 2010

A few years ago, I was talking with my neighbor, Tom Hunter, and our conversation turned to the topic of movies. It was Oscar season, and Tom and I were discussing his picks. I think he mentioned Clint Eastwood for best actor—or maybe best director. I'm fuzzy on the details.

What I do remember is that Tom seemed to know a lot about the film industry. He knew about producers, directors, screenwriters, and actors from long ago with square shoulders and slicked back hair and ruggedly handsome looks that could snare a dame for the night.

I think he mentioned the name Robert Mitchum. I'm pretty sure he called him Bob.

One thing led to another and before you know it, I had a stack of old movies in my arms that all had one actor in common: Tom, better known on the big screen as Thomas Hunter.

If you're a movie buff, you've probably heard of Spaghetti Westerns, Italian-made films that emerged in the 1960s and were shot in inexpensive places that resembled the American Southwest, primarily Spain and Italy.

One of the films Tom gave me was *The Hills Run Red*, produced by the Italian filmmaker Dino De Laurentiis. I watched it that night after my sons went to bed. It had all the ingredients of the genre: covered wagons racing past the mesquite; dark-eyed women with luscious black hair; a tuneful score by the great Italian composer Ennio Morricone; gunfights; bad guys; heroes. Tom was the good guy—and the star.

It's easy to forget that someone lived a life before you met them. Maybe the mother running after two toddlers on the playground took a case to the Supreme Court. The old man walking his sway-backed mutt might have stormed the beaches of Normandy. The tailor could have been a college track star.

Until that late-night viewing of *Hills*, I thought of Tom as my kind and courteous neighbor who always tipped his baseball cap and waved and who liked to take daily walks down Blackstone Boulevard and play tennis on the courts at Brown University with his wife, Isabelle.

Now I was seeing him in another light, as a young man with a chiseled face and baby blue eyes and a two-day stubble that he didn't seem to give a hoot about because he was out to get the lousy good-for-nothing who killed his wife. I was seeing him as a Spaghetti Western cowboy.

"It's Tom!" I shouted to myself when he appeared on my Sony, sweaty-faced with a red kerchief tied around his neck and a soiled cowboy hat with a three-pinch crease perched on his head. I couldn't help but smile.

By the end of the week, I was something of an expert on the filmography of Thomas Hunter. His movies were irresistible. More sidewalk chats ensued, and I soon came to discover that Tom, uh, Thomas O'D. Hunter, was writing a book, *Memoirs of a Spaghetti Cowboy: Tales of Oddball Luck and Derring-Do.* He gave me a copy to read.

He began with his idyllic childhood in Savannah, Georgia, where one Sunday morning, while still wearing his sweetpea nightie, he walked barefoot three blocks to the Savannah River to sail his toy boat.

From there, he charged through life like a wild Appaloosa. He graduated from the University of Virginia and found work as a model in New York. On a whim, he auditioned for Uta Hagen's acting class. He eventually landed a two-month job on the Blake Edwards film, *What Did You Do in the War, Daddy?*

At the end of the shoot, he figured his movie career was over. But one day he was rushing down a hallway at the William Morris Agency, a talent agency in Beverly Hills, and bumped head-on into De Laurentiis. The call came a few days later: Do you want to star in Mr. De Laurentiis's first Western?

"Geez," said Tom.

The role in *Hills* led to 17 more movies, among them:

Death Walks in Laredo, another De Laurentiis film, this one about three half-brothers who inherit a secret gold mine from their philandering father. Tom plays Whity Selby, the brother with the smoking four-barreled colt.

Battle of the Commandos, a war film about a tough Army colonel (Jack Palance), who leads a group of ex-convicts on a mission to destroy German-built canons. Tom plays Captain Burke, who gnaws on a cigar butt while dismantling a mine. (Tom was well-suited for the role; he served as a Marine Corps Captain in the mid-1950s.)

Anzio, a film based on the 1944 Allied assault on a small Italian port in World War II. Tom is Private Andy, who takes a bullet in the neck far too early in the film. Mitchum is a news correspondent.

And don't forget *The Amsterdam Story, X-312 Flight to Hell, Escape from KGB*, and *The Cassandra Crossing*, which starred Burt Lancaster, Ava Gardner, and O.J. Simpson. (Tom was Simpson's acting coach for a week.)

In his free time, Tom wrote scripts: *The Human Factor*, a thriller starring George Kennedy, and *The Final Countdown*, a sci-fi adventure with a young Kirk Douglas and a very young Martin Sheen, shot aboard the USS Nimitz aircraft carrier.

Then there was that book he wrote about the end of civilization, *Softly Walks the Beast*, which went into three reprints, selling more than 50,000 copies.

Along the way, Tom met other actors. "Do tell," I said one day.

Jack Palance liked to warm up with pushups, the one-arm

type. "The idea is to get your energy up," Tom said. "After all that sitting around in Spain's hot weather, waiting for the next scene to be filmed, you get listless. I'd do pushups while he did them. Same number."

Martin Sheen was friendly. He liked Tom's *Countdown* script and told him he'd like to star in the movie. "I remember bouncing 7-month-old Charlie Sheen on my knee, doing my best 'trot, trot to Boston' routine," Tom said.

Tom sat next to Ava Gardner during Cassandra: "In her 50s, still beautiful, still warm and interesting to talk to."

Robert Mitchum had a "great swagger," and always looked stoned, with his hooded eyes. During *Anzio*, Tom shared a trailer with the then-fledgling Italian actor, Giancarlo Giannini—yes, that one.

"Mitchum had a bad hangover and refused to work, playing cards in his trailer instead," Tom said. "The director comes over and asks us to work, and we have to pass by Mitchum's trailer. Mitchum gives us the finger for being scabs. Giancarlo and I answer with the 'up yours' Italian arm salute."

Finally, there was Clint, another Spaghetti Cowboy. He took Tom and Burt Reynolds ("incredibly athletic") out to dinner one night in Rome. At a wild party a few days later, Clint and Tom watched as an Italian actor slashed a German actor's face with broken glass.

"Blood went everywhere," Tom said. "Clint and I are sipping our beers when he turns to me and says, 'Cut. Print.' Very cool, this guy."

Now we have another cool guy among us. Maybe you've seen him. He's that lanky fellow in a tan cap walking the boulevard, moving so fast he's kicking up dust in his tracks.

CHAPTER 6

....

Bluebird
December 2010

My mother-in-law was not a sentimental woman, but she kept everything that came from someone or somewhere: a painted rock from Maine, her brother's ball of twine, Uncle Harry's stick matches.

After she died my husband and I emptied out her house and found boxes filled with her possessions, and soon we began the process of trying to decide what to keep and what to discard.

In the end, nothing much was thrown out except maybe a paperclip and, even then, we were tempted to keep it.

Carol's belongings were too precious to give away. No one else would understand or care about their history. They wouldn't know that the walnut turned into a thimble-size flower basket was carved by her grandfather, Thorvald Sorensen, or that the rusty, hand-operated eggbeater was owned by her mother, Sophie, who made everything from scratch, including her beloved mince pies.

One box in particular piqued my interest. The top flap said in big orange and blue letters: Electronic Jet Fighter. There were illustrations of planes and bombs, and one side had a sketch of a radar scope that promised to "fire 1-2-3 rocket guns at moving targets!"

My husband noticed the box immediately. His paternal grandmother, Ruth, gave him the jet fighter as a Christmas present when he was 9, and he spent many Sunday afternoons on his living room floor flying at supersonic speed. The toy disappeared long ago, but Carol kept the box to store her Christmas ornaments. I looked inside.

No Christmas is complete without ornaments. They doll up a scrawny tree or make a grand tree look even more majestic. Sadly, most ornaments today are mass produced and bear no resemblance to their unique forebears. Now you're more likely to find a dull red ball of plastic, than a hand-made gold pear with a curled green stem.

Carol's ornaments were relics of bygone days. Half a century old, maybe older, they were all made of glass and wrapped in tissue-thin paper, yellowed by time. I don't think it would be a stretch to call these wondrous decorations works of art.

I have no idea who made them, but I imagine he must have been a heck of a craftsman, maybe a shy old man with bad posture who owned a trinket shop on Broadway and displayed his creations on a wilted evergreen in a dimly lit window he never bothered to clean.

Did Eddie, the neighborhood dreamer, press his pug nose against the pane every holiday season and calculate how much penny candy he'd have to forgo to buy the toy soldier with the red drum?

"Par-rum-pa-pum-pum," Eddie hummed. "A week with no licorice."

Nothing is truly yours until you use it, until you roll it around in your hands. You can inherit all sorts of things from a doting aunt, but if they remain in a box, untouched, they are museum pieces tucked away in storage for an exhibit that will never happen. They are safe, but unloved.

If you have children, as I do, you worry that these heirlooms could break. I am the mother of two energetic boys. The latest mishap around our house involved an antique captain's cabinet whose glass door was shattered by a football tossed by my 10-year-old son Peder, who was aiming for the sofa and missed.

I suppose I could have made a good case for keeping Carol's ornaments in the box, at least until my sons go off to college, but I decided to risk it. The decorations were too charming not to share with family and friends and, anyway, what misfortune could befall an ornament dangling from a top branch, out of reach of small hands.

I took the box downstairs, and we trimmed the tree with Carol's stuff: a reindeer in snow-capped mountains; a genie lamp with a long stem; a gold vase with arched handles; a bluebird with a tail of yellow feathers.

In all, there were more than 50 ornaments, some still in their original boxes, including one that contained 12 hexagons in various shades of blue and, according to a sticker on the box, went for 49 cents at McLellan's, a five and dime at the corner of Medway Street and Wayland Avenue that closed its doors decades ago.

Other Christmas decorations were in the box, too. I found a package of Christmas tree bulbs, gold, blue, and green, and although they no longer worked, I kept them anyway and put them in a fruit bowl.

I found a candle holder carved from a birch tree and a foot-high cutout of Santa from a shop called The Tin Woodsman. I found a Santa piggy bank from the now-defunct Old Stone Bank and a string of tiny paper Norwegian flags that Carol hung across her tree in honor of her heritage: God jul.

We trimmed the tree and celebrated with eggnog and sugar cookies. Later that night, after my sons went to sleep, I went downstairs and plugged in the lights.

It was quiet, and the room was dark. I stared at the lit-up tree, and the ornaments from Christmases past. I searched the thick branches for my favorite, the bluebird.

It was perched high, just below the star. But it was crooked, so I decided to straighten it. I reached up and gave it a tap, and it tumbled through the branches to the wood floor, shattering into pieces.

I swept up the shards of glass, and put the feathers in a drawer, but one day I tossed them, too. The bluebird had been out of the box, if only for a short while, and now it was time to let it go.

Charlie

February 2011

My friend Charlie has moved to town. He's the friendly guy in a Sox cap and red suspenders picking up an order of lox at Davis Dairy or sitting at a table at Starbucks poring over some of the four newspapers he reads every day. Once a news junkie, always a news junkie.

His full name is M. Charles Bakst, and if that doesn't sound familiar to you then you've been living under a rock for several decades. Charlie was the legendary political columnist at *The Providence Journal*, writing three, sometimes four, columns a week from 1995 until his retirement in 2008.

Now he is living in our midst. Charlie and his wife,

Elizabeth, left their Barrington home after 42 years and moved in November to a condo on the East Side, over there, beyond the treetops, to a place that will remain a secret. The couple liked what the East Side offers: great restaurants, arty shops, Brown University, a real community.

"It felt like we belonged here," he said.

Charlie spent his career writing about other people; now it's time to take a look at his life.

He'll turn 67 on February 22. Born and raised in Fall River, he graduated from Phillips Academy, Brown University, and the Columbia University Graduate School of Journalism. He worked as a summer intern at the *Journal* and joined the paper full-time in 1968. He started covering politics in 1972 and never looked back.

He wrote about gay rights, abortion rights, immigrants, baseball, the dangers of smoking, voter apathy, and corruption. His holiday greeting poems were utterly unique.

One of his favorite articles was "A Flight to Destiny," a reconstruction of when President George H.W. Bush was shot down over the Pacific in 1944. Rhode Islander Jack Delaney, a crew member, was killed. Charlie interviewed President Bush by phone.

In all those years, he missed only one deadline, in 1963 when he was an intern.

"I was crazy about accuracy," he said, "and the integrity of the column."

In September 2008, he decided to call it quits and accepted an early buyout. He'd had a good run; now it was time to take it easy. He spent time with his three granddaughters. He went to Bruins' and Celtics' games. He gave away or sold hundreds of his books. He donated his personal papers and memorabilia from four decades of reporting to the Brown archives.

Who knows? he thought. *Someday, a student will walk into the library and say, "I heard there was something once called newspapers. Did anyone from Brown ever have anything to do with that?"*

In March of 2009—about seven months after his retirement—he went by himself to Fort Myers, Florida, for his annual pilgrimage to Red Sox spring training. In the past, he'd gone for six days, but this time his plan was to fulfill a lifelong dream and stay for a month. He even rented a condo.

Several weeks into the visit, trouble found him. His teeth started to hurt, and he had a burning pain in his throat. Most alarmingly, he was short of breath. Through a combination of confusion and denial, he put off seeing a doctor.

But things eventually came to a head. He almost collapsed walking home from a market less than two blocks from his condo. Leaning on a shopping cart for support, he felt like "a feeble old man."

He knew something bad was happening. He drove himself to a hospital and staggered into the emergency room: "I don't know what's wrong with me," he said, "but I can barely breathe."

As he lay on a gurney, with tubes traveling from his arms to a machine, it occurred to him that he might die. His reporter's instinct to document events took over, and he snapped a photo of his face—puffy eyes, pale skin—with his iPhone.

An hour or so passed. His jaw throbbed, his throat burned. He called for help. The machine started to beep wildly. "You're having a heart attack," the doctor said. Charlie's first thought: "I'm alive."

An ambulance raced him to another hospital, where

doctors inserted two stents to open his blocked arteries. But more agony awaited him. He lost consciousness and awoke the next day to hear frightening news: his heart had stopped twice, and he had to be revived.

Charlie still remembers a doctor's funny way of saying hello: "You don't look so bad for a guy who tried to kill himself twice yesterday." The patient laughed—a good sign.

The recovery was slow. The fatigue lingered. Once, he had to leave a Paw Sox game just after it started. When he got home, he had a light dinner of a bowl of Cheerios, but he lacked the energy to slice a banana to put on top. In time, he regained his strength.

"A heart attack definitely drives home very vividly the fact that you're mortal," Charlie said. "At first it almost obsesses you. It's like a demon. You have to put it out of your mind and not let it overwhelm you."

Still, his life has changed. Pastrami sandwiches are out. Hummus is in. Easy on the salt. He exercises on a treadmill every day. He's slimmed down to 145 pounds. He takes four prescribed pills a day; his nitro tablets are in a tiny metal bottle on his keychain, just in case.

"You have to tell yourself that you have a lot to live for and that you can do almost anything you did before, yet in moderation," he said. "You just try to get as much out of life as possible."

In the old days, Charlie worked around-the-clock in the newsroom writing stories on his computer, his small tape recorder spewing out the musings of the state's famous and near-famous pols. Now he happily lingers over coffee and a slice of whole wheat bread, no butter.

Does he miss his column?

"I miss the camaraderie in the newsroom," he said. "I miss the ringside seat at the political scene, but I don't miss running around, and I don't miss the deadlines and the writing. A column is an all-consuming experience. You're always thinking about it. It's a great, great job, but it's a lot of work."

Welcome to the neighborhood, Charlie. And thanks for all those years of telling us things we didn't know. Now go have fun. Live.

Henry B.
March 2011

I am not a cold person. I am a warm person. I love sweltering days with thick and still air that never moves, except for the sudden breeze that comes in like a rogue wave.

Growing up in St. Louis, where the August temperatures soared to 100 and beyond, I learned to revel in the heat. Move slowly. Wear sleeveless shirts. Leave the shoes at home. Walking barefoot on toasty sidewalks was a family tradition.

Up here, in Rhode Island, I go inside for the winter months, all nine of them. I put on my uniform—long underwear, a turtleneck, a sweater, a vest, a down coat—and sit by a hissing radiator in the parlor, reminding myself that nothing lasts forever, especially the weather.

This is not the case with New Englanders. They embrace winter.

Take my friend, Henry B.

His favorite season is winter. I know this for many reasons. He spends hours climbing snowdrifts in front of his house. He's got a pretty good slider when he throws a snowball. And he likes to kick up the white stuff on his way to the bus stop.

Once I took him sledding at Moses Brown School. Not only was he fearless on the icy slopes, but he also didn't seem to mind, on descent, that his calves were exposed to white-frosted winds. I shivered just looking at him.

This year, Henry took his fondness for the cold to the next level. If I were writing a book called, say, *Bold in the Cold*, I would tap Henry for the introduction. Don't let the cold run your life, he might write. You have to brush your teeth, but you don't have to wear pants.

But I'm getting ahead of myself.

Henry lives up the street from me in the house with the River Birch. He is 11 years old. He has blue eyes and a mop of unruly blond hair. His dog, a Bluetick Coonhound, is named Magnolia, but everyone calls her Maggie. Henry is crazy about sports: soccer, baseball, football, hockey, squash, tennis, badminton, ping-pong. He is an avid skier.

"It gets my—what's that called—adrenaline going, especially when I go off jumps," he says. "You look down and everything's smaller. It just seems like you're the king of the world."

In early fall—September 10, to be exact—Henry was walking to the bus stop two blocks from his house when an idea came to him that was so perfect, he wondered why he hadn't thought of it earlier.

He had recently read an article about a boy who went an entire year without wearing shoes to find out what it would be like to be homeless. As he scurried down the sidewalk to catch the 7:28, Henry thought: *I wonder what it would be like to wear shorts all year, even during the winter.*

"I wanted to do something different," he says. "I could have worn a short sleeve shirt all year, but that wouldn't have been as hard. You just wear your coat."

Thus began a shorts-only pledge that has captured the attention of all who know and admire him and turned him into an iconic figure among his classmates at Henry Barnard School, where he is a pupil in Miss P's fifth-grade class.

"It's kind of unbelievable," says my son Peder, a classmate. "The cold can be painful, but Henry attacks it in the best way."

It hasn't been easy.

September, Henry reports, was a manageable month, as far as shorts go. The weather was mild, the wind gentle. He fluctuated between his khaki shorts and midnight blue gym shorts. November, however, proved to be more difficult.

"The coldness was like—bang—it just came at me," he says. "It felt like I was swimming in really cold water."

One morning he woke up and looked out his window. The trees were bare. The sky was gray. The wind sounded like a roaring locomotive. His pants stared at him longingly. The temptation was powerful, but Henry reached for his shorts.

"I started wearing shorts and I wanted to finish wearing shorts," he says.

During the Thanksgiving break, he had a brief reprieve when he went to visit his grandparents in Florida. Henry used the visit as an opportunity to "de-thaw" his legs. The balmy weather was "soothing" and "relaxing." He came back invigorated.

Arctic temperatures are unkind to bare skin, and such was the case with Henry. Chapped calves started to appear in December and stayed with him through the winter months. Still, Henry forged ahead. He rubbed "creamy stuff" on his wounds at night and by morning his legs were healed and ready to face yet another frigid day.

The East Side is a small community. I know, for example, that Noah scored the winning goal for his hockey team in the final 9.1 seconds of a game on January 20, a Wednesday. I know that Zack got white Jordan's for Hanukkah, and that Theo once put red highlights in his hair.

Most people in the neighborhood know about Henry and his shorts. There are exceptions. The other day, Henry was alighting from my car and another boy, unaware of Henry's pledge, commented about his scantily clad legs.

"Why are you wearing shorts?" the boy said.

"Cuz," said Henry.

Henry's answer to inquiries of this nature is usually "Cuz," which is another way of saying, "Because I want to. Case closed. Period."

Without a doubt, Henry has pluck. If he has the determination to get through a winter without pants, imagine what he can accomplish at NASA, Google headquarters, or the White House.

"Just do it," Henry says, offering advice to others who also believe less is more. "On really cold days, you just have to put on shorts. It's not that hard. The bus is heated and so is the classroom."

The challenge, he says, is staying warm at recess. Like all great thinkers, he has a solution: a rousing game of football.

Well Done
April 2011

Not long ago, my son Peder walked down to the neighborhood convenience store with a buck fifty in his pocket to buy candy. Instead of taking a right at the corner, he went straight, past the mailbox and bank, and ended up at an upscale market that sells fine meat and fish, as well as pastrami sandwiches.

He'd been in the shop before, usually for a breakfast of Belgium waffles, but this time he strolled up to the meat counter and directed his queries to a butcher, bedecked in a white apron tastefully stained with, well, whatever.

"Got any scallops?" Peder asked.

The butcher seemed surprised. Maybe he didn't hear right. It's not every day that a kid walks into your shop and asks for scallops. A bag of chips, sure, but raw shellfish? The butcher plopped a few slimy chunks into a plastic container and weighed them. The cost was far more than Peder could afford.

"All I have is a dollar fifty," said Peder.

"What are you?" said the butcher. "A comedian."

First, let me apologize to the butcher. My 11-year-old was not mocking you. He spoke the truth. On that brisk afternoon in February, his pockets were not deep.

Second, his desire for scallops was as sincere as his desire to play middle infield for the UCLA Bruins.

He is not a comic. He is a cook. Actually, he is the sous chef, a fancy way of saying that he's second-in-command in our kitchen, my husband being the executive chef. I am noticeably absent from the lineup.

I have the same relationship with cooking as I do with the makeup counter at Nordstrom. I know I should go there for a short tutorial, but I'm not going to do it. I can't muster the interest.

Cooking skills are inherited, passed down through the gene pool. They also have a visual component. If you grew up seeing a parent stir the pot, chances are you'll do the same. My mother didn't like to cook and neither did her mother, so it's no surprise I turned out the way I did.

I make no apologies and neither does my mom. Peggy spent a lot of time at home with her six kids, but she was not domestic. She mixed whites and colors and dusted with a wet paper towel now and then. We still joke about how I walked down the street to ask Mrs. Doxsie to sew a button on my shirt.

My husband was aware of my ineptness in the kitchen when we got married. Thankfully, he is an excellent cook and took over those duties, especially after the births of Peder and his younger brother Henry.

A typical evening in the baby years: I'm upstairs trying to put Henry to sleep while Peder and his dad are in the kitchen preparing a feast. One of my favorite childhood photos is of Peder, then 3, standing on a chair with a plump black olive stuck on the tip of his pointer finger.

Peder would toss greens and peel potatoes and gab with his dad about this and that—how to get to the heart of an artichoke, the rising price of fuel oil, Tonka fire trucks—unaware that a passion for cooking was taking root while the pork chops festooned with capers sizzled in the frying pan.

One thing led to another and pretty soon, Peder's birthday list included can openers and wooden spoons and cookbooks, which he happily devoured, including the latest, the 397-page *Good Eats* by celebrity chef Alton Brown, who hosts a TV show by the same name.

I am thrilled Peder has assumed the No. 2 spot. When my husband has to work late, I simply cede the kitchen to the Little Man, who specializes in whipping up meals with what's available in the fridge and pantry. No need to rush out for ginger root.

During meal preparation, Peder is a whirling dervish, spinning from stove to cutting board, measuring, slicing, stirring, tasting, and stopping every so often at *Good Eats* yawning on the table.

"Why do you like to cook?" I asked one day.

"When people eat my food, they're happy," Peder said. "I like making people happy."

Earlier this month, with my husband absent, Peder planned the meal. At first, he selected cheeseburgers and fries, but scrapped that after inspecting the meat, which had been sitting in the freezer too long and had the gray pallor of the ailing tubercular.

"This meat is horrible," he said, as he removed the ground beef from the cellophane. He quickly switched gears, this time to stir fry—carrots, celery, snap peas, and chicken sautéed in two cups of soy sauce. The meal was salty, but delicious. Henry and I asked for seconds.

On his birthday Peder made cornbread and while it did not rise to the occasion—literally—it still had a unique consistency and buttery flavor that proved to be the perfect pairing with our main course of roast.

Peder takes his cooking seriously. He's browsing the internet for a wok. He is also assuming some responsibility for grocery shopping. Good cooks know their way around the produce aisle and fruit stand. You need to smell the cantaloupe and so on.

That trip for scallops taught Peder that good food comes at a price. When he returned home that day empty-handed, I reached into my tin can and gave him a fin. He went right back to the shop and put in a respectable order.

"The first butcher was very engrossed in some other activity, so I got another butcher," Peder recalled. "He asked me what I was making with the scallops. I said I was going to sauté them for the Super Bowl."

That evening we set out a buffet of chili, nachos, artisan bread, and a scallop dish Peder retrieved from the internet: Randall's Ordinary Scallops. There was nothing ordinary, however, about the dish, an unexpected complexity of scallions, garlic, paprika, and salt.

Our guests gobbled it up.

Well done, son. The wok is in the mail.

Wild Things
May 2011

A few weeks ago, my son and I pulled into our driveway and discovered a mouse attempting to mount our stone wall. He was up on his hind legs, poking his whiskered nose into an airy crevice, oblivious to the headlights showcasing his feats. He looked well-fed, but not plump. His coat was shiny, and he seemed perky.

"Look," I said to Peder. "A mouse."

He got all jittery and wondered whether he should tiptoe or bolt into the house.

"Oh please," I said. "It's just a mouse."

Peder knew what we all know: If you have one mouse, you have a dozen and they are all scurrying around your grounds, sniffing their way through pin-size openings in your ancient windows to reach the trash can, stinky from those pitiful kidney beans you tossed out the night before.

To be honest, I can't get too uptight about mice. Spring has sprung. This is the East Side. The critters are out.

I dare any East Sider to come forward who has not had a harrowing experience with a wild thing. Every spring, I hear stories about the frantic squirrel with the bad fur that sprinted through an open kitchen door or the loony bat that mistook the boudoir for a dank cavern.

The woodsy town of Foster probably has a lot of critters, but I suspect the men and women up there, in their steel-toe boots and flannel shirts, catch the creatures themselves, probably luring them to their doom with leftover shiners. Around here, we call the experts for help. We call Critter Control, known affectionately at our house as CC. The guys—always guys—race over with their putty guns, ladders, and nets to calm us. You will part with thousands before they drive off.

My earliest memory of a critter was back in '02, when Peder and his younger brother, Henry, were still in diapers. I was nodding off when I heard a scratching noise inside my chamber walls. I didn't think much of it, until I heard it again the following night and the night after that. The next morning, I called CC.

Dave was a gentleman. I described the noise—"tiny claws on a treadmill"—and he asked me to direct him to the backyard. He winced when he looked at the top of a picnic table: Bat guano. He poked a few droppings with the tip of his pencil. The news was not good: Bats in the belfry. He eyed Peder and Henry waddling around in their Pampers and casually tossed out a word guaranteed to instill panic: rabies.

"Cream in your coffee?" I asked.

He caulked a few holes in the eaves, covered the vents with wire, and disposed of eight dead bats that he said had "mummified" in our attic. I don't remember the exact cost of the job, but I do recall that it was more than the tangerine-orange Golf I bought in 1986 from an environmental lawyer who lived on Long Island.

Later in the week, I called my friend Denise to apologize. During a visit years ago, she claimed that she had been jolted awake by a bird fluttering around her face while she slept at night. "Sure," I said dismissively, certain she had had a bad dream. Thanks to Dave, the truth suddenly revealed itself: Denise's bird was a bat.

Another time, I was lying on the sofa and noticed a mass moving swiftly under the insulation on our outside-the-wall water pipes. I screamed, but by the time my sons and husband arrived, the creature, uh, mass was gone, and no one believed me.

I called CC anyway. Dave rushed over with soothing words, assuring me that, no, it was not a rat, more likely a mouse. I can deal with a mouse. A rat would have sent me over the edge and into a hotel. Dave inspected the house from top to bottom and then did something in the basement that would not go over well with the PETA people.

My most disturbing encounter with a critter involved squirrels. We have two century-old towering silver maples in our backyard that squirrels inhabit throughout the year, nesting inside the gutted-out parts of the trees and frolicking like schoolboys amid the branches.

Years ago, I was playing in the yard with my sons and a squirrel fell from a branch and landed at my bare feet, plop. It died instantly, which I confirmed by its stillness and a smidgen of blood. I am skittish when it comes to dead squirrels, so I called my husband's uncle, Gordon, who ended his gin game prematurely to assist. He showed up with Uncle Alfie's wooden-handled shovel and nudged the squirrel into a trash bag, which, mercifully, he took home.

A few weeks later, the same thing happened. This time, I performed the grisly task myself.

Not all critters are a nuisance.

Take Rocky, our family raccoon. He lives inside the maple so close to our house we can practically pet his nose from our third-floor window. He emerges at dusk when he smells the bacon sizzling on the skillet and at dawn when the boys are getting ready for school.

One morning, we saw Rocky and his significant other, Ruby, scaling the tree together, strolling back to their nest, a picture of domestic bliss. Henry snapped a photo and took it to school. He wowed his classmates with our new neighbors. Pretty soon, we saw little ones peeking out from the nest. Babies.

I did not call CC.

I'm a mom, too.

Aw Shucks
June 2011

Driving down Elmgrove, I saw the fire truck barreling past the cherry tree and thought, once again, of a kitchen fire. I always think of kitchen fires when fire trucks come through our neighborhood. I imagine that a pot boiled over and everyone panicked and then Freddie reached for the phone: 9-1-1: Uh, our house is on fire. Can you come?

I was cruising at my usual snail's pace, which is to say I was going 10 miles an hour, 12 max. I always drive slowly on the East Side. I savor my alone time, and I want to hear the end of the National Public Radio report. If I drive too fast, I'll reach my destination too soon and never find out how it all ends: Did she finally tell her mother about the tattoo?

Elmgrove is pleasant on a spring night. The streets are mostly empty of the loud-mouthed buses, and the spry walkers are out with their Springer spaniels and long-tailed mutts.

The turn off Elmgrove onto my street, Irving, is wide, and I usually look both ways several times and then some to make sure no cars are coming my way. The intersection is notorious for accidents, so it's wise to exercise patience.

That night, I saw a fire truck racing down the road and I pulled off to the side. To my surprise, the truck took a right onto Irving and, to my bigger surprise, stopped in front of my house, the one with the hockey sticks sprawled across the driveway.

My husband had been preparing dinner while I was out, but he is such a seasoned and careful cook, a kitchen mishap never crossed my mind. I thought much worse and braced myself for life-altering news. I was wrong on both counts.

Peder emerged from the house, his face ashen, his hand wrapped in a blood-soaked towel. He sat down on the top step. I couldn't get close. He was surrounded by a gaggle of firefighters, all ministering to him with utmost care. I had to shout over the roar of the truck's idling engine.

"What happened?" I asked.

"Oysters," he shouted back.

The dinner had been carefully planned by Peder for our guest and next-door neighbor, Tom. It was Tom's first time over, and Peder wanted to serve something special. For the main course, we would have chicken meunière (lightly breaded cutlets sautéed in butter and finished with parsley), along with a side dish of fresh asparagus.

Tom likes seafood so Peder chose hors d'oeuvres of shrimp, smoked mackerel, and oysters. Who can resist an oyster? I could slurp down a dozen on a lonely bar stool and still beg for more. I like mine with a dash of hot sauce mixed with horseradish.

When they are in season, oysters are as common in our house as, say, baseballs or poorly sharpened pencils. My husband prides himself on his ability to shuck the rock-hard shellfish, a skill he honed during his bachelor days sailing the ocean blue. Oysters beckoned at every port.

Shucking is an art that involves some risk. Usually, Peder wraps his left hand in an old rag to shield it from the knife's sharp blade. On this evening, his hand was unprotected. The knife slipped and slashed the palm of his left hand. I wasn't there but was later told that "a fountain of blood shot up—you should have seen it, Mom."

"Oh no," my husband reportedly said. "It hurts."

The call to 911 was placed.

We live a few blocks from a fire station, so the big red truck arrived in seconds. Tom saw all the commotion from his study and rushed outside, long before his expected arrival time for dinner. The firefighters cleaned the wound and wrapped Peder's hand in a bandage.

It was settled. Tom would stay with our two boys, and I would take Peder to the emergency room. In the past, we've gone to Rhode Island Hospital for our emergency care. This time, we decided to stay in the neighborhood and visit Miriam Hospital.

Emergency room visits often involve a long wait in a stuffy room with a lot of people sneezing, but, in this case, Peder was seen immediately. No doubt it had to do with the blood dripping onto the tile floor.

"Get him to 1C," a nurse shouted.

Within minutes, Peder was whisked off into a separate room, where his wound was cleaned and examined by two nurses and a chatty and remarkably calm emergency room doctor named Dr. Cummings.

The knife had nicked an artery, hence the gushing blood. Dr. Cummings closed the wound with three grand stitches and sent Peder on his way with a prescription for antibiotics. The discharge papers minced no words: "Since you impaled yourself shucking oysters, your wound is at risk for infection."

We left in a buoyant mood. Only two hours in the ER.

Back home, we found Tom and the boys with full bellies, thanks to my oldest son, who cooked the dinner that my husband had started but never finished. Our hospital adventure was recounted over a touch of the grape.

A short time later, the hospital called.

"Your husband left his book here," a nurse said.

I thought back. I remembered seeing John Sandford's crime novel, *Heat Lightning*, on a medical cart. How could I return to the ER now? I was tired, even tipsy. And then an unexpected gesture of kindness: Dr. Cummings offered to drop the book off on her way home to her East Side house. Her shift ended around midnight; she'd leave the book on our front steps.

I gave her our address, hung up and realized we removed the numbers when we painted the house last summer. I wrote a large "75" on a piece of paper and tacked it to a post on the porch. On another sheet of paper I wrote, "Thank you, Dr. Cummings."

I listened for her footsteps but fell asleep.

Heat Lightning was there in the morning.

Clogs
July 2011

I'm sorry to admit that I know Maria and Arnold have split. Maria grew tired of Arnold's womanizing, which included fathering a child with a household maid and groping, a truly detestable offense.

I know about this celebrity breakup because it was on the front page of the greatest newspaper in the world, just below a story about those courageous rebel fighters in Libya getting killed by pro-Gadhafi forces.

The Shriver-Schwarzenegger story was an all-time low for *The New York Times*. Mixing the trivial with death rankles me, but these are tough times for daily papers.

With a decline in the number of people reading newspapers (or anything involving the printed word), editors across the country are scrambling to sell their product. Hence, we see drivel.

We see stories about Angelina's bump.

We see stories about Pippa's slinky dress.

We see the weekly yoga pose.

The most egregious example of this vacuous journalism is a new column in the *Times* called "What I Wore." Women prattle on in exhaustive detail about the clothes they wore during a week in their hectic lives, what with all those gallery openings and charity dinners. No detail is spared.

I nearly dozed off reading a recent post by a 27-year-old editor for *Marie Claire*: "I was still kind of groggy from being in Europe for the shows, so I woke up trying to figure out a way to incorporate flats into my outfit. I just can't deal with heels anymore. So I put on black Chanel boots over ribbed DKNY tights and a blue and white batik-print Zara tulip skirt with an ivory short-sleeved turtleneck sweater from Michael Kors. I headed to a Core Fusion class at Exhale, for which I wore black Lululemon leggings with a white American Apparel tank top."

Let's all take a deep breath for this young woman.

So many choices. What to do?

If it's any consolation, I, too, have had it with heels. It's impossible to herd 11 boys off the playground wearing my black grosgrain Kate Spade pumps with 6-inch glitter spikes that light up a room when I make an entrance. Fed up, I chucked the shoes one day into the forest behind Patterson Park, where they sit in a bed of daisies.

"What I Wore" should be called "What A Bore."

I don't care about Miu Miu flats or Jimmy Choo totes or Akris shirtdresses with blue watercolor prints of Capri on them. Most days I look like I just stepped off the midnight train from Fargo, North Dakota. My beloved uniform consists of cords, clogs, and a turtleneck, which I wear year-round except in August, the only warm month in New England.

Clothes are not a big priority in our house. My two young sons wear the first thing they touch in their dresser drawer, usually a stained Red Sox T-shirt and jeans roughed up at the knees. Now and then, I encourage them to put on a clean shirt for church. That pleading is inevitably met with, "Mom, I'm not changing. It's my life."

I've taught them well.

When did this obsession with clothes begin? Sure, some grown-ups have always enjoyed getting dolled up, even for a trip to the market. But over the years this preoccupation with dress has trickled down to the masses, most notably to teens and young adults, who spend far too much time and money worrying about the way they look. Do they really need those $250 Ugg boots for a math class?

When I was kid, jeans, flannel shirts, and desert boots were our go-to clothes. We wore peacoats in the winter and cut-offs in the summer. Prom queens were the only ones who wore lime-green Pappagallo flats and plaid wool skirts with big safety pins on the side.

My advice to all, young and old alike, is to resist the temptation to be stylish. Do not search for your aesthetic. If we all dressed like slobs—jeans, comfy tops, shoes with no elevation—imagine how much time we'd save, not to mention money. A boardroom of ladies and gents in Levi's.

To help others make the switch to simplicity, I've started my own blog about attire:

I woke up feeling achy all over, so I decided to wear clothes that barely touch my body. I retrieved from the banister my black cotton sweats from Bob's with a risqué phrase on the tight-fitting part. My sons begged me to change. I did. I put on my black cords from GAP and discovered that they had a large white spot on the right knee, marred during a tub cleaning with Clorox-laced Soft Scrub. I called my best friend in Cleveland, and she suggested coloring the spot with a black marker. Brilliant idea. Go Indians!

As usual, it was freezing in our house, so I put on my pink

striped long-sleeved undershirt from the Layabout Laura line and a gunbolt gray turtleneck from L.L. Bean. I looked out the window. Torrential rain, again. I would need more. I picked up off the floor my two-tone orange fleece from Ocean State Job Lot and my marine blue puffer coat I found in a box on our front steps one winter morning with the note, "Return to Building 19 if unsuitable."

I usually get dressed in 15 seconds, but today it took only four.

My son said, "You look great, Mom."

My son said, "You look great, Mom."

I said, "Thanks guys. So do you."

Close Call

September 2011

Up, up, and away, and here we go over amber waves of grain and purple mountains, majestic and utterly American at 10,000 feet. They are down there, where I want to be, but it's too late.

I'm stuck.

I am surrounded by passengers gabbing about their great aunt in Kansas or eating stale peanuts in between sips of flat Coke.

I've got the jitters.

I am double crossing my fingers and asking the Hound of Heaven to delay the inevitable. I have that tingly feeling that comes from sheer terror. I dig deep into the front pocket of my jeans and rummage around for a pin-size white pill. My sweet lady. A valium. I don't even ask for water.

I love to sing, but I hate to fly.

A long time ago, I didn't mind zipping through the air at 580 miles per hour in an aluminum tube with low ceilings and cramped bathrooms. When I was only 9 years old, I flew alone from my hometown of St. Louis to the Delaware coast to spend the summer with a friend and never panicked during the three-hour flight. The breakfast of scrambled eggs and sausage was delicious.

But then along came that train wreck and the sky turned from robin egg's blue to steel gray. The deadly experience made me realize that those big objects that take you places and the people who drive them are imperfect.

Flashback to the winter of 1987: After visiting my sister Emily and her husband Bill in Washington, D.C., for the New Year, I boarded Amtrak's Colonial to Connecticut, where I lived during my early months working as a reporter for *The Providence Journal*.

The train was packed with holiday travelers, so I ended up sitting in a rear car in a seat next to a window. We left around noon, and I remember thinking that I should go to the café car to get a cup of coffee to perk me up for the six-hour ride.

But the crowd was thick, and I decided to stay put.

Less than an hour later, just outside Baltimore, the train jolted to a stop. The lights flickered and then went out. I heard a deafening screech. I lunged forward, hitting my head and leg on the seat in front of me.

I got up to investigate and bumped into a man with a bloody gash across his forehead. I ran outside and screamed for help and soon realized the enormity of what had happened. The cars in front were piled on top of each other in a horrific jumble of twisted metal.

Passengers, most with gaping wounds, were walking

around in a daze. Residents living in quaint West Twin River heard the blast from their houses and ran to the track to pull people from the burning wreckage.

I was one of the lucky ones. My decision to sit in back and to forgo coffee probably saved my life. It was one of the worst crashes in Amtrak's history. Fifteen people—many of whom were in the café car—were killed, as well as an Amtrak engineer and café worker. Hundreds of the 600 passengers were injured.

I stayed in the town for four days, sleeping in a family's house near the track and filing stories to the *Journal.* I also took photos that ran all over the world. Back then, there was no such thing as a laptop. I dictated my stories over the phone to the newsroom:

Passengers with bloody foreheads and swollen eyes called out for loved ones still trapped inside. "My husband went to get some food," one woman said, crying and pacing frantically. Some gathered on a road nearby, clinging to each other with their heads bowed. A train conductor, his face splattered with blood, sat on the ground with his legs splayed out in front of him and a blanket over his shoulders. He stared ahead vacantly. A woman held his hand.

I even received treatment for my wound: a gash on my leg.

Rescue workers soon figured out what had caused the crash. Moving at more than 100 mph, the Colonial had rammed three Conrail locomotives that had run a caution light and failed to slow down. Months later, the Conrail engineer admitted to smoking marijuana and eventually served time in prison for his role in the crash.

Traveling for me has never been the same.

It took a decade before I would ride a train again. Even

now, when a train speeds up, I clutch the arm rests and count the minutes until we arrive—safely—at our next stop. I always sit in a rear car, and I try my best not to get up while the train is moving. I refuse to go to the café car.

Flying is a challenge too. When the pilot hits the brakes on the runway my back presses against the seat and, for a moment, I feel like I'm on the Colonial again, speeding down the track. Will we make it?

Minutes after the collision, I met Eric, who lived with his parents near the tracks and rushed from his house to help. I slept on a hide-a-bed in his family's basement for days while I reported the story.

Back home weeks later, Eric, who was 23, wrote me a letter saying that he was having anxiety attacks and nightmares. He said his life would never be the same. "The trains give everyone the chills when the whistle blows," he wrote. "The feeling is a tense feeling like you might feel when you hear a car slam on its brakes just before an accident or in a close call."

He told me he was going to be an architect.

I wonder if he made it.

I wonder.

Pawn Stars
October 2011

Pawn Stars is making us happy.

There is nothing naughty about the program other than the title, which is too predictable to be offensive. It's good family entertainment. My 10-year-old son Henry, a student of contemporary culture, discovered the show during one of his channel surfing exercises a few weeks ago.

I walked into the TV room and there he was, sitting in the brown chair, remote in hand, blue eyes riveted to Rick "The Spotter" Harrison delivering the news ("first the good, then the bad") to the pleasant woman from the Catholic charity: Yes, that's Al Pacino's loopy inscription in your leather-bound script of *The Godfather*, but, sorry, I'm only giving you 400 bucks. Tops.

"Gosh," the woman replied. "I can do better at the church auction."

When the show was over Henry asked me if I wanted a peanut and then he asked me if I wanted to watch a second episode. (All of the 100-plus shows are available to us through On Demand.) By evening's end, we had watched four 30-minute episodes, all reruns. We even ate our dinner in the TV room. I won't apologize.

The show is what's called in the biz a reality show. It's probably scripted, but I don't care.

The series is filmed in Vegas at the Gold & Silver Pawn Shop, a family-owned joint run by "The Spotter" and his dad, also known as "The Old Man," a rascal with well-tended hair and snake eyes who can spot a fake Rolex a mile away. Their sidekick is Chumlee, a lovable young man who seems guileless, but is not. Everyone wears black.

It's no surprise that in this sputtering economy the show is a hit. I can only imagine the joy that comes from strolling into a Vegas pawn shop and discovering that the rusty buck knife from your great uncle will pay the heating bill.

After our marathon session in front of the TV that evening, Henry asked if we had goods to pawn. Hmm. I thought about all that stuff I lugged home from my mother-in-law's house five years ago. Carol never threw anything out and neither did her mother, brother, uncle, and aunt, so we own a truckload of oddities that might interest Gold & Silver.

My husband's uncle, Gordon Alf Lawrence Johnson, was a huge fan of the funny pages, especially the Peanuts comic strip, which he read up until the day he died, at 83. He took great pleasure in giving Peanuts books and memorabilia as presents on birthdays and holidays.

We have a dozen or so musty-smelling books by Charles Schulz from the 1960s, as well as a porcelain bobblehead of my favorite depressive, Charlie Brown. Time has been kind to him. He has a rough patch on his big head, but otherwise is in excellent shape. The red tag on the bottom of his stand says, "Fine Quality Lego. Japan."

There's nothing better than a good John Hancock. Bob Dylan might titillate some; others go for Pauly D, the North Providence deejay and star of the reality show, *The Jersey Shore.* In our house we have Douglas Fairbanks, and his wife, Mary Pickford. In the 1920s, Fairbanks and Pickford were the Brangelina of Hollywood. Their Beverly Hills mansion was called Pickfair.

We are in possession of five signed photos of the stars. They came to us through Carol, who received them from her mother, Sophie Johnson. Sophie's husband, Capt. Peder August Johnson, was a tanker captain for Esso, now Exxon, from 1920 to 1943.

Family lore has it that he befriended the actors when his ship was docked in Long Beach, California, for a few days. Maybe they had a drink together. Maybe they had a few drinks together. Captain Johnson, as smitten with the couple as the rest of the country, asked for autographs.

A few weeks later, Sophie received a package in the mail at her house in Smithfield, Rhode Island. "To the nautical Johnsons and their tiny crew—Best wishes from Douglas Fairbanks, 1927," the mustachioed swashbuckler wrote, referring to Peder and Sophie Johnson's three children, who, in addition to Carol and Gordon, also included Stanley.

Then there is the fine but gloomy art from Stanley. In the early 1950s, Stanley, a graduate of Brown University and raconteur fluent in Russian, worked as a reporter for the Associated Press, in Moscow. When he returned home, he brought back lithographs of barges on a fog-shrouded Volga River. Is Vegas biting?

What about Aunt Gert's glass knife? Or Uncle Harry's six-inch wooden ruler from the "Providence Electric Blue Printing Co., 86 Weybosset St., Providence, R.I. Established 1905"?

What about the tin match box? The chrome flour sifter from Benny's, with the 68-cent price tag intact. The Australian boomerang with carvings of kangaroos? The armadillo basket—too dreadful to reveal details.

Maybe there's interest in my husband's collection of racetrack programs and losing pari mutuel tickets from Lincoln Downs, Narragansett Park, Hialeah Park, Marshfield Fair, and AK-SAR-BEN, which is Nebraska spelled backwards, a fun fact grasped only by those who know the difference between a filly and a colt.

The Vegas boys look like a betting bunch, but, who knows, maybe they don't play the horses. If that's the case, we will go elsewhere. I bet Saratoga has a pawn shop.

RUK?

November 2011

I don't have much time to write today. My phone beckons. I've had the phone for a year, but I just expanded my coverage plan to include texting. Unlimited texting.

For those of you still tethered to land lines, texting is a cell phone perk that allows you to misspell words on purpose—I cant pik U up—and talk in code. That's stuff like R U K? a perky phrase my 11-year-old taught me.

It means, Are you okay?

No, I texted back.

Unlimited texting means you are piloting a plane in an endless stretch of blue.

I know what you're thinking. Distraction. Car accidents. Juvenile delinquents.

You are wrong on all counts.

Texting is like a shot of espresso. It charges me up. It makes me feel connected to everyone: Denise in faraway Cleveland; my sister in Washington, D.C.; my son roaming around like a gypsy:

where R U?

playng ftbll

K. chik for dinr

For years, I derided texting and tried my best to speak and write in complete sentences.

Silly. Me.

This new technology first gave me pause after reading a story in *The New York Times* a few years ago that began thus: "They do it late at night when their parents are asleep. They do it in restaurants and while crossing busy streets. They do it in the classroom with their hands behind their backs. They do it so much their thumbs hurt."

Teenagers sent and received about 2,272 text messages per month—or 80 a day—in the fourth quarter of 2008, the paper reported. Doctors and psychologists were worried. The phenomenon was leading to anxiety, bad grades, sleep deprivation, distraction in school, and repetitive stress injury from too many what ups?

What really got my teeth grinding were the comments of a psychologist who studies texting among teenagers. The MIT professor claimed that teens who text have trouble breaking free from their parents as they mature into adults. "You have adolescents," the professor said, "who are texting their mothers 15 times a day, asking things like, 'Should I get the red shoes or the blue shoes?'"

It's a no-brainer. The red shoes.

OMG, I said to myself. I will never let my son get a cell, and if I ever cave, I will never let him get a cell with texting. He will communicate with me the old-fashioned way—calling from a friend's house:

Mom, it's me.

What up?

Don't say that.

OK.

I'll be home at 5.

The request came a few weeks before the start of middle school. My son wanted a cell. No, I said, citing the professor's findings, you're too young to have a phone. Being a persistent kid, he pressed on. He did the research. He suggested a GoPhone, a pre-paid cell. You buy the minutes for texting and phone calls (remember those) and when you run out, you buy more.

I'm a sucker for kids who do the research.

The fellow at the AT&T store at the mall was really nice. My son got a phone that sounds like the iconic game Pac Man, and I added texting to my iPhone. We were kids in a candy store as we exited the shop. We decided to do a test run over ice cream cones:

hi

hi

Where does all the time go? They walk off to middle school, turn the bend, and you're left on the front steps, waving goodbye. You might stand there for a while, watching the cars pass. You might pick up a twig and toss it aside. You hope they're safe and happy.

School ended at 2:40. 2:41, no text. 2:42, no text. 2:50, no text. And then it came: im walkin home with Noah. Minutes later, he fired off another: at bahras. Then, yet another: on my way home.

I texted back: grate

I have a bone to pick with the professor. Texting does not impede emotional growth. If used properly, it gives kids more independence and parents more peace of mind. I don't want my son to text me every five seconds. I just want a hi-it's-me text after school and an on-my-way-home text after football.

The truth is, I'm the one who's texting compulsively. I think it's the greatest invention since tights. I knew I had really cracked up when I texted my friends to let them know I was a convert and that going forward, I could be reached in this way.

text me! I wrote.

When no one responded, I texted again.

pretty pls

Bullygirl

December 2011

When I was girl, I lived with my family in a small Midwestern suburb. Our red brick house was in a neighborhood called Wydown Forest, a cluster of houses nestled among oaks and maples that towered over rooftops. In winter the trees were bare, and icicles hung on the branches.

Christmas was an especially festive holiday for us. Wreaths entwined with berries decorated thick wooden doors and lit-up Christmas trees sparkled in windows. I loved being inside, curled up next to a hissing radiator.

On rare occasions I left the warmth of our house, usually to build a snowman in the backyard or trek through knee-deep drifts to play Clue at Peggy's around the corner.

One winter, I was invited to go Christmas caroling. We would walk door-to-door, singing "Deck the Halls" and "O Come All Ye Faithful" to generate holiday cheer. No one else in my family wanted to go—I had four sisters and one brother—so I had to venture out alone.

That wasn't an easy thing for an 11-year-old from a big family to do. We moved as a unit and that strength in numbers provided some protection from life's cruelties. The bullies dare not approach our sibling army.

Winters in the heartland are harsh. The wind howls off the Mississippi and sweeps down to the suburban valleys, with no respect for wool coats or mittens. In the darkest days of winter no one goes out unless it's necessary.

My mother had to push me out the door. I had committed to a night of merrymaking and couldn't cancel now. Besides, my friend Mignon was expecting me. I buttoned up my navy peacoat, all the way to the top.

Mignon lived a block away in a white house with two small columns that framed her red front door. She was the oldest of three girls and her father worked as a reporter for the local newspaper. He smoked a pipe and tended to an old-fashioned mustache that curled up at the end, making him look like the tenor in a barbershop quartet. Her mother was a painter.

Susie was my best friend; Mignon was my second-best. Some friendships among children are based on proximity, not kinship, and such was the case with Mignon. Despite all those afternoons hanging out in her bedroom listening to David Bowie's "Ziggy Stardust," I knew we didn't have much in common. She was an artist. I was a tomboy. She wore billowy skirts and heels. I wore jeans and desert boots. We were friends because she lived down the street.

I joined the carolers—parents and their children—in front of our house as they belted out "boughs of holly" and "holy night," making perfect O's with their mouths on the drawn-out notes.

I tried to feign enthusiasm. I felt self-conscious singing in public—after all, I was just a kid—so what came out of my mouth was more of a whisper. My shyness didn't help. Who were these people? Neighbors, yes, but did I know them?

Mignon connected with us halfway down the block. I could tell something was amiss. She seemed uncharacteristically silly, poking at her younger sisters, who had come along. Her clothes were different too—a black wool cape that fit her arty image and made her look exotic.

By the time we got to the Mills' house, I was miserable. I was wearing sneakers, not boots, and my feet were wet. My toes were numb. My peacoat was so helpless against the wind

I might as well have been wearing my pajamas.

Still, I proceeded with the carols and fought my mutinous instinct. I sang but didn't mean it. A few notes into "Silent Night," I noticed Mignon was missing—no longer by my side. Our group was big, so I assumed she was on the periphery and would appear later.

Suddenly a holly bush, with sharp and pointy leaves that could draw blood from the careless, shook as if a frenetic squirrel were lost inside. Out popped Mignon, her cape flapping in the lamplight. It came with no warning: a snowball as hard as a baseball hit me in the eye.

Mignon laughed.

The pain nearly knocked me over, a sting unlike anything I had experienced before. The holly disintegrated into a blur of green. Dizzy with a ringing in my ears, I felt sure the damage was permanent.

My pride kept me from running home, and I pressed on with the tra-la-las, blinking back tears, getting no apology from my second-best, only more teasing and laughter.

Later that night, I soaked a washcloth in hot water and placed it over my wound. My eye healed, but not my friendship with Mignon. Very young, I learned the difference between a mischievous person and a mean one.

Mignon eventually moved to Texas—or maybe it was Italy. I can honestly say that I never missed her. Not once.

I can't remember my favorite toy as a kid or a single birthday party, but I remember Mignon's heartless shot, so much so that I always offer a bit of advice to my kids before a snowball fight.

Never the face. Aim low.

Just Ducky

February 2012

On a recent afternoon, my son Henry and one of his best buds, Oren, gathered for a business meeting on the third floor of our house. A nosy reporter (me) had requested the meeting to find out about the boys' new company, zazogratiffi, a maker of finely crafted duct tape wallets.

The first order of business was to set the ground rules: One, no somersaults on the bed when responding to the reporter's questions; two, no take-back statements along the lines of, I know I said this, but I want you to say that; and, three, no ukulele playing by Henry during the interview.

The questions were fast, sometimes furious.

Me: "How did your company get started?"

Henry: "Well, everybody was making companies in school."

Oren: "Except it wasn't duct tape companies."

Henry: "Jason was making sticky notes with cool lettering."

Oren: "Everybody would put them on their desks so they knew exactly who they were."

As so it went for nearly an hour, the words tumbling out in all their existential glory, revealing what I had suspected from the beginning, that zazogratiffi was a start-up destined for greatness, at least in the neighborhood.

It's encouraging to see a small business thriving in our sputtering economy. In bad times, customers usually bypass the mom-and-pop shops and head to big-box stores like Target. A pity—small businesses have so much character. The owners are usually convivial people pursuing their passions on a modest budget with no guarantee of financial success. Consider Oren and Henry. They work long hours, taking conference calls late into the night, and they just barely break even, what with duct tape going for $5.49 a roll.

Unless you've been living in Modesto for the last decade, you probably know that these imaginative 10-year-olds have been hanging out with each other for years. They like to make stuff. After one of Oren's visits, our kitchen table is usually piled high with rubber bands, orphaned LEGO pieces, twisted paperclips, broken pencils, and the sliced-off tips of erasers.

On the way out the door, the latest creation, maybe a sling-shot or mini catapult, is usually deep in a little boy's pocket. That creation makes its way into a school backpack and onto the desktop of a 5th grader equally enchanted by the bones of things. Classroom chatter ensues: "Did you see Henry's thing-a-ma-bobber?" "How did he make it?" "I want one."

This fall, Henry's fifth-grade class was abuzz with the capitalist spirit. Jason's handmade sticky notes were a huge success, and there was talk of making friendship bracelets. Henry wanted to get in on the action.

One night he was "traveling through videos" on the inter-net when he came across a site about how to make duct tape wallets. Duct Tape Stuff, created by a college student who likes taping himself to trees with duct tape, was soon on favorites. Night after night, Henry would retire to the computer room with a roll of duct tape and a pair of scissors and watch the site's tutorials, rewinding on the hard parts.

His first wallet was the "magic," a no-nonsense black-and-green wallet the size of a baseball card. He showed it to Oren one day after school. He was wildly impressed and bought his own roll of duct tape.

"I was so amazed that you could take something that

seemed so dull and stupid," said Oren, "and then make something so cool out of it."

A company was born. Oren settled on the name. "Zazo" stands for the first letters of four boys' names—Zach, Aidan, Zack, and, of course, Oren—and "gratiffi" is what happens when you are 10 years old and typing really fast. Company titles came next. Oren was appointed CEO; Henry, president and creative director. The board's vote of two was unanimous.

"I consider myself more of a businessperson in this company," said Oren. "When I grow up, I want to be a CEO or the general manager of a baseball team."

Like all innovative entrepreneurs, the boys started exploring how to sell their goods online. Henry was skeptical, but Oren convinced him otherwise, especially after Henry's big brother wowed middle-school kids with a purple-and-green "zazogratiffi" wallet customized with the initials of the buyer, still a mystery.

"After that, we pursued the idea of a website," said Oren.

With Henry's help, Oren worked feverishly to create a site that was both functional and attractive. He took photos of the wallets and together the boys wrote captions to entice customers. The skateboard wallet is a "singular square with a flip-up part," the staircase wallet "just keeps on going like a staircase."

The company's site debuted on the web in mid-November. Sales are expected to climb as word gets out.

"My orthodontist is interested," said Oren.

"My dad is interested," said Henry.

Expansion plans are in the works. Seven rolls of duct tape in various colors—purple, green, red, orange, black, yellow, and zebra print—are stacked in a corner in Henry's room, awaiting deft fingers. Henry has also upgraded to an X-Acto knife and portable plastic cutting board that allows him to make house calls.

Since zazogratiffi is a mouthful, the boys are mulling over a name change.

"Our name's a little cheesy and corny," said Oren. "We might hire a phrase director."

"No, Oren, we don't need a phrase director," said Henry.

"Okay," said Oren. "Never mind."

"We can come up with a new name," said Henry. "What about something French?"

CHAPTER 7

....

A Beautiful Life
March 2012

How does she say goodbye to hair ravaged by chemo?

First, she dyes her beloved locks purple. Why not? Any sane person would. Then she strolls through her neighborhood, pulling out clumps and letting them float to the ground like rose petals.

I know everything Kim Turner Clark wants to tell me about her breast cancer. Every night, I click on her blog, "BadMannersCancers (so rude it just shows up without an invitation)," to read the latest post about an illness that has turned her life upside down and proved in the harshest way that life is luck, good and bad.

It's so incongruous that I had cells in my body dividing madly, surreptitiously, and as healthy and good and powerful as I felt, I was horribly sick, my body going haywire trying to kill itself. I didn't have any symptoms. Cancer is the great deceiver, the trickster.

For most of us, cancer is a concept, an illness that happens to other people. We are told (and see) that chemotherapy causes fatigue, nausea, and hair loss, but do we really know how that feels. No, we do not. Nor do we know how a head must spin when mortality knocks, especially when children are in the front parlor.

Kim's blog is a memoir in the making, searing and heartfelt

without being sentimental. And it's beautifully written, with haunting imagery that will make you shift in your comfortable chair. What makes the work even more special is that Kim is an East Side resident, a local artisan, and the single mother of two boys, 10 and 16.

The November diagnosis comes from nowhere and whacks Kim silly—stage 3 breast cancer, invasive ductal carcinoma, the kind of cancer with "wanderlust." She soon learns that the tumor is large—one and a half inches—and that the cancer is triple negative, the quickest-growing and most aggressive type of breast cancer, a cancer that does not respond to the hormone-blocking treatments so effective today.

I thought cancer-schmancer sucks, yeah, but I'm tough; it will be a god-awful year and then I'll be fine. One year. I was willing to give up a year of my life to cancer. I didn't expect it might want a whole lot more than that.

The narrative of Kim's early posts fluctuates between anger, defiance, and paralyzing fear, a mounting "free floating anxiety" rooted in her feeling that "everything is out of control, that I can't keep up." A flurry of visits ensues with oncologists and nurses. She feels overwhelmed by the new information in her "chemo class" and diligently reviews her "two-inch thick, 12-pound" chemo binder at night.

Good news comes. An MRI reveals that the cancer has not spread. A bone scan is clear. A CAT scan shows no evidence of metastases. To prepare for chemo, she is "portified," a surreal procedure in which a medical device is inserted under her skin to administer the chemotherapy drugs.

The procedure went smoothly, but I'm more than sore and I feel like Frankenstein with a slit stitched up the base of my neck. They told me not to shower for a week. LOL. Not shower for a week.

That's funny. This girl doesn't go a day without a shower.

To Kim's surprise, the first day of chemo is a "breeze." The nurses are sassy and smart, the chair is comfortable. Five hours of drip, drip, drip. But by evening's end, she is nauseous with a pounding headache. The next day, she can't get off the sofa.

I think I was overly optimistic about this week. I'm queasy and woozy, dizzy, befuddled, confused. My vision is blurry, the lights too bright. I'm tired and teary and just want to sleep. I've heard about chemo-brain.

Kim is so wiped out over the next few days she considers lying down during her shower. She has "axe-lodged-in-head caliber" headaches. Her gums bleed. Her guts churn. And then the inevitable. Her luscious hair falls out—in one day.

She reports that she has "two jars full of hair, much hair in the trash and down the drain" and promptly embarks on her "ceremonial walk" in the neighborhood, letting go of the tufts left behind. Later in the week, Kim instinctively reaches for a comb after showering and stops herself, blaming "old habits."

I'm afraid of how disconnected from any sense of the norm I'll be when I don't recognize myself in the mirror.

Still, through all the uncertainty and discomfort, she strives to be optimistic.

When I got in bed last night, I was tired—depleted, but happy. I wasn't worried or scared or pissed. This is my life and it's still a beautiful life.

Kim's most poignant posts are about her 10-year-old son, her "love bug," whose courage is heart-rending. He asks her if she "will be better by Christmas." With a knot in her stomach, she explains the "longevity" of her illness.

One day, love bug spots a sign that says, "After Cancer Every Day is a Great Day" and tells his mother he's excited about what most certainly lies ahead, for signs don't lie. "Isn't that great, Mom?" he says. She wants to say yes.

After months of chemo, Kim will undergo surgery to remove the tumor, and then comes the burning of radiation. Her journey is long. She is asking us to bear witness, and for that we should be grateful.

No Ukes at the Table
April 2012

My son Henry plays his ukulele in the morning, before the sun rises, before the curtains open, before the coffee maker purrs. I'm in bed, dreaming of dandelions, when I hear strumming so sweet and happy that gray skies turn blue and birds cease their back-and-forth to listen.

He might play for 30 seconds or 30 minutes, depending on his mood and the endurance of his dancing fingers.

Around our house, we call it the "uke." Initially, we used the full name, but that was a mouthful and anyway it's more fun to talk in abbreviated form. "Where's the uke?" "No ukeing during dinner, please." "Yes, the uke will fit in your backpack."

If you walk into our house on any day, you'll probably see the uke leaning against a cushion on our sofa, with that full-of-beans attitude reserved for politicians and jazz singers.

The uke knows it's special.

Serendipity played a role in Henry's discovery. I took a left into the fudge shop; he took a right into the music store.

"I was on Martha's Vineyard," said Henry, "and I went into a music store and saw an unusual instrument and figured out it was a ukulele. It sounded really good. I wanted a guitar at the time, but a guitar seemed like you needed a teacher, and I wanted to do something in my free time, so I decided a uke was the way to go."

Most people associate ukes with Hawaii and hip-swaying hula dancers festooned with leis. That might have been the case long ago, but not now.

According to my friends at Wikipedia, ukes originated in the late 19th century in Portugal. Portuguese immigrants from Cape Verde and Madeira introduced the uke to the Hawaiian Islands.

The instrument eventually made its way to the mainland, where it was picked up by vaudeville performers, including Roy Smeck, nicknamed "Wizard of the Strings." And let's not forget the frizzy-haired eccentric who came along in the 1960s, Herbert Khaury, better known as Tiny Tim of "Tiptoe Through the Tulips with Me" fame.

Ukes took a back seat to electric guitars in the 1960s, but emerged once again in the 1990s, thanks to the Hawaiian musician, Israel Kamakawiwo'ole, whose moving medley of "Over the Rainbow" and "What a Wonderful World" touched millions.

After yet another lull, the uke is making a comeback. Eddie Vedder, the lead singer for Pearl Jam, released a solo album last year called "Ukulele Songs," a collection of tracks performed on what he calls his activist instrument: the uke.

CNN recently reported that uke lovers are on the rise throughout the world, including New York City, where a uke subculture is thriving in bars and restaurants among people seduced by the instrument's intimacy.

"Ukuleles are the most global instruments in the world," said Ken Bari Murray, who solos during open-mike night at

Maui Tacos on Fifth Avenue in the shadow of the Empire State Building. "We like to notice that and foster it."

For the record, Henry, who just turned 11, picked up the instrument long before the patrons at the taco joint.

After that enlightening trip to the Vineyard music store, he parked himself in front of the computer for days and surfed the Web for uke players.

He did not find Vedder.

He found Sungha Jung, a music prodigy from South Korea with a Justin Bieber haircut and the intense focus of someone fully absorbed in his art. His interpretations of popular songs—the Beatles' "While My Guitar Gently Weeps," for one—are astonishing. Henry also found Jake Shimabukuro, a 34-year-old Hawaiian sensation who compares uke playing to a long yoga session.

Henry decided that he would have a uke and that he would buy it with his own money. Fair enough. He researched ukes and settled on the Guitar Center, in Warwick.

The ukes were displayed by the front door, not far from the Strats, way far from the snares. Henry sat on a bench and strummed, just for the heck of it. He bought the light-brown one with the white edging made by Lanikai.

"I picked out one that was cheap enough that I could get it with my own money, but would also fit my beginner level," he said. "At the time, becoming a professional was not on my mind."

At first, he was lost. What's a chord? What's fingering? How to strum? Again, he sought help with the technology that had propelled him to mastery many times: YouTube music videos. For hours, he'd watch a tutorial from, say, ukeflip, on how to play Jason Mraz's "I'm Yours," until he felt he had it down.

"The strings started to loosen up a little," Henry said. "My fingers started to get stronger. In the beginning I struggled to get a clean chord, then it turned into a walk in the park."

Ukes are shaped like pears. The instrument is easy to carry to a friend's house or to school. Not long ago, Henry brought his uke to his fifth-grade class for "Hawaiian Day" and serenaded students while they sipped pineapple smoothies.

What makes the instrument really special is that it only has four strings. Henry likes that; less is more. A scarcity of strings makes it easier for him to improvise and pursue his passion of composing his own tunes, like the ditty he came up with just after reading the morning paper's headlines:

I am bored.
The sun is shining no more.
The town is frowning all around.
I think it needs a merry-go-round.

Playground apparatus won't do. Give everyone ukes. That'll perk them up.

Garden Peppers
May 2012

He'd peek over the fence during his daily walks, until one day he decided to speak up. He had never seen such a lush garden in his South Providence neighborhood and wondered how he could get a plot of his own.

He asked around and discovered that it was a community

garden, a place by the people, for the people. By the spring, Cabreja Aquilino, who did not turn the soil, not once, during his boyhood in the Dominican Republic, was doting over his vegetables like the proud parent of a newborn.

Now the 73-year-old grandfather is unstoppable. His days involve weeds and watering cans. His peppers are green and glossy. He is amazed that he can pluck one in the morning and eat it for lunch.

"If I stay home, I do nothing," says Cabreja. "Here, we smile, we wave. We all get along."

The East Side is filled with community gardens, but so are other neighborhoods nearby. Cabreja's second home is Somerset Community Garden, off Broad Street, in one of the city's poorest neighborhoods. The one-acre of land—the site of a former chop shop—is a refuge in a tough section of town.

Nothing goes to waste. Many of the gardeners grow enough so they don't have to buy produce in grocery stores. Not even one pea. They often freeze food to save for the winter months.

Somerset is also known for its diversity. Once called a "Little United Nations," the garden has members from all over the world, including Laos, Cambodia, Liberia, and Ireland. Many families are Hmong refugees who resettled in Providence in the 1980s.

Behind a fence smothered with vines are 72 plots of raised beds divided by chicken wire and bamboo. The garden is magical in full bloom, with narrow paths that lead to secluded spots shaded by arbors of branches and faded boards. Cats lurk in the tall lemongrass.

Southside Community Land Trust, a nonprofit organization founded in 1981 by a Brown University student trying to rejuvenate the neighborhood, supervises the garden. With a private donation, the student bought a few cheap vacant lots and encouraged residents to turn them into gardens. Somerset was born.

Over the years, the land trust has flourished. The organization now has 15 community gardens, including Somerset, an urban farm that provides food to farmers' markets, and educational programs. Every year, the land trust holds a plant sale.

All the gardens are unique, but Somerset is special. It's the oldest garden and just a few steps from the land trust's offices. The three city blocks of green provide residents with a respite from urban life.

"A garden stabilizes the concept of hope," says the land trust's executive director, Katherine Brown. "Every year, you plant a seed hoping for a harvest."

That peacefulness is why many gardeners come back to Somerset year after year. Many fled violence in their countries of birth and appreciate the community they find at the garden. They meet for workshops on everything from composting to canning and begin each session with a group chant: My plot, our garden, our neighborhood. In mid-September, they hold a harvest party.

Phil Edmonds, a native of Ireland and a member of the celebrated local band, The Gnomes, has been planting peas at Somerset for two decades. He recalls dancing to Bob Marley tunes with gardeners from Laos and Liberia during a potluck at the Amos House soup kitchen years ago.

"It was quite a sight," says Phil. "To see these gardeners with big smiles on their faces was so beautiful."

Cabreja visits his plot in the morning, walking the ten blocks from his high-rise apartment. On this day, he unlocks the front gate and enters his tidy bed of vegetables. At first, he planted everything too close together. Sara Smith, another gardener, offered advice over her cornstalks: Don't crowd your plants.

She should know. Farming was a way of life in Liberia, where she grew up and fled in 1994 to escape civil war. She grows sweet potato leaves to simmer in sweet potato soup, a Liberian dish.

"My lady, how are you?" Cabreja says to her. He holds up one of his peppers. "Looks good," she says. She lives in the yellow house across the street. Her young grandson carries the harvest back home in his arms.

"You make a garden, you eat," says Sara, bending over to cut plants for the day's meal. "It's that simple."

One year, she was sick and couldn't clear the plot to seed. Phil sifted the earth for her. He's the go-to guy in the garden. He knows everyone and laughs often.

Growing up in an Irish village on the banks of the River Shannon, he tended carrots, cabbage, and potatoes that he dug up with his bare hands.

Phil has been a member of the Somerset garden for two decades: He's the wiry guy in a wool watch cap who gives away bouquets of collard greens and plays the pennywhistle by the yellow cosmos on summer nights.

"I get to feel a connection to the earth," he says. "And I get to eat organic, fresh food."

In the back, by a creeping morning glory, is Chantay Kingvlay, a gardener since opening day in 1981. She and her husband, Phan, tended their plot of bitter melon, long peas, and pak khao tong, a pointy-leafed plant that is a staple in the cuisine of Laos, her homeland.

A storm swept through one day, nearly toppling her bamboo fence. Phil came to the rescue, again. He tied the fence to the arbor with frayed netting, left behind by Phan, who died not long ago.

"I miss for my husband," she says, under the shade of her wide straw hat. "I come here and feel happy. Garden, garden, are you okay?"

After The Snip
June 2012

My locks are gone, shorn on a whim. If only I had read that article, you know, the one in *The New York Times*, which said, in short, that long hair on mature women is a "mark of liberation."

I've always wanted to be a feminist, and now it's too late.

I spent months living with unruly hair, only to decide, in the end, that those wavy strands cascading down the nape of my neck looked stupid. I glimpsed myself in the mirror and saw the scraggly tail of a sickly squirrel.

I called my salon: "I can't stand it. Book me."

If only I had done the research. I always do the research. If I had Googled "long hair on middle-aged women" or better yet, "long hair is the new black," I would be celebrating the growing season.

Instead, I called Michelle, a Picasso with scissors, and, in a few days, my mane was a bob. Don't get me wrong. The cut she gave me was superb, as always. It is full of bounce and vigor. But it is less; the glass is half-empty.

I was hasty and failed to pick up on the long-hair trend

sweeping the country.

The 2010 story in the Gray Lady was penned by Dominique Browning, a writer, blogger at slowlovelife.com and mother who lives in New York and on the Rhode Island coastline, hence the scratch-and-you-will-find Little Rhody connection.

She is pushing 60 and proudly sports long hair, not the kind that simply brushes her broad shoulders. No, we're talking hair "long enough for a ponytail with a swing to it, long enough to braid." Her agent thinks she's hiding behind something. Her sister frets over it. Her mother hates it.

Browning isn't listening. She is crazy about her hair and hangs steady despite all those judgments from people who can't zip it. Long hair is too rebellious. Long hair is an attempt to relive one's girlhood. Long hair is high maintenance, what with all those wisps flying hither and thither in a mad dash to the grocery store.

Are these complaints true or false? Who cares when Browning exhorts us to consider the "wonderfully sexy way our grandmothers, those women of the prairie, or concrete canyons, would braid their hair up in the morning and let their cowboys unravel it at night."

Patience. If only I had exercised patience.

There are many things to worry about in the world today, but even the most ardent feminist, the one for whom personal grooming is a patriarchal conspiracy to oppress women, must agree that one's day cannot proceed if the hair is uncooperative. Hair is a topic from the board room to the soccer field, from the professor's office to the kitchen table. Hair is the great equalizer among women.

When I was a skinny little girl, I had a pixie. My hair

was so short an elementary-school teacher once directed me to the boy's bathroom. "No, you belong here," she said, gently pushing me in line with Billy, Brant, and Sam. "I'm a girl," I replied, but the damage was done. I would never succumb to the shears again.

I still have the photo from high school. I'm sitting on a picnic table with my elbows propped on my knees and my hands cupped around a Marlboro. I'm wearing my favorite piece of clothing, a black Mexican-style T-shirt embroidered with the sun. My hair falls over my shoulders like a tent. Curls and more curls. It must weigh a ton.

Amy had a bob, but she was the exception. Most of us had long hair that we rarely pulled back in ponytails or swept up in buns. We happily wore our hair "down," even during gym. The goal was to obscure the face, not all of it, just the sides, in the way of Neil Young, back when he had hair.

I had long hair in college and in my early years as a reporter for a newspaper, no small feat considering that I was always in motion, often outside, sometimes in front of a burning house spitting sparks. In my late 30s, I decided to go for a trim. My friends said I was too old for long hair. I got a mid-back cut, which led to a shoulder-length cut, which led to a bob. I felt lighter, more swift-footed.

But then middle age came, and a pang of regret swept over me. Were those comments from my elders that long hair looks "silly" on older women the musings of ladies who parked the car and cut the engine at 50? I began to long for my long hair: I let it grow. And then doubts mounted, and I called Michelle.

If only I had read Browning.

Long-hair foes accuse her of "living in the '70s." Browning gives her mane a flip and responds: "And why not? I like being

55 going on 15. As far as I'm concerned, we never did get better role models than that gang of girls who sang their hearts out for us through lusty days and yearning nights: Bonnie Raitt, Joni Mitchell, Linda Ronstadt, Cher."

I'll pass on Cher, but gladly take the others, especially Joni, who is 68 and still has long hair. It's a healthy gray, and, to steal from *Blue*, as long as a river to skate away on, long enough to make my baby cry.

Helicopters
July 2012

I had a great Mother's Day.

I know, it's a market-driven, hyped-up holiday. Much worse, it's offensive to the millions of women who have made a choice not to have kids. And even worse than that, there's nothing more boring than parents gushing about their children.

But, please, let me indulge.

Just this once.

Mother's Day is my favorite holiday. I like it better than Valentine's Day (too forced), Christmas (rampant consumerism), Gaspee Day (too far away in Warwick), and even Halloween (always a Poe fog). The sun usually bursts through the clouds on Mother's Day, and we know who has a hand in that. It's a day to kick back and let your kids dote on you.

I've had a dozen Mother's Days. The early ones were fairly uneventful. I got a fistful of wildflowers and rocks and then went back to changing diapers. As my two boys got older, I got more sophisticated presents: feathery bookmarks; sculptures of penguins; cards with their mugshots. Still, after the offerings, I went back to supervisory roles. The little guys were simply too young to plan the dinner meal.

That's all changed. They're 11 and 12 now; practically grown men. They can mop the kitchen floor, whip up an omelet, wash their Little League uniforms, and even plan a Mother's Day during which everyone hustles but Mom.

My day started when my son Henry tapped my shoulder at dawn and whispered in my ear, "Happy Mother's Day." He asked me what I wanted for breakfast. I said, "Coffee and buttered toast." He said, "Dark coffee?"

I heard dishes clattering in the kitchen and a few minutes later Henry appeared at my bedside holding a tray, with my black coffee and a special treat: a mise en place bowl filled with orange marmalade. As I ate my toast, he serenaded me with his uke, playing a little ditty he made up on the fly.

"Bravo," I said, when he plucked his last string.

Presents followed: white tulips, a book for worriers called *Anxious Gardening*, and a poem penned by Henry that I'm not at liberty to divulge in full, but let's just say the eyes welled with the words "loving heart," "peanut butter sandwich," and "napkin in my lap."

Henry and his older brother, Peder, asked me where I wanted to go next, and I said the shower. After that, we hopped in the car and drove to Seven Arrows Farm, in Seekonk. If a nursery exists in heaven (fingers crossed), I hope it looks like Seven Arrows, an oasis of serenity.

Magic is at every turn—the climbing hydrangea hugging the pine, the rows of hosta sprouting like green fountains, the bamboo swaying in the breeze. For that alone, it's worth the trip, only a 15-minute drive from the East Side. I bought pots of Thai and Red Rubin basil for my herb garden.

Back home, I ate a turkey sandwich, carried home from the deli for this special day. I made the mistake of reading the paper. Never read the paper on Mother's Day. Editors like running anti-mother stories.

I read a review of a book written by a woman novelist who hates being a mother. One of her kids is a "tyrant," the other a "Dracula." As if that weren't bad enough, the reviewer was a big whiner too, which was obvious from this sourpuss remark: "What is interesting is that despite the mind-numbing boredom that constitutes 95 percent of child-rearing, we continue to have them."

Them? No one forces you to have kids. Why is it always the writer types who are miserable parents? Self-sacrifice is part of the package, and what a relief not to think about yourself all the time. I tossed the review aside and took a sip of my lemonade.

A friend stopped by and asked the boys if they wanted to play baseball. They said it was Mother's Day and that they would have to check with the lady of the house. We're big on baseball in our family, so I said, "Heck yeah." I told them I'd see them after a few homers, and off they went.

Earlier that day, I had made two Mother's Day requests: clean the bathroom (accomplished promptly) and sweep up the helicopters from the backyard. We have two century-old maple trees that unload millions of annoying seeds every spring. It's labor-intensive to dispose of them.

I secured a broom and a leaf bag and got to work. My husband took pity on me and helped out. When the boys got back from the ballfield, they also pitched in. Later, the boys and their dad went to the grocery store. I knew things were going my way when Henry called to ask if I wanted triple-crème brie.

I had requested a meat-free dinner and that's what I got: oysters, shrimp, and smoked bluefish, with my husband's secret dip. The homemade clam chowder soothed the soul. Mango sorbet for dessert. I didn't have to clear the table, scrub a pot, or take out the trash.

"Are you happy, Mom?" Peder said.

"Yep," I said.

"Did you have a good Mother's Day?"

"Yep," I said.

"Good," he said.

I curled up on the sofa and summoned the boys to the room.

"Thanks for being my sons," I said, sounding all mushy.

"Aw Mom," said Peder.

Thumbs-up signs all around.

Hello Saturn

August 2012

Watch your step. It's dark, as it should be. After all, we're looking at the night sky, and we can't very well see Saturn, Jupiter, or that cluster of stars way older than Buffalo nickels if we are carrying flashlights or fired-up iPhones. Keep them in your pocket. This is sacred land.

Welcome to Seagrave Memorial Observatory, in Scituate, a mere 20 minutes from the East Side and one of the state's best-kept secrets. Not only is it free, but it's also bursting with brainy volunteers who can give grown-ups and kids a quick lesson in dark matter.

I'm here with my sons, Peder and Henry, and their friend, Jozef, on a summer night when Saturn is so crisp and clear it looks like one of those images on a sci-fi poster from the 1950s, rings and all.

"It's amazing," says Jozef, peering into a telescope for the first time in his brief eleven years on this planet. "It looks like a cartoon picture."

Nestled among trees on a one-acre clearing off Peeptoad Road, Seagrave has plenty to spark curiosity about the universe—two computerized telescopes that can locate celestial objects if you press a few buttons, and the observatory's treasure, the Alvan Clark Refractor, a 134-year-old telescope that used to sit on the East Side.

That's right—in our neighborhood.

Back in the late 19th century, a boy named Frank Evans Seagrave was captivated by the celestial realm. His father, a textile mill owner and bank president, bought him a telescope for his 16th birthday. In 1878, young Seagrave set it up in the backyard of his house at 119 Benefit Street.

Eventually, he grew weary of the light pollution from gas lamps and, in 1914, built the still-standing observatory in Scituate, taking along his telescope. He was an astute astronomer. That same year, he received an honorary degree from Brown University for his three years of precise and groundbreaking work on the orbit of Comet Halley.

Not long after Seagrave's death in 1934, Skyscrapers, an amateur astronomical society founded by a Brown professor, bought the Scituate property. Today the group has 90 members, mostly amateur astronomers who share a passion for the night sky.

Among the members are a toolmaker, an engineer, a web

designer, a former Brown administrator, and a 12-year-old boy from Glocester whose backyard is dark enough for night viewing. You don't need to be an astronomy expert to sign up at Skyscrapers. You don't even need a telescope.

"You just have to have some interest in looking at the sky," says David Huestis, a former senior programmer analyst for CVS and a member of Skyscrapers since 1975. Huestis, who also teaches an astronomy class at Bryant University, says he's happiest when he can get people to "look up."

The group is making a special effort to recruit "junior" members. That's a fancy term for kids, many of whom would rather play video games than spend an evening gazing at Saturn.

Peder first dabbled in astronomy in his sixth-grade science class when he wrote a report on Saturn, gathering information online. As he read about the sixth planet from the sun, he veered off into other territory and links.

He soon read about the exploration of Mars, possible life on Venus, and what lies beyond faraway Pluto. Comets? Black holes? Then he discovered videos of the heavens on YouTube and there was no turning back.

Peder talked his dad into taking him to Wheeler Farm, in Seekonk, to attempt a glimpse of Saturn and the phases of Venus with binoculars salvaged from a closet. He allegedly spotted the rings of Saturn, but in all likelihood, they were probably a Southwest flight to Palm Beach. No sightings of Venus.

From there, he jumped to Google to find observatories in Rhode Island. There are two besides Seagrave: the Ladd Observatory on Hope Street, here on the East Side, and the Frosty Drew Nature Center & Observatory in Ninigret Park, in Charlestown.

Word spread about Peder's new passion, and we soon came into the possession of a nifty portable telescope, thanks to my husband's boss, Dan, who loaned it to us. We can stargaze every clear night for years.

Peder used to read Sox stats in the paper every morning. Now he's reading in *Sky & Telescope* magazine about "self-destructing clumps of ice particles that are changing the face of Saturn's bizarre F ring."

All this stargazing has inspired him to ask some heady existential questions: Where are we in time and space? Why are we here? What or who lies beyond?

His argument, delivered to me in writing, goes something like this: "We are just one planet in a star system with eight planets. Our star is one of over 400 billion stars in our galaxy, the Milky Way. Our galaxy is just one galaxy in thousands, maybe millions of galaxies. With this amount of possible planets and stars in our known world it is very improbable that we are the only life out there."

I guess we're just a speck, a humbling idea from which we could all benefit.

"Before I got into this, I always wondered what's up there," says Peder. "Now I've turned this wondering into learning. I can tell you one thing: we are definitely not alone. No way, no way in the world."

Henry Wennmaker
September 2012

I spent a lot of time this summer going back to my old haunts.

My son had baseball games close to towns where I used to live, and I couldn't resist checking out the territory again to see if things had changed.

One of the places I visited was Norwich, Connecticut, where I had my first job as a reporter for the local paper, *The Norwich Bulletin*. When I was there, in the mid-1980s, the town was a dump. Flophouses galore, a failing Woolworth's, a seedy tavern. For a cub reporter, it was heaven.

The Mashantuket Pequots had just received approval to build an enormous bingo hall. That was big news. Bigger news was to come, long after I left. Bingo led to slot machines, craps tables, and Wayne Newton at Foxwoods, that monstrous casino a hop from Norwich.

Foxwoods workers had to live somewhere, and my guess is that they all set up house in Norwich. I barely recognized the town during my drive-through. Coffee shops, restaurants, and upscale shops were everywhere. My old apartment building on Jail Hill, named for the prison that stood there a century ago, was gone.

I like Norwich better the way it was, down-and-out. I couldn't wait to return to the ballfield.

I also took a drive to nearby Ledyard. My beat was town government, but my most probing story was about a stubborn Swamp Yankee named Amos Banks. One day, Banks noticed a pool of black stuff bubbling up in his front yard. "Fuel oil," he said. He held up his greasy, callused fingers.

He blamed a faulty pipe installed by a hot shot oil company. The company insisted the culprit was a buried oil tank that had cracked. Many front-page stories later, the company was vindicated. The tank was removed, and Banks had a bathtub-size hole in his yard for weeks. He never apologized to the oil company and made sure the executives picked up the removal bill.

My most memorable trip, though, was to Westerly.

After a year at the *Bulletin*, I moved to *The Providence Journal*, where I started out in the Westerly bureau, covering the region. Westerly is a fine historic town, with a Romanesque public library and a sprawling Wilcox Park.

On that day, I drove down High Street and stopped at Immaculate Conception, a Catholic church founded in the 1880s. I thought of Henry. Henry Joseph Wennmaker IV. His mother, Mary Dolores, would sprinkle holy water on his face when they went there to pray. Henry couldn't reach the font.

He was born with Werdnig-Hoffman disease, a genetic disorder that paralyzes the nerves that activate muscles. Needing a wheelchair, he could move only his forearms, thin as reeds. He was 4 feet tall and weighed 38 pounds. His bed was an 850-pound iron lung.

I met him through a friend and thought he had a story to tell.

Self-pity is destructive and Henry, at the very young age of 14, knew this. He had no time to ask, *Why me?* There was so much to accomplish: trips to the park to feed the pigeons; chats with Ernie, the parking lot attendant; books to read. His mother turned the pages.

Henry played the drums. Drumsticks were too heavy for him to hold. Mary Dolores came up with another idea: chopsticks. She wrapped tape around the tips so he could grasp them. They were a team. She called him Hen.

Henry had a crush on the rock star Stevie Nicks of "Landslide" fame. Posters of her hung on his wall. Once he dialed random numbers in Beverly Hills to track her down.

The phone bill was $200. "I just fanned the bill—all 14 pages," Mary Dolores said back then. "He got the message."

My story helped spread the word about Henry's lady love. A short time later, he got to meet Nicks through the Wish Come True foundation. Photos of the two are still on the internet. Henry couldn't move, but his eyes danced. They said to the songstress: *I adore you.*

I knew Henry was a special teenager, but I got so wrapped up in my job I lost touch with him after I moved to another beat for the paper, in another town. Reporters swoop in to get the story and then make a hasty exit, a shameful downside of the profession.

Back in Providence, after the baseball tournament, I dug up my Henry story. The memories came flooding back. Sitting in his dining room as he taps his snare. A grilled cheese cut into tiny squares for lunch. His mother gently wiping his mouth with a tissue.

"I want to go somewhere exciting," Henry once said. "Different."

He died in the winter of 1991. He was home, watching TV, when he inhaled a sip of water into his lungs. Too weak to cough up the fluid, he died an hour later at the hospital. He was 18 years old. All those years battling infections, and a sip of water kills him.

A selfless optimist, Henry would say life is fair, but from my perch, I would say it isn't. Now I see how gutsy he was. He taught us something about how to live. Each day, fresh from his iron lung, was a gift. Cynics bored him.

I once asked him what his favorite subjects were in school. Vocabulary and algebra, he said. He hated social studies. "I don't know why you have to know what happened in the past," he told me. "I figure that was then, this is now."

He's buried at Saint Sebastian Cemetery, in Westerly. Next time I'm down there, I'm going. I'm going to see Henry.

Zaid
November 2012

The holidays are upon us. What to do? You can drop a C-note on useless things that never move—fancy glass bowls and decorative pitchers come to mind—or you can buy a bag of granola. This fresh, mostly organic granola is special because it tastes good—and is made by refugees trying to start over in a country that can be tough to figure out.

The Providence Granola Project was founded by Keith Cooper and Geoff Gordon during a late-night talk about how to reach out to people who come to America with nothing more than a suitcase.

Keith, a Yale University graduate and former campus minister at Brown University who lives with his family on the East Side, had one of those aha moments. He'd been whipping up batches of granola for years in his kitchen. Why not turn his hobby into a business and mobilize refugees too? The two friends shook hands. A company was born.

That was five years ago, and Providence Granola is still going strong. In rented space at the Amos House soup kitchen in South Providence, the company makes 1,000 pounds of granola a month. With the holidays approaching, Keith hopes to sell even more, and with a robust website and offerings that are as whimsical as they are tasty, he's sure to hit his goal.

My sons love the granola, especially Keith's Originola. If

you want more variety, check out the Granola of the Month recipe. Looking for something to snack on at the playground? Try Maple Rosemary, with organic fresh rosemary from Keith's garden. Stomach of steel? Try Caramel Apple Corn, with popcorn caramelized in Sucana, a natural cane sugar. Want a lift? Try Ginger Zinger.

The granola is delicious (the indie actor Mary-Louise Parker is a fan) and ubiquitous (it's available at Whole Foods and Eastside Marketplace, among other places), but what makes the company truly special is its commitment to refugees from Iraq, Burundi, Eritrea, Myanmar, Liberia, Bhutan, and other countries.

For years, Keith worked at the International Institute of Rhode Island, now the Dorcas International Institute, helping refugees make a start in Rhode Island. The next time you're feeling sorry for yourself because you can't afford a puffer coat from North Face, think about what it's like to step off an airplane in a foreign country with a duffle bag and, if you're lucky, a few family photos.

Keith was moved by what he saw at the Institute—dignified and hardworking men and women who want to succeed. With so many obstacles in their way—no money, language barriers, a different culture—you'd expect them to give up. But they do not.

Providence Granola is all about opportunity. The refugees learn how an American business operates, improve their English, make money to support their families, and connect with two guys who get up every morning and think about how they can make life better for some of the most vulnerable men and women in our community.

Refugees get the experience and confidence they need to

progress to other work. That's important. The nonprofit is a stepping stone to full-time work. Many have found jobs in hotels, restaurants, and laundry shops.

All the workers are amazing, but one in particular has touched me deeply. His name is Zaid Wadia, a 35-year-old Iraqi refugee. He was born in Bagdad to a middle-class family. Life was progressing predictably and with pleasure; then the United States invaded Iraq and his world crumbled. His wife's brother was killed by a bomb. Zaid dodged bullets.

He fled to Syria, but it was too dangerous. He went to Sweden, where he spent a year selling hotdogs from a cart outside a bar.

Dejected, he went back to Syria. Just when he was about to give up, Zaid and his family won approval to come to the United States. In 2010, Zaid and his wife, Zena, and their two children arrived in Providence. Keith was one of the first people he met.

Zaid says he would be lost without Keith, whom Zaid calls, "Teacher." Zaid has worked his way up to shipping and payroll positions in the granola company and found a part-time job inserting ads at *The Providence Journal*. He is looking ahead and dreams of running his own business.

What makes Zaid even more remarkable is that he feels no resentment toward the United States. The invasion ripped his country apart. Still, he is thankful every day for his life here.

"Zaid is such an ideal Rhode Islander," Keith says. "Our state was built as a place of refuge for people to come and have opportunities. It seems important to our identity to give refugees a chance to get started here."

Not long ago, Keith had another aha moment. Why not expand the concept of Providence Granola to reach out to other people, not just refugees, who also live on low incomes and face language and cultural barriers. Keith calls his new nonprofit, Beautiful Day.

The organization would be a training center and business incubator. Keith wants to build a co-op kitchen to train workers, and he wants to team up with businesses.

He needs two things: money, either through grants or personal donations, and space, maybe in an old mill building. Keith is also looking for volunteers to help out with everything from marketing to mentoring.

I hear about projects like this and wonder why our city and state officials and business leaders don't jump at the opportunity to provide support. So much money is wasted on dead-end projects that benefit the politically connected.

Granola made by Zaid.

You can't go wrong: good food for a good cause.

The Rocket
January 2013

Dr. Ed is back. In between trips to Italia, sips of espresso, heaping plates of Bolognese pasta, gatherings with friends, and an occasional game of golf, Edward Iannuccilli has managed to write another charming book about growing up in an Italian-American family in the 1940s and 1950s. *What Ever Happened to Sunday Dinner? and Other Stories* is a gem, a must-read for anyone longing for simpler days or an escape from our turbulent times.

If Ed's name sounds familiar, it should. A retired gastroenterologist, he's a former chairman of the board at Rhode Island

Hospital. He's also a member of that rare and distinguished club of physician writers. Ed can turn a phrase, evoke a tear or two, make you smell the meatballs sizzling in garlic and olive oil on the rear burners of his grandmother's Barstow Stove.

I wrote about Ed two years ago following the release of his first book, *Growing Up Italian: Grandfather's Fig Trees and Other Stories*, which also vividly describes his childhood in Providence's Mount Pleasant neighborhood, where he roamed the streets in his high-top Keds searching for his next adventure that he would happily conceal from his loving parents. In his time, kids were expected to wander—and they did.

Ed and I met for coffee one snowy day back then and laughed a lot. He's a friendly and gracious man who is thrilled—and a little amazed—that he has found a second career as a writer. After he retired in 2001, he submitted an essay to *The Providence Journal* about his childhood. To his delight, the paper published it. Flushed with confidence, Ed sat down at his walnut desk and wrote more essays, all compiled in his first book.

The essay in *Growing Up Italian* about Vincent Troiano, Ed's grandfather, burying his fig trees in the fall to preserve them for the spring is one of his best, a touching portrait of immigrant life in America. Vincent would dig a ditch by the tree, wrap cloth around the trunk, pull the tree into the ground, and then cover the grave with dirt, leaves, and boards. Peering down to the snow-covered garden from his window, Eddie imagined he was looking at the hump of a sleeping elephant.

Over the years, Ed and I have kept in touch. His first book was such a huge success—he sold 5,000 copies in a few months—he realized that he might be onto something. He discovered that people were drawn to personal essays about an America that seemed less harried and impersonal than it is today.

Ed says it best in his *Sunday Dinner* preface: "Growing up in a neighborhood of family and friends was a journey to cherish. That neighborhood and the people living, working, and playing there, though from diverse ethnic backgrounds, had strong traditions of family, caring, and mutual respect. I am grateful for the simplicity of the time."

He was raised in a three-decker on Wealth Avenue, with his family—his parents and younger brother, Peter—on the third floor, his grandparents and great-grandfather on the second, and his aunt and her family on the first. Laughter and the smell of brewing coffee filled every corner. I see Ed racing up the well-swept back staircase to taste his grandmother's "gravy," or pasta sauce; I see him hiding in a basement clubhouse made of old coal bins; I see him playing hide-and-seek late into the night, using the streetlight as base.

Ed's new book gives us more sweet details about his idyllic life. Where to begin? Maybe with a list. This curly-haired towhead who used Emu shoe polish to make his Buster Browns shine loved Holloway's Milk Duds, Peter Paul Mounds, Root Beer Barrels, Nehi soda, and Hoodsies, whose covers he licked clean to reveal pictures of movie stars.

He liked the smell of the ink wells, library paste, and oiled wood floors in his public school, a short walk from home. A free present during grab bag day at The Outlet store was a highlight of his week. He dreaded waking up early on Sunday morning to deliver the newspaper but looked forward to dressing up in his pressed white shirt and bow tie for Sunday dinners. His favorite TV program was the *Howdy Doody Show*, sponsored by Hostess, maker of his favorite snack, the Twinkie.

He wore out the 78 rpm of Jack and the Beanstalk. His cousins jitterbugged to big band music on an RCA Victrola.

In the summer, he cooled under a sprinkler or at Waterman Lake, in North Smithfield. The Woonasquatucket River, in Olneyville, smelling of leather and metal, was his swimming hole. He made balls from hot tar scrapped off streets and killed rats at the local dump with his slingshot. He played baseball with taped-up balls on a sandlot at Valley Street Playground and spied on teenagers kissing in the "big barn," a decrepit garage owned by a grump. On sticky nights, he caught fireflies.

His bike, a maroon and silver Monark Rocket Royale with sleek red, white, and blue streamers on its handlebars, filled his 10-year-old belly with butterflies when he found it by the blue spruce on Christmas morning. The fenders glimmered with chrome. The horn honked with one squeeze. It had a kickstand.

"My bike had nothing but speed," Ed writes. "I rode it everywhere—on the neighborhood's streets, to the brook, to sandlots, rivers, and stores, pedaling with little effort. There were no boundaries. My world opened up beyond the neighborhood, and I explored."

His remembrances of those long hours away from home on The Rocket under the roomy sky gave us two wonderful books. Alone, far from grown-ups, the little boy's imagination soared. He stored those memories away, until now. We should all be so lucky.

CHAPTER 8

....

Winter Clamming
March 2013

I don't know about you, but I'm going clamming. Baby, it's cold outside, and the water is a tub of ice, and the wind is whip-sharp against my cheeks, but my kids are out there in the ocean blue so I'm going.

My 12-year-old son Peder is trudging along in the muck in his snow boots, clutching the household hoe, a rusty Uncle Harry relic that sowed a few corn kernels back in the day and is now doing duty as a clamrake. If you don't know what a clamrake is, then you are from Iowa.

We are family of clammers. It started with my husband, who learned how to clam from his father, Walter, whose idea of a good meal was something fresh from the sea. My husband first took Peder and our other son, Henry, who is 11, clamming when they were toddlers.

"It was just so unique and adventurous," says Peder. "It was so cool to be catching your own dinner. I couldn't believe that the food I could eat was right under my own feet."

We were soon digging up bivalve mollusks on a regular basis. Most of the time, we went clamming in the summer at low tide. Why then? Let's ask the young expert. "For clams to survive they must be submerged in the water for a majority of the time," says Peder. "But during low tide, for a few hours, they can be exposed to air without dying off. This is the time to strike."

Clams—quahogs, little necks, cherrystones—soon lead to other discoveries: oysters, mussels, and crabs. I still remember the mussels we pulled from the reeds off Prudence Island back in '07, tender morsels with the flavor of celery. And how can I forget that oyster retrieved from Narragansett Bay two years ago. On a dare, I slurped it down, on the spot. We are fearless.

Our clamming spot is top secret. Don't be offended. Real clammers never reveal their locations. What could be more disappointing than discovering that your spot has run dry, thanks to loose-lipped Larry who had one too many at the local watering hole. I will say this: we clam at a tidal flat in East Bay, not far from a potato field. That's as far as I'm going.

If you're about to write a letter asserting that we are break-ing the law, put that pen down and walk the dog. I have been assured by my lawyer that it is legal for Rhode Islanders to go clamming in Rhode Island. Mr. Smith, attorney-at-law, cites Article 1, Section 17, of the Rhode Island Constitution: "The people shall continue to enjoy and freely exercise all the rights of fishery and the privileges of the shore, to which they were heretofore entitled." Translation: go to the muck and pluck. People from out of state, I'm not sorry to say, need a license to dig clams here.

You can't go hog wild and take home every clam that you find. There are size restrictions. The hinge—you know what I'm talking about—has to be one inch wide. We know this because not long ago we were clamming at our secret site and an enforcement officer with the Department of Environmental Management approached us. He had a walkie-talkie. He explained the rules and showed us a device that measures the hinge. He suggested we get the contraption. We did. Hello, Lucky's Bait & Tackle.

Clam digging is for people who don't get manicures. Roll up your pants. Grab a bucket. Wade into the water and probe the bottom with your feet until you feel something solid. If it's a rock, throw it back. If it's a clam, reach down with your hand and pull it up. If it's legal, put it in the bucket.

Another clamming method is to kneel on the shoreline and dig down with a garden tool, such as a hoe, a pronged trowel or a kitchen fork. Drag the trowel through the muck, pulling out any clams that surface. If you find a gold doubloon, keep that, too. Sand and mud might accumulate under your fingernails. So what? Grit is good.

If you see blood, it's probably from a toe cut. "I've had plenty of wounds," says my husband. "It goes with the job." The salty ocean promotes healing. Back home, apply an anti-biotic ointment, cover with a Band-Aid, and brag about your wound to co-workers and neighbors.

Clamming is a great winter sport, and it's cheaper than skiing. My husband came up with the idea. His motives were practical. After a successful dig in late January, we celebrated with a dinner of clams and mussels steamed in a garlic and white wine broth. Raw oysters were served on crushed ice.

"On our cold clamming adventure in January, I forgot to bring my hat," says Henry. "This resulted in an unhappy Henry. Right when I tasted the clam at the dinner table, I knew the trip was worth it. A clam by itself doesn't satisfy my tongue. But if you slather on Dad's special sauce, it's the best thing in mankind."

One thing we've never found during our digs is the elusive scallop. "I am constantly researching where they might be in

Rhode Island," says Peder. "I've never come up with a defin-
itive answer. I'm always turning shells over, hoping it's a live
scallop. It never is. If anyone knows where I can find these
mysterious bivalves, please let me know."

I promise, he won't tell.

Ink Spots
May 2013

The Ink Spots were a popular vocal quartet in the 1930s and
1940s that paved the way for rhythm and blues and rock 'n' roll.
I know this because my 11-year-old son Henry likes pens as
much as, say, baseball or French films. Henry is especially fond
of fountain pens, the kind that can be messy and leave—you
guessed it—ink spots on the white sheets. I have no idea how
the Ink Spots came up with their name—maybe they were
pen enthusiasts too—but I do know that a smart company on
the other side of the Atlantic is using their songs to sell pens,
hence the Ink Spots-Henry connection.

Not long ago, Henry was browsing the internet for information about pens when he came across a website called
Kaweco, a 130-year-old German pen company. He entered it,
and the Ink Spots, Orville, Ivory, Jerry, and Charlie, started to
croon: "I don't want to set the world on fire. I just want to start
a flame in your heart." I was smitten and not by the pens. The
next day, I bought the "Ink Spots Greatest Hits" and thanked
Henry for introducing me to the singers. He thanked me for
promising to be a patron of his new hobby.

It's unusual for a kid to show an interest in pens. Most
boys collect rocks or Red Sox T-shirts. For a while, he was

charged up by yo-yos, and we have a shoebox of Duncans to prove it. Then he moved on to making duct tape wallets, even launching a business that boomed for 23 days. The pen fascination began in the fall. Henry and his friend, Theo, were searching about for something to collect. "How about pens?" said Henry. "Sure," said Theo.

Trips to Staples ensued and, in less time than it takes to click a Bic, Henry had pens from all walks of life: Uniball Jetstream, a sleek black pen with a fine tip; Dr. Grip Roller Ball, a chunky pen with a comfortable grip; and Pilot G2, a popular pen with, according to Henry, a "smooth writing experience." One day, Henry walked into the Brown University Bookstore with a $10 gift certificate in his pocket, expecting to buy a paperback. "I saw a giant wall of pens," Henry recalled. "I was like, 'Whoa!'" He settled on a Parker Jotter. "I really liked the click of the pen," said Henry. "I took it to school the next day and started clicking. Now I click the pen if I can't remember the answer to a question. There are a lot of good things about pens—put that down."

By winter, our house was the pen capital of the East Side. Pens in pickle jars. Pens in old coffee cans. Pens in empty water bottles. One morning, I opened a drawer in the bathroom and found a Pentel EnerGel X Roller Ball next to a tube of Crest. Henry is a tinkerer and soon discovered that one of the joys of pens is taking them apart. They are complicated creatures, what with all those cartridges and tiny coiled springs. Putting them back together is not as fun. Springs and little tubes of plastic soon dotted our domestic landscape.

Collectors are expansionists by nature, and Henry is no exception. The ho-hum G2 soon gave way to more refined pens, a shift accelerated by Henry's discovery in a lonely living room drawer of a gold-plated Cross pen inscribed with his name. A friend had given Henry the pen years ago. Henry was beside himself. "It was a good pen," he recalled. "I thought about taking it to school but knew 14-karat gold and middle schoolers don't go together."

Fountain pens came on the scene during an evening stroll to the East Side's Wayland Square, where he spotted a poster of a Lamy in the window of Runcible Spoon, a charming shop that sells stationery and luxury soap. Henry was with his dad. They were talking about moon tides and then, well, I'll let Henry take the microphone. "I walked in the store and felt out of place," said Henry. "Most 11-year-old boys don't end up in a shop of fine—whatever. But seeing the writing instruments I felt more at home. The Lamys had a totally different design than your normal click pens." Henry exited a satisfied customer, a Lamy Safari in hand.

Henry and Joan, the owner of Runcible Spoon, became fast friends. With his birthday money, Henry also bought an ink well and a converter for his Lamy. He has his eye on the Lamy Studio, a step up. I'm sure there will be more trips to the Square this summer. Henry says he likes pens because he loves to write and because they are amazing tools. Think about it. "It all started with a feather and ink, and now it has moved up to Roller Ball pens, and who knows what's in the future," Henry said. "Computers are everywhere, but a pen is more personal. It's one with you."

Henry has an especially personal connection to one writing instrument that surfaced in a dusty box during an attic cleanup: an antique pen passed down from his great-grandmother, Sophia. Henry did some research and identified it as an Eclipse desk pen, minus the base. The find became more precious when I told him that the ink spots staining the green felt on our old desk, also from his great-grandmother, were made by Sophia's pen. That set his world on fire.

Buttercups
June 2013

Once upon a time, there was a park with trees and swings and not much else. I took my two sons there when they were toddlers and, boy, did they have a good time. Off they went, running over patches of stubby grass to a grove of pines in a corner far away, out of sight of overbearing parents. I'd sit there on a rickety bench eating a peach, knowing full well that the guys would come racing back when tag was over.

We called this glorious piece of public land on Humboldt Avenue The Baby Park, and so did everyone else in the neighborhood with young children. As far as I was concerned, it was the best park on the East Side for little people uttering phrases like "Juice peese" and "Where's my sand bocket?"

The park I knew and loved is gone. It's been replaced by a park so littered with cast-off toys, mostly plastic, it looks like a landfill. My sons are older now, and we haven't visited the park in a few years. I don't want to. Maybe that unsightly playhouse the size of a backyard shed that someone dumped there over the winter is keeping me away.

We're a civilized bunch on the East Side. Restraint is expected and appreciated. But now and then it's good to speak up. Those worn-out toys, visible from the street, have turned a once-charming spot into an eyesore. Call in the recycling trucks. The plastic needs to go.

How did the park take such a wrong turn? Parents probably started leaving their toys overnight so they wouldn't have to lug them around in their cars. Word got out, and I suspect people figured no one would mind if they dropped off a Little Tikes Cozy Coupe after the kids outgrew it. This is not healthy.

The toys are filthy. They've gone from Dick's to Jane's, probably without a solid scrubbing. The toys land in a public park swarming with teething tots who like to gnaw on hard objects, leaving behind their germs. What's worse, the tots are nibbling on plastic, which might be toxic.

This is not fair to the abutting homeowners. I'm guessing that in the evening, when the playground visitors are tucked in bed dreaming of Tonkas, Mr. and Mrs. Prescott would rather see a warbler tugging at a worm than a squirrel feasting on a grapefruit-pink Sweet Petite Trike. Even worse, the toys occupy the grounds in all seasons, including winter. It's just plain ugly.

Consider that this is a public park open to all, including people without kids. Maybe two lovebirds out for an evening stroll are looking for a place to plop that's free of toys. Maybe a teen seeking solitude would like to walk to the park alone after dinner and sit on a swing, without looking at stuff.

If parents want new playground equipment or want to expand what's there now—a slide, for one—they should ask the city to help. Surely, the city can come up with money or a grant. Public playgrounds are vital to the East Side, where we essentially live on top of each other.

I miss the old park. I remember many things. I remember the sandbox—nothing fancy, just a square. I remember the tree stumps, great for climbing and holding forth on the virtues of

Batman. I remember the jungle gym, with a covered slide. I'd catch my sons at the bottom. Sometimes I'd miss. Plop, bottom-first into the dirt. "Shake it off," I'd say.

I remember that it was almost impossible to escape from the park to the uncertain world outside, thanks to a stately wrought-iron fence with heavy gates that clanked shut. The gates had knobs as big as baseballs.

"The park was our getaway," says my son Henry. "It was our baseball field, our scooter park, our football stadium. Good times."

"I remember the leaves," says my other son, Peder. "There were a lot of leaves, more leaves than I've ever seen in my life. I'd hop in the leaves, play in the leaves."

We brought back whatever we took, even if we had to make two or three trips. Once, we mistakenly left a tricycle and other toys at the park but didn't realize what we'd done until after dinner and baths. My husband returned later that night, cramming everything into the trunk of our car. That's what trunks are for when you have kids.

I liked the park because it was simple, free of the pretense that seems to plague so many public spaces today. Parks are too studied now. I call them designer parks. Doesn't anyone appreciate an open field anymore? What could be more calming than looking out over a slope covered in buttercups.

The Baby Park was our second backyard, a place filled with wonder and possibility.

Bring it back.

Vodka

July 2013

Pat Herlihy likes her vodka "neat." That means she likes it without embellishment. No orange juice or heavy cream, in a glass and no ice, thank you very much. On occasion, she will drink a vodka tonic or a vodka martini, but it has to be a really big party. Her favorite vodka is Russkiy Standart, known on this side of the world as Russian Standard. "It's smooth," she says, with a grin.

Pat is 83 years old with white hair cut in a bob and gray eyes that light up when she laughs, which is often. Maybe you saw her latest YouTube video, a seven-minute gem that chronicles her travels to different "watering holes" on the East Side and beyond to imbibe. And Da, she lived to tell the story.

But this Brown University historian is more than an internet sensation. She has also written a charming book about this most versatile of spirits, *Vodka, A Global History*. The book takes us for a ride through vodka's history, from its origins in a Slavic country in the 14th century to its global popularity today. Along the way, we get clever illustrations and tidbits like these: Bison Grass Vodka, a favorite among Poles and Russians, is reputed to enhance virility; and vodka demand spiked in the United States after James Bond, uh, Sean Connery, uttered those famous words, "shaken not stirred," in the 1962 film *Dr. No*.

I'm not much of a drinker, but I love this book. I like the author just as much. How lucky we are on the East Side to have her in our midst, holding forth on both Russian history and a seemingly unremarkable clear liquid without color, odor, or taste that marketing wizards have cleverly promoted. Surely, you've seen the vodka in a bottle shaped like Marilyn Monroe with her skirt billowing up.

Pat is charming crowds at local bookstores and restaurants, as she did one night at Waterman Grille at an event hosted by the liquor store Bottles. Her talk included a power point presentation and "tasting" of five different vodkas, among them, Hammer and Sickle and Sons of Liberty 9, made here in Little Rhody. The veggies, bread, and smoked salmon were not optional. Pat explains: "Russians, unless they're really, really far gone, never drink without food. You toast. You eat."

All roads lead to the East Side, and so it is with Pat. She was born in San Francisco and moved to China in 1930 with her newly divorced mother, Irene, who had planned on a brief visit, but instead stayed five years. Pat's first language was Mandarin, her second, pidgin English. She graduated from Kaiser-Wilhelm kindergarten in Shanghai. (We should all be so lucky.)

The two returned home in 1936, settling in San Francisco's Haight Ashbury neighborhood, long before it became a hippie haven. Pat graduated from the University of California, Berkeley, with a bachelor's degree in history and married another historian, David Herlihy. They met at a high school debate in 1945 about socialized medicine. Pat was in favor, David against.

They raised five boys and a girl while pursuing academic careers. David received his doctorate in medieval history, and Pat earned her doctorate in Russian history from the University of Pennsylvania. "I preferred studying to housecleaning," she says.

David taught at colleges throughout the country, including Harvard, eventually becoming a world-renowned Italian medievalist. Pat made her mark too; her expertise is 19ᵗʰ century Russian history, especially in Ukraine. They moved to Providence in 1986 to teach at Brown University, where David was a professor until his death in 1991 of pancreatic cancer. "We were great pals," says Pat.

The Herlihys lived on Keene Street, in the house with the turret. Pat's son-in-law, an émigré from Albania, worked in the fish department at Eastside Marketplace in the mid-1990s. Her son, Maurice Herlihy, is a professor of computer science at Brown. A grandson graduated from Brown last year, and a granddaughter will graduate from there next year.

Pat taught at Brown until 2001 and moved a few years ago to Cambridge to be closer to her children. She commutes to Brown's Watson Institute for International Studies, where she's an adjunct professor. From her sun-drenched office on Thayer Street, she does research, meets with students, guides professors from Tajikistan, and engages all with her wit and warmth, raising her charka, a Russian vodka cup, only after hours.

Her fascination with vodka began while researching Nicholas II's ban on the spirit, in August 1914. The czar thought Russians were turning into alcoholics, and he wanted his troops to be prepared for World War I. That work resulted in a book, *The Alcoholic Empire: Vodka and Politics in Late Imperial Russia*, published in 2002. It took her four years to write *Vodka, A Global History*, partly because the Russians were skittish about providing information, fearing that she might portray them in a bad light. She did not.

In between visiting her six grandchildren and following her beloved Celtics and Red Sox, Pat is cranking out two more books, a memoir and a book about Eugene Schuyler, an

American diplomat who served in Russia. Pat is also a three-time cancer survivor: breast cancer in 2009; chronic lymphocytic cancer in 1994; and kidney cancer in 1978. If you want to hang out with an optimist or to chat about the Bolsheviks, check out Room 315 at the Watson Institute. The door is always open.

"I've always found that life is fun," says Pat. "I told my kids to put on my grave, 'She had a good time.'"

One last thing. She prefers red wine over vodka, but don't tell her publisher.

So True
August 2013

When I was a cub newspaper reporter with more of a purr than a growl, I read a lot of fiction to teach myself how to write. I was more interested in how words sounded on a page than in what they said. Investigative journalism is hard work. You have to decipher complicated financial documents and people hang up on you all the time. I just wanted to write a beautiful sentence.

This is a roundabout way of saying that I read the novels and short stories by Ann Hood. If you live in South Dakota, you may have heard of her, but if you live on the East Side, you most certainly have heard of her. She is one of our most celebrated writers. It seems every time I visit a bookstore or pick up a magazine, I see her name. She is prolific. By far, her most searing work is *Comfort: A Journey Through Grief*, a memoir about the death of her 5-year-old daughter Grace and, as one reviewer said, Hood's "climb back to wholeness."

I have never met Hood, at least not formally, although my son Henry did meet her, and he reported back to me that she is "really nice." He's 12 years old and has freckles and strawberry blond hair. But I'm getting ahead of myself.

My story begins in 1987, the year Hood published her first novel, *Somewhere Off the Coast of Maine.* I bought the book at the College Hill Bookstore, the Thayer Street landmark, which closed years ago and is now a shop that sells bangle bracelets and other trinkets from India.

The novel is about three friends and the paths they choose after college. I devoured every page, paying special attention to the rhythm of Hood's sentences and to her description. I still remember the character Sparrow's Day-Glo green VW. I even wrote my name on the title page to document this latest addition to my shelves: Elizabeth Rau, October 1987.

Reading Hood's work and the books of other authors from that time—Raymond Carver, Susan Minot, and Ann Beattie, among others—helped me as a foundering reporter. Their writing was spare, fluid, and accessible, and they wrote about lives truly lived. I read their work and thought, well, maybe I can do that.

Back then, I traveled a few times a year to St. Louis, where I grew up and where my parents and sisters and brother still lived. These visits were always bittersweet, a mixture of sadness about leaving my big family and excitement about returning to a reporting job that I loved. Often I would land in Rhode Island with a frown.

My exits from the plane were usually uneventful, dignified scrambles to breathe fresh air. One exit, however, was memorable for what it brought later. I was standing in line, holding my bag in one hand and a book in the other, and a flight attendant leaned in and asked me what I was reading. I held up a collection of short stories by William Maxwell. Her face lit up. I could have said "Terrific book!" or even "$24.99, Barnes & Noble!" but, instead, I didn't utter a word. I remember being surprised that a flight attendant would be keen on a literary giant like Maxwell. I was young and understood nothing about life, especially the writer's life.

A few weeks later, I was flipping through my beloved *Somewhere Off the Coast of Maine*, and reread the author's page, which included a photograph and this snippet: "She is currently a flight attendant." I stared hard at the photo. Hmm. My flight attendant and Ann Hood were one and the same.

Ashamed of my behavior, I wrote her a long hand-written letter apologizing for my rudeness and telling her how much I liked her book. I probably rambled. No, I am sure I rambled. I'm not sure if I sent the letter to TWA or to her publisher. I am also not sure if I included a return address. For all I know the missive was lost in a mailroom in Poughkeepsie.

Over the years, I followed Hood's writing career as it soared. One winter, from my car window, I saw her sitting on a chair during a reading at Books on the Square on the East Side, and I thought about stopping in to divulge my secret but didn't.

Henry finally brought us together. He came home from school one day and told me that Ann Hood was coming to give a writing seminar. "Really," I said. His sixth-grade English class had read *The Treasure Chest: Angel of the Battlefield*, the first book in Hood's new series for middle school readers. I wrote the date on my calendar.

Henry loves to write. He takes his craft seriously. He knows how to build suspense, and his dialogue is pitch perfect.

He's not afraid to take risks. Now and then, he lets me read his work, but rarely lets me edit. "It's my story, Mom," he says.

The morning of the event, I asked Henry if he would take *Somewhere Off the Coast of Maine* to school and ask Hood to sign it. He put the book in his backpack. I couldn't help but wonder if he would remember to remove it and hand it to her. He did. "For Liz, Ann Hood," she wrote in big loopy cursive. Since the seminar had turned into an impromptu book signing, they also talked. "I remember writing this," she told Henry. "Look at the yellowed pages."

They might be brittle, but they are well thumbed.

I once heard someone say that we are all connected. So true.

Baseball Forever
October 2013

I went to a lot of ballparks over the summer. We took a trip to the Midwest to visit family and decided to squeeze in as many games in the Bigs as we could along the way. Our seats were good, especially the ones at Camden Yards, in Baltimore, where the Sox played the Orioles. It was a thrill to see David Ortiz hit a homer. I stood up and cheered in a very undignified way. It was boiling hot, so I turned the sleeves of my black T-shirt into a tank top. A lot of other people did the same thing. It's dress-down day every day in a ballpark.

Baseball came to me late in life. I played softball in middle school and then there was a big gap until I went to a Red Sox game at Fenway when I was in my 30s. My companions were three friends, all guys familiar with the sport. They knew what a walk-off home run was; I did not. I was bored and couldn't wait for the game to end. The only thing I remember is that one companion was a vegetarian who called his body a temple. He was eating a bag of greasy chips. I thought, "Why is a vegetarian eating a bag of greasy chips?"

Fast forward many years and I am married with two boys who know the difference between a change-up and a knuckle ball and can throw the pitches with some authority. In no time, baseball gear is as common in our house as Legos and toy firetrucks. Little League, Fall Ball, and AAU dominate our evenings and weekends. Our one television is tuned to MLB games and the chatter of sportscasters around-the-clock. I am learning something about the game; I am learning to love it.

My husband arranged our trip. He reserved the airline tickets, booked the hotel rooms and, with my older son, Peder, bought the baseball tickets. This is something they like to do together. You can see what a ballpark looks like online now, so it's easy to pick out seats. It always takes the two of them a long time to decide, sometimes days. The father-son bonding is at its peak. I don't get involved, although I do get updates at the dinner table: "Dad wants left field. I want first base." Two stubborn guys haggling over baseball seats. Music to my ears.

America is filled with major league baseball parks—30, to be exact. I've only been to a few. "What will you do with your one wild and precious life?" the poet, Mary Oliver, asks. My response: Hit every ballpark before the heavens open. I'm sure the pale pink sands of La Digue island in the Indian Ocean are stunning, but I'd like to see a moon ball sail over the bleachers at AT&T Park in San Francisco and land in the Pacific with a quiet splash. I'm sure the snorkeling is fine at Kahaluu Beach Park, in Hawaii, but I'd rather marvel over the ancient ivy walls at Wrigley Field and eat a Vienna Dog smothered in mustard and onions.

We visited three ballparks: Camden Yards, which, as I said, is in Baltimore, home for a while to Providence's beloved Edgar Allan Poe; U.S. Cellular Field in the great city of Chicago, where I am living in my next life; and Busch Stadium in my hometown of St. Louis, which I left decades ago for the East Coast to work as a reporter. Each game was memorable in its own way. I cheered like a schoolgirl at a high school basketball game, and I ate a lot of junk food. The cement floor beneath my seat was littered with peanut shells and empty cups of Coke. No one uses a trash can at the ballpark.

It was unseasonably cool at Busch Stadium. Most summer evenings in the Gateway City are sweltering. Not that night. The cool breeze off the Mississippi kept everyone in a good mood. My husband and sons found three seats together, and I managed to find one a few rows up. They watched the game; I roamed the ballpark, in awe of the majestic arch looming overhead in the twilight. Everyone was wearing a red T-shirt to honor the Cardinals, who clobbered the Phillies. It was a blowout or, as my son used to say when he was a toddler, a "blowup."

Our best seats were at Camden Yards in the Sox vs. Orioles game. First base was within spitting distance. I got to see one of those acrobatic double plays by the unflappable and dogged Dustin Pedroia. The night before, Ortiz had smashed a phone in the dugout with his bat, so everyone booed when he walked to the plate at this game. Success is the best revenge. It was Big Papi's 20th homer of the season.

By far my best experience was at Cellular Field. The White Sox were playing the Braves. Peder scored the game, a task that requires focus and patience. He made a lot of squiggly marks on a score sheet he bought for a buck at a kiosk. Our seats were on a deck behind centerfield. We sat on stools at a table. We'd sip our lemonades and I'd say, "Where do you think he'll hit it?" and Peder would say, "Left field." I'd say, "Good catch," and Peder would say, "Hmm." It was a balmy summer evening, thanks to Lake Michigan, a glistening blue that seemed to go on forever. One hour passed, then two. I was hoping we'd go to the 10th, but we didn't. I never wanted the night to end.

Magic Cards
December 2013

I know what to get my boys for Christmas this year: magic cards. No, not the pick-any-two kind owned by white-gloved magicians. I'm talking about cards from Magic: The Gathering, the fantasy trading card game that is taking our youth by storm and turning my dining room into a poker parlor, minus the cigars and whiskey. A recent conversation between my son and a friend proves my point:

Friend: I'll swing at you for 2, so you're at 18.

Son: No, you're at 17.

Friend: Yeah, you're right.

Son: Okay, now I'll tap 1, and I'll regenerate him. I'll swing at you for 5, and I'll gain 5.

Huh? The game is far too complicated for my wee brain. I'll leave it up to the young ones to explain: "You're trying to take away the other person's life pretty much."

In its purest form, the game pits two players, usually best friends, against each other. Each player has a deck of cards representing magical lands, creatures, and spells. The first to reduce his or her opponent to "0 life" or below wins.

One of the best things about the game is that players get to customize their decks, often through trades, hence those late-night phone calls in our house: "I'll trade you Trostani Summoner for an Advent of the Wurm and a Rancor. No. Then how about Call of the Concave for Axebane Stag?" The game's publisher, Wizards of the Coast—all MIT graduates, no doubt—is always releasing new cards to enrich collections. Rite Aid even sells $3.99 booster packs.

Some parents might scoff at a game involving sorcerers and raven-haired vixens, but I like it. To play, you need a razor-sharp memory, an analytical mind, and a competitive spirit. You also must be able to translate strange sentences: "Nighthowler. Enchantment Creature—Horror. Nighthowler and Enchanted Creature each get +X/+X, where X is the number of creature cards in all graveyards."

Again, I say, "Huh?"

Funny how things change as your children grow up. One minute they're playing with Legos, the next minute they're shuffling through their Magic cards to prepare for an all-nighter at the yellow house east of Elmgrove.

When my kids were toddlers, they swooned over firetrucks. I'm ashamed to admit that we had more than a dozen toy firetrucks back in '05. I'll never forget my mother-in-law's response when a Christmas present that should have gone to our house mistakenly went to hers and she opened it, only to find yet another firetruck. She called immediately.

"I was thunderstruck when I opened the package," she said. "They have enough fire trucks."

"But this one is made of wood," I said.

Firetrucks soon gave way to Legos, which gave way to stuffed animals, which gave way to yo-yos, which gave way to sports gear, which gave way to bigger sports gear. We kept the yo-yos and a few toys for sentimental reasons, but most of the stuff has been handed down to the next generation. I don't miss anything. We had too many toys. Maybe my mother-in-law was right.

Magic crept into our house this year. The game, delightfully compact and light, came to us as all things come to us—through a friend, in this case, Eric. In the beginning, our guests played on the coffee table. When that got too small, they progressed to the dining room table, which provides a perfect surface for gaming: smooth as ice. The cards float across the top.

Weekends are especially good for Magic. A boatload of boys come over, each with cards bearing distinguished names like Slime Molding and Slaughterhorn. The cards pop with illustrations that are fantastical and ghoulish: a castle on a sun-dappled hill or a mutant flashing pointy pearly whites that could eat you alive.

There the fellows sit, bartering, exchanging minutiae, mulling over their next move, until, abracadabra, someone is victorious. Give him a piece of Dubble Bubble. Popcorn and Shirley Temples for all. Let the next game begin.

Parents who worry that Magic is becoming more than a harmless pastime for their children can rest easy. Players who are really good can get college scholarships, thanks to a nonprofit organization called Gamers Helping Gamers.

The New York Times reports that the group was founded by Jon Finkel, a longtime Magic enthusiast. "There was just nothing enjoyable or fun about high school, so I got my mental stimulation elsewhere," he told the newspaper. "I would play Magic until midnight and never do my homework."

No slacker, he. He ended up graduating from Rutgers and is now a partner in a hedge fund. He lives in a spacious apartment in SoHo. Did I say he's only 35?

Finkel and his Magic pals look for highly intelligent kids who might not have a long list of extracurricular activities that dazzle admissions offices. One scholarship recipient is now at Yale Law School. Think about it: a Gruul creature helped him get there.

Merry Magic to all.

Alfie

February 2014

His name was Alf Mads Andreas Thorvald Sorensen, but everyone called him Alfie. I never met him, but I know a lot about him. He was my husband's great-uncle, a hardy Norwegian who tilled the soil and ate Gjetost cheese with crispbread during Christmas gatherings.

He made an entrance years ago when I was sorting through my mother-in-law's things. She had died and left behind a house filled with stuff, from rose-patterned teacups to letters her father wrote to her when she was a little girl. "My Darling Daughter," he'd begin.

Carol never threw anything out. When she was alive, she rarely talked about her possessions, but I see now that she treasured them. They were all weighted with history—her brother's red agate cigarette holder, her father's porcelain shaving bowl, her mother's crocheted sewing bag with a spool of thread still attached to the handkerchief she was embroidering before she died.

Alfie's box was in the eaves. I remember dragging it out from a cobwebbed corner and opening it under the slanted ceilings on the top floor of Carol's Nisbet Street house. Here were the contents of a man's life, neatly packed away in a cardboard box and, in some cases, even labeled: Alfie's letters. Alfie's war photos. Alfie's papers.

Looking through a person's past takes patience, so I sat there all day, alone, piecing together Alfie's life, from his boy-hood days in Providence, to the battlefields in France, to his farm in Smithfield and, in the end, to the hospital bed where he died.

He was born Dec. 8. 1893, the child of Thorvald Fredrik Sorensen and Emilie Jorgensen, who came to the United States from Norway in 1876. The Sorensens raised Alfie and their six other children in a clapboard house in Providence's Valley neighborhood. I know this because I found a metal nameplate that Alfie nailed to the family's door for the postman. "Alf. Th. Sorensen, 39 Lisbon Street," it said in fanciful cursive.

I opened a green-cloth photo album. There he was as a boy sitting next to his mother on the steps of their front porch, a medal pinned to the lapel of his Sunday jacket. Did he win a spelling bee? His hair was cut short enough to show off a cow-lick, and he had a radiant smile. He seemed like a happy kid.

Everything in the photos spoke of nature—a picnic in the side yard, a blossoming dogwood, the sun shining through lace curtains and bathing the front parlor with light. Life seemed simpler back then. I wondered if small gestures brought great joy: pruning the hydrangeas by the latticework in the yard, or petting the fluffy cat, which, in one photo, was curled up on a velvety chair.

After high school, Alfie worked as a machinist at Gorham Manufacturing Company, one of the largest makers of silverware in the United States at the time. On his 24th birthday, he signed up to fight in World War I and began a great adventure—or so he thought.

Here are the facts: He served from 1917 to 1919 in France with the 19th Co., 2nd Regiment of the Air Service Mechanics. He worked on aircraft and fought in the Champagne-Marne Defensive, the St. Mihiel Offensive, and the Meuse-Argonne Offensive. He was entitled to wear two gold chevrons.

But there was so much more.

I found the pocket watch that he carried with him throughout the war, with his military identification tag looped through the watch's ring. Engraved on the watch were his initials: ATS.

There was a miniature painting of a sloop sailing on a lake framed by verdant mountains, and on back was the artist's signature: "Hand-painted by Pvt. Blair Cleveland in Nettancourt, France." Inside an old powder-blue Air Mail envelope were French postcards and a program from The Folies-Bergère, with Miss Shirley Kellogg on the cover. Alfie's military buttons, plucked from coats, trousers, and lapels, were linked together with string.

I counted 169 letters. They were censored, so few, if any, battlefield details were revealed, but they were poignant in their simplicity. Artillery "rained down." The explosions were "loud, so loud." He talked of "muddy trenches," and how his contingent camped in the woods to hide from air raids. Still, he told his "folks" not to worry. He wrote of returning home to Little Rhody in America—God's country. A black leather scrapbook he put together later, and which I found in the box that day, was filled with photos from the front lines, with soldiers hunkered down in trenches, wearing gas masks, and clutching bayonets. They must have been terrified.

After he was discharged, Alfie returned to Providence. He lived again with his parents on Lisbon Street and then moved to a small farm in Smithfield to live with his sister Sophie— my husband's grandmother.

But he was never the same. The bombing and shelling in the French countryside split his eardrums, and he lost his hearing. His mind suffered, too. Back then, it was called shell shock. Today, it's known as post-traumatic stress syndrome.

He was reclusive and mostly kept to himself. Children played quietly when Alfie was in the room. There were whispers about his nerves. A lifelong bachelor, he tended to his corn field and vegetable garden as he withdrew, over time, into a valley of lonesomeness.

On Feb. 4, 1954, he died of colon cancer at the Veterans Administration Hospital, across the street from the house he lived in as a little boy. I found a condolence letter from the hospital's medical director, still in its envelope, the flap sliced open gently with a penknife.

"I wish to offer my deepest sympathy to you," Dr. William J. Sullivan wrote to Sophie. "May you find consolation in the knowledge that he served his country and died honored and respected by all of us."

Things from the past clutter our houses and turn yellow over time. Why do we keep them? It's hard to let go. Love inspired Alfie's mother to pack a box a century ago. I'm grateful that she did. Everyone deserves to be known.

Acme
March 2014

Not long ago, my husband Peder rushed into the house and told me he had some bad news. His face was white, and he looked so sad I prepared for the worst. Death perhaps, or a grievous illness.

A long, uncomfortable pause stilled the room and then he let it rip: "Acme shut down." He had made a Saturday afternoon run to the video store on Brook Street to get a movie and encountered a "closed" sign in the window and darkness inside. Clerks at the nearby wine store confirmed that, yes, another local business—and a revered one at that—had closed its doors.

It's probably safe to say that anyone who has lived on the East Side for any length of time has rented a movie from Acme. Maybe you were a regular, stopping by every Saturday night for an obscure film from France or, even better, Korea. Maybe you patronized the business one measly time, renting a movie for an unexpected visitor.

If you never visited Acme, my condolences. You missed out on the joy of discovering a great movie by doing something called browsing, a lost pastime in today's high-tech world. You could hold the movie case in your hands, look at the art and photos, read the summary on back. So much for the fine art of sizing up a movie in 150 words or less. Oh, the delight we experienced coming across a fringe movie so touching that scenes lingered for days, long after the final credits. Off-beat movies and documentaries were bountiful. Where else could you find a documentary about the iconic *New York Times* fashion photographer Bill Cunningham?

Another thing I liked about Acme was the shop. I'll call it a shop because it looked more like the sitting room of a tilting Victorian, not a sanitized video store on a strip mall. I remember the wavy floors that seemed perilous to navigate. And what about those doors? They had knobs that turned—no push-button or automatic doors at Acme. A movie was usually playing on a TV across from the register so the employees—rather than the customers—could watch the drama unfold. What better way to educate your workforce.

My husband the cinephile is heartsick over the closing. He's an old-fashioned kind of guy who still goes to the library every Saturday—his beloved Providence Athenaeum—and enjoys talking to the librarians about the latest legal thriller by Phillip Margolin or any other new arrival. Imagine that? A face-to-face conversation with a human being about a book. It's downright thrilling.

In his bachelor days, my husband lived on Williams Street in Fox Point, a few blocks from Acme. It started off in the 1990s as a hole in the wall—my husband's words—and took up less than half of its current, uh, former space. To put it in layman's terms, the left side of Acme was a bookshop. After the bookshop closed, Acme expanded.

Peder said that, in a few years, the shelves were packed with gems. He said Acme was so popular it was a challenge to hold your position in front of the "New French" or documentary sections. Owner Ralph Goudreau happily shared his immense and impressive knowledge of motion pictures. Atomic FireBalls, a spicy jawbreaker, sat in a bowl at the front desk for customers.

"I know for sure that Acme introduced me to the actress Sandrine Bonnaire and the director Patrice LeConte," Peder said. "One of my favorite movies was LeConte's *Intimate Strangers*. I started watching off-beat movies in my college days. Acme kept me current. It was a library of movies."

Peder also remembers the doors. One said IN; the other said OUT. Peder, a stubborn New Englander, always went in the OUT door and out the IN door. Ralph didn't mind. After 25 years, he didn't need to see Peder's video rental card. "You have a low number," he said. "One of my early customers."

Acme probably fell prey to on-demand movies like the vacuous *Meet the Parents*. A pity. I fear we all might drown in mindless mainstream dribble, turning into Stepford moviegoers.

One of the last movies I rented at Acme was a Polish film about Nazi atrocities in the Warsaw ghetto during World War II. It was horrific and disturbing, but I watched to the end. Acme's movies were like that; they told us about the world in all its pain and glory. They tested our endurance. They made us feel alive.

Clear Curbs
May 2014

Spring is in the air, and it's time to step out to your curb. Go on, it's safe—no plow trucks speeding by, no cars kicking up rock salt. Chances are you'll find a patch of crabgrass and a cement edge that probably survived our bitterly cold and offensively long winter.

Gaze upon that edge. It's a lonely stretch of cement that needs something to place you in the universe. You could scrawl out a peace sign or the abbreviation for Finland (fi!), or you could set down your home address, in which case you need to reach out to the CEO of Clear Curbs. His name is Peder. Tell him his mother says hello.

Here's how it works: You call Peder's secretary—me—and ask to make an appointment to get your curb dolled up. He comes over with paint, a brush, stencils, and his security detail. He thoroughly cleans the curb, then works his magic. The UPS truck will never get lost again.

I know what you're thinking: lawlessness. Take a walk around the block with your dog Happy or your tinkling G&T to cool down. This is a legitimate business sanctioned by people in high places. Enough said. On to the particulars of a cool idea from a kid with big dreams, and you can't fault him for that.

Not long ago, Peder was kneading bread in the kitchen, and he casually mentioned that he wanted to start a business. I thought that was a swell idea. I envisioned a landscape service, but he wanted a project that required some thought, even a "business plan."

"Let's not get too complicated," I said.

"I like complicated," he replied. "Complicated is good."

The next thing you know a flyer was sitting on the kitchen table: "Clear Curbs delivers reliable and useful curb number painting to the East Side. We provide a clear address so friends, emergency personnel, and delivery people can quickly and easily find your home."

When I was a kid, a century or so ago, life was simpler. I made money babysitting and working as a soda jerk at Velvet Freeze, the neighborhood ice-cream parlor. I was 13, clearly underage, but back then everyone ignored child labor laws, especially Mr. Martin, the gruff owner who barked out my last name, "Rau," when he put in an order for "scoop of Rocky Road."

Today, kids are more entrepreneurial, mimicking what they see and hear in the media and on the street. Those heady TEDx conferences come to mind with the message that you can succeed if you come up with a good idea and some capital from your great-uncle in Buffalo. And let's not forget the value of hard work.

The lousy economy weighs heavily on kids, too. Think about it. They were in diapers when we lived in a bubble and renovated our kitchens every five seconds, and now they see headlines about a sputtering economy that might never rebound. They must rethink the world as we know it.

Kids all over the East Side are launching start-ups. The products and services are impressive: duct tape wallets, string bracelets, tailoring, errand boy, greeting cards, cookies, home-made bread, Rice Krispy treats, and, of course, old reliable—the lemonade stand.

Customer service is the key to success in any business, and such is the case with Clear Curbs. Peder's clients are satisfied, even giddy—"You're sick!" "Great colors!" "Thanks for the play-by-play on the Brown hockey game while you worked!" Peder is so conscientious he will return, free of charge, to his clients for touch ups.

Where are the profits going? Back into the business, of course. More paint, more brushes, more stencils, more flyers. Any good businesskid knows the only way to succeed in this country is to grow.

Broskies

October 2014

The other day, my son told me I was "sick." If you have kids, hang out with kids, or eavesdrop on kids, you'll know that means you do not have the sniffles. It means you're a decent person and might even be groovy, although teenagers today would never utter that word. Groovy was popular when I was a wayward teen in breezy peasant shirts and hip-hugging bell-bottoms, but I'll spare you a back-in-the-day lecture.

Teenagers and James Dean have always had their own lexicon and the early 21st century is no different. Spend some time in our house on Irving Avenue and you will hear an earful of unfamiliar words and phrases that are a far cry from, "Your tennis shoes are very attractive." I am here to clarify.

Let's start with Mr. Nesquik, my favorite long boarder and nice guy. He was sitting on our sofa one day, cradling a comely Sector 9 board, when he announced to a packed room of teenagers that an acquaintance of his was "bombdiggity." Immediately, I thought of "hot diggity," which is what young people said in the South back in the 1950s when they were bubbling with enthusiasm.

Mr. Nesquik informed me that I was way off course. Taking a cue from Webster's, I suggested he use it in a sentence. "I'm the 'bombdiggity,'" he said. "It means I'm cool." He rattled off more: "sweet," just plain awesome; "broskie," a reference to friends as in, "What up, my broskie?"; and "swag," cool but not in a showy way.

Versace, another guest, came up with the word "dope," which means good. I asked him to use it in a sentence. "Those sunglasses you're wearing are NOT dope," he said. "Dang," is another word. No explanation necessary.

"Fresh" was proposed by Dragon. "It means something looks cool," he said. "Like, those shoes are fresh." Skechers are not fresh; Nike Jordan's are. Collared shirts are not fresh; a T-shirt emblazoned with the upright Henderson Bridge is. "Noice" is another gem. If you're thinking of kind, you were born on Long Island. "Noice" means amazing. Again, the shoe reference is appropriate. "Mom, your clogs are really noice."

A-Train's contribution was "sweet bruh," which in a Cheeveresque world means, "Well done, my friend." Locomotive also suggested "tots." This one is complicated. "It means totally, but it's pronounced like the word totes," said A-Train, referring to the bag. "My sister says it all the time."

What's so great about having your own lingo? "We can talk in code," said Jean Pierre. "Vous comprenez?" Dragon piped up. No secrecy intended, he said. "It's not, like, a giant conspiracy," he said. "It just happens."

Teen texts also need to be translated, not that I'm peeking at my sons' missives. LOL (laugh out loud); OMG (oh my God); NVM (never mind); THX (thanks); IDK (I don't know); TTYL (talk to you later); Sk8bording (skateboarding); M2 (me too); U (you); Gr8 (great); YOLO (you only live once); YOLOUYBIR (you only live once unless you believe in reincarnation); M.C. (you'll have to ask Dragon); K (O.K.); and my favorite, JK (just kidding).

That shorthand makes me want to roar to my boys: "It's your turn to mop! JK." Really, so much in life can be a JK moment. "Chicken livers for dinner. JK." "We're moving to Seekonk. JK." "There's a fisher cat in the backyard. JK."

I'm sure that I've left out plenty. My bad. Help is on the way. The Urban Dictionary is a web-based dictionary that has nearly 8 million words, mostly slang, but readers beware: the definitions can veer into the dark side. As a parent of teens, I find the dictionary invaluable. I'm a click away from figuring out what my sons and their best buds are talking about—and that's really "noice."

CHAPTER 9

....

Chess Whiz
March 2015

William Ruiz was kicking around a soccer ball one day and doing other stuff little boys do when he decided to take a serious shot at chess. He had dabbled in the game before but never fully understood it, and his opponent always won. He asked his mother, Rosa, to sign him up for the school chess team. She did.

At first he wasn't, as he puts it, "very good." He thought about quitting. Rosa would have none of that. She encouraged him to stick with it. She told him he was smart enough to do anything, and he believed her. William started to practice with his classmates, his friends, and the chess team's coaches, Gina Dufresne and Frank Delbonis.

Today, the 11-year-old is a chess whiz, beating other players who are older and more experienced. He also beats the grown-ups, including Central Falls Mayor James Diossa. "I was excited to win," says William, also known as Junior. "It was nice to meet the mayor, too."

Chess has shaped William into an ambitious boy with dreams. Chess, he knows, could open doors to an excellent university, as well as to tournaments in distant places with the best players in the world. "I'm proud of him," says Rosa. "He's a good boy."

Rosa was born in Guatemala, fleeing the impoverished country in 1988 to live with her brother in Central Falls. It hasn't been easy. She's a single mom raising William and her daughter, Stephanie, a college student. To make ends meet, Rosa cleans houses and works as a nurse's aide. "My kids see me working hard, so they work hard," she says.

William is in sixth grade at the Segue Institute for Learning, a charter school. His best subject is math, but he says, "I like all of it—gym, science, the humanities." He gets A's and B's. His favorite magazine is *Chess: Life for Kids*, which is mailed to him monthly because he is a member of the United States Chess Federation. He plays soccer and basketball, and he goes to church at Holy Trinity.

Toys are scattered throughout his bedroom—Legos, Woody from *Toy Story*, a stuffed brown bear—but they're outnumbered by his chess memorabilia: 19 trophies, 8 medals, and 14 certificates, all laminated and taped to his wall. One trophy that he is particularly proud of says, "Level of the Knights of the Square Table." "Look," he says, picking it up. "Look at this one."

He has two chess sets—one from his mother, the other from Stephanie. William also plays chess with his computer and usually wins. For his birthday his mother bought him a chess journal, *100 Game Scorebook*, to record his wins and losses and even his moves during a match: "When I get home from a tournament, I read it and check the mistakes I made," he says.

His passion for chess started when he was an 8-year-old student in fourth grade at Veterans Memorial Elementary School. Coach Dufresne offers the details: He played his first tournament Aug. 17, 2013, at the Providence Invitational, at Roger Williams Park, placing 16th out of 32 kids in the

10-year-old and under category.

In fifth grade he played in a dozen competitive tournaments, hence his medals and trophies. A year ago, he placed fifth out of 26 kids at the Scholastic Blitz Tournament. He also competed in the State Scholastic Chess Championships. And not long ago, he started working with chess master Bob Salvas at the prestigious Monastery Chess Program, in Cumberland.

Last April, Central Falls sent its first elementary school team to the Junior Chess Nationals, in Atlanta, and William was one of the competitors. He was 103 out of 355 kids and helped his team place 24th out of 57 teams. William had a blast. "We got a hotel, ate, went to the Coca-Cola factory, saw the fish," he says. "It was fun."

William can't wait for his next match. "Chess is good for me," he says. "It helps with my mind. I concentrate more. Chess is a mind sport. You've got to think before you move. I don't touch the piece until I know what I want to do."

Even so young, he knows each move counts—on the board and in life.

David and the Green House
May 2015

The story begins with the green house on Elmgrove Avenue. Many East Siders know it as the former house of Governor Gina Raimondo. She lived there with her family for many years, and then one day a For Sale sign appeared on the lawn, signaling a move, eventually to Morris Avenue. The sign came down, and I wondered about the new owners, especially after a ramp went up in front. I thought it was an older couple.

Wrong.

The new occupants are Jeremy and Marina Goodman and their three children, including David, who has physical and developmental challenges and moves about in a wheelchair, hence the ramp. "He's a lot of fun. He loves people," says Marina. "He's the mayor of the neighborhood."

David is also a member of Congregation Beth Sholom, the Orthodox Jewish synagogue at the corner of Camp Street and Rochambeau Avenue. He has been going there since his family moved to the East Side two years ago when Jeremy, a veterinarian, started a job as director of the Roger Williams Park Zoo, in Providence. David loves the synagogue, and so does his family, but there's a problem: only the upper level of the building is accessible to wheelchairs. The lower level, where all the social events take place—kiddushes, dinners, and festivals—is not.

Marina wants to change that. She and other members of the congregation have launched a campaign to raise money to install an accessible entrance for David and older members and parents pushing strollers. It's a fund drive born out of love and devotion, and she's graciously asking for your help.

David was born 17 years ago with severe disabilities—cerebral palsy, cognitive challenges, and autism. Marina spent years trying to make things better, even exploring alternative treatments in Canada. In time, she made peace with his limitations and, with her husband, focused on making his life as comfortable and fulfilling as possible.

His success is impressive. He's a student at Cornerstone School, in Cranston, a school for people with disabilities. He can read and write and is making strides in math. His attention span is improving by day. His memory is superb. "When you meet him, he'll ask for your name, phone number, even your extension," says Marina. "When you see him again, he'll repeat everything."

With renovations, the green house has become his palace. His bedroom is on the first floor. The bathroom is fully accessible. His parents even installed a ceiling lift so he can be moved easily from his wheelchair to his bed. "It's a wonderful house for us," says Marina, a graduate of Cornell University who works as a portfolio oversight manager for a financial institution. "We're very happy there."

Now the family is concentrating on the project at Beth Sholom. When David first joined, four men carried him in his wheelchair down a flight of stairs to the lower hall after Saturday services. "It's just become too dangerous," says Marina. "You're talking 200 pounds, with the wheelchair." David remains upstairs while his parents take turns going down to the lower hall with their other children, Jack, 14, and Dina, 10, both students at Providence Hebrew Day School.

Last fall, the congregation took steps to help David. East Sider and Beth Sholom member Grace Novick called contractors to get bids for an entrance and met with an engineer. Marina started a campaign to raise $30,000, the cost of the project. So far, she has collected $7,000.

David has helped Marina and her family zero in on what's important. "Don't sweat the small stuff," says Marina. "Take one day at a time. Be kind. Smile." She is amazed by how much compassion "the world" has shown her son, from bus drivers and home health aides to teachers and social service workers. "What has my son taught me about life?" she says. Turns out, everything.

Call Her Jessica

July 2015

As I write, my friend Jessica Brand is on her way from Rhode Island to San Francisco to get gender reassignment surgery. She's been taking the hormone estrogen for years, and the surgery is another step in her journey to become a woman. Before she left, I gave her a jewelry bag to keep her favorite necklace safe during the trip. I also gave her a hug. She's a remarkable 22-year-old—whip-smart, brave, funny.

A few weeks before she left, we talked at her home in Exeter. Transgender Americans are on the forefront of the next great civil rights debate in our country. Jessica wanted to tell her story so other transgender teenagers don't have to endure the pain she went through, "ever."

Right off, I told her that the directions she had given me were perfect, that I didn't get lost. "Great," she said, walking into the kitchen. I saw a large family photo hanging on the wall and asked about it. The Jessica in the photo had no resemblance to the one I was seeing today. That Jessica was a frowning boy in khakis and a navy polo shirt. The Jessica before me was a radiant young woman in a pale-blue shirt with lacey sleeves. She told me that the family portrait was the last photo she let anyone take of her for years. "I hated my appearance then," she said. Now she adores the camera. She loves the way she looks and feels.

Three people, she said, saved her life: her mother and late father—Susan Trostle Brand and Stephen Brand—and a Rhode Island pediatrician. When Jessica was in middle school, she begged doctors to give her estrogen. They refused, insisting she was too young. "They had never seen anyone like me," she said.

She knew at 2. Toddlers in her day care center were telling secrets. One boy said he didn't have a bellybutton. "I'm a girl," said Jessica. She slogged through elementary school, hoping her feelings would go away. Adolescence, with puberty, facial hair, muscles, and voice changes, sent her into a deep depression. She tried to kill herself. "I never left my room," she said.

One day Jessica was sitting in a restaurant parking lot with her mother. The pressure was so intense she thought her head might explode. She asked her if she loved her. Yes, said Susan. Jessica took a deep breath: "I'm a girl and have to live like one." Her parents' response: We love you; let's do this. They made the rounds of doctors, but no one "got me," said Jessica. Then she found Dr. Michelle Forcier, a pediatrician at Hasbro Children's Hospital, in Providence, who specializes in helping transgender youths and who prescribed hormones. The changes were swift: breasts, hips, soft skin, full cheeks and lips, and less facial hair. "I could finally look in the mirror," said Jessica. "I was seeing the real me. It was thrilling." She emerged from her shell, and started telling her story to other transgender teens, reassuring them that they could get through challenges and be themselves.

We chatted all afternoon at her house that day, even sharing a pizza. I ran out of questions to ask and started bringing up mundane things, like the weather. Looking back, I see that the shift to small talk was a good thing. Jessica is another young woman navigating the world. "I just want to blend in," she said.

She's been dreaming—literally—about gender surgery for years. After two weeks of recovery, she'll return to Rhode Island, where she'll meet up with two New York filmmakers who are making a documentary about her and other young people who are transgender called, *What I'm Made Of.* Her body didn't fit with her mind and now it does. She finally has what we all want: happiness.

Bill's Jacket
August 2015

One of my least favorite things to do is shop. Clothes are not a top priority in my life, and that's obvious. My duds at work are jeans, a turtleneck—in all seasons—and clogs. My duds at home are jeans, a turtleneck—in all seasons—and clogs. This is a long way of disclosing that I am a fan of no-nonsense clothes that make the morning ritual painless and swift. The just-right jeans. The trusty turtleneck. The basic blazer.

Which brings me to Bill Cunningham's jacket. Cunningham is a photographer for *The New York Times.* Actually, he's a fashion photographer, although I'm not sure he would like to be called that. He's too modest. "I'm not a good photographer," he says. "I just love to see wonderfully dressed women." He roams Manhattan on his Schwinn, taking photos of people with his battered Nikon for his street-fashion column, "On The Street." He also maintains a society column, "Evening Hours." Both are snapshots of the city in any given time, and sometimes that time is downright embarrassing. A reptile-skin trench for April showers? Poor boa.

He's been doing the columns for years, long enough to gain a following among fashionistas like Anna Wintour, longtime editor of *Vogue*; society types who dress up for flower shows; and everyday people looking for a brief distraction from the heaviness of life. I am not a regular reader, but I know, for example, that Cunningham wrote a column not long ago about the revival of wide-brimmed felt hats in New York and orange clothes, which I eagerly read because that happens to be my son's favorite color. Cunningham, who was 86 at press time, also narrates short videos of his work. I enjoy them, mostly because I like his Boston accent, which he never abandoned, even though he has lived, since 1948, in New York.

Which brings me to Cunningham's movie, *Bill Cunningham New York*, a 2010 documentary about the elusive photographer, his enormous body of work and his charming habit of calling people under 65 "kid," as in, "Nice work, kid." I recently watched the film on Netflix. Cunningham is shy and doesn't like talking about himself, so the film is more entertaining than revealing, until one of the final scenes when he bursts into tears for a few seconds and a lifetime of heartache pours forth.

We learn from the film that Cunningham is an ascetic. He lives in a tiny apartment in the Carnegie Hall building, with no private bathroom, kitchen, or closet. He doesn't need a closet, since he wears the same thing every day: straight-legged khakis, a solid button-down, black dress shoes, and a blue worker's jacket from France. I covet his coat, a loose-fitting, four-pocketed, slump-shouldered smock designed for French factory workers in the 19th century to protect their shirts from grime. The "bleu de travail" is Cunningham's signature piece. If only I could get my hands on one, I'd be, well, très content.

As the story goes, Cunningham bought his jacket years ago for $20 during one of his trips to Paris to shoot the catwalk. Good luck securing that price today. I started with Google. So many knockoffs—too stiff and the blue hailed from the Crayola hue. Cunningham's coat is faded, more of a gray-green. I tracked down a fashion blog that critiqued a few of the offerings, including a $500 jacket from Tokyo, no thanks, and a "vintage" version—translation: used—with holes and paint stains. Again, no thanks. I finally found a reasonably priced version from a New York store called Hickoree's.

I checked out the store's website. Sold out. I fired off an email to customer service: "Do you expect any more Bill Cunningham jackets?" Kristen wrote back the next day: "Hi Liz, We aren't stocking this brand any more, unfortunately, but hopefully will soon replace them with another French moleskin jacket—stay tuned."

I don't want "another" jacket. I want Cunningham's.

Je suis triste.

Bill, if you're out there, reading this piece during a pass-through of Providence, do a kid a favor. I'm a small.

Pink Balloons
September 2015

The balloon was pink and said, "It's a Girl!" A baby wasn't born, but there was a rebirth, as far as Jessica Brand was concerned. The balloon was a present from her mother after Jessica's sex reassignment surgery to become a woman. I should rephrase that. Jessica said that even though she was born with a man's body she has always felt like a woman. Gender affirming surgery is a better way to describe the operation. "Finally," said Jessica, "my body fits with my mind."

A few months ago, I wrote about Jessica and the pain she went through as a child and a teenager when she knew she was transgender. Jessica's awareness surfaced well before puberty, at age 2, when she tried to remove her male genitalia with a toilet lid and toy saw. Puberty was a dark period. She hated looking in the mirror and spent much of her time, alone and unhappy, in her bedroom. She tried to kill herself. One day, she found the courage to tell her parents that she was a woman. Hormone treatments followed and, eventually, surgery.

We talked at her home in Exeter after her surgery. In her jeans and purple T-shirt, she looked healthy, content, and relaxed. Dark curls framed her heart-shaped face. Her porcelain skin was flawless. She told me that she has never been happier. The suffering, she said, is over. Her body is now a source of joy. She looks at it with a mixture of delight and curiosity. No wonder, then, that her mom, Susan Trostle Brand, bought her a bikini for her 23rd birthday.

The surgery was at Mills Peninsula Hospital in Burlingame, California, a suburb of San Francisco. In early May, Jessica flew out by herself and stayed in a hotel near the hospital. With a few days to spare, she decided to do some sightseeing. A longtime baseball fan, she went to a game at AT&T Park. She ate dinner with a relative and met a friend who had the surgery 20 years ago.

Her mom and two younger sisters, Faith and Fiona, joined her at the hotel the day before the surgery, flying in from Providence. Jessica said she slept soundly the night before the operation. No last-minute jitters? "Not at all," she said. "My life was about to begin, not end." Dr. Marci Lee Bowers, who specializes in transgender surgery and is also a transgender woman, performed the four-hour operation. Contrary to what most people think, the male sex organ is not removed. It is "reshaped," Jessica said. The results, she said, are amazing, a testament to the brilliance of gifted, caring surgeons.

After the operation, Jessica knew she was fine when she started cracking jokes with her family. The first night she needed morphine, but in the ensuing days she was mostly pain-free. In late May, she returned to Rhode Island and visited Dr. Michelle Forcier, the pediatrician at Hasbro Children's Hospital, in Providence, who prescribed the hormones that Jessica said, "saved my life." Without them, she says matter-of-factly, "I'd be dead."

What's next? She's young, bright, and, finally, fulfilled. She talks about finding work in finance or attending graduate school someday. Now she's content being a public advocate for transgender people, especially children and teenagers. "They need so much guidance and support," she said. "I want them to know they're not alone."

Her story might be told in a movie. Two New York filmmakers, Jenn Hallam and Jane Renaud, are making a documentary, *What I'm Made Of*, about Jessica and other transgender youths. Dr. Forcier is in the film, too. The trailer has already been released. One scene in the final cut might show Jessica modeling her new bikini. "I made it through," Jessica said. "Others can, too."

The Maple
December 2015

This summer we cut down an ancient maple that towered over our house. I was sorry to see it go. Actually, I was devastated, but I'm in the final stage of the grieving process, working through denial, anger, and depression to finally reach acceptance. Well, sort of. I still miss it like crazy. How can I feel so much loss for a tree?

Our backyard is about the size of one of those carports that popped up in the 1950s. Most of the ground is covered by a patio—dull cement bricks in varying states of decay, compliments of our brutal New England winters. The trees were the stars—two majestic silver maples.

My guess is that they were either planted when the house was built more than a century ago or were saplings that grew over time. Some people call them swamp maples. That sounds undignified to me, as if they're dime-a-dozen trees that have no aesthetic value. I don't care what the experts say. I like them.

I'll start with the maple still standing, the one that spreads over Jay's house. The main trunk is as wide as a kid's plastic swimming pool. Your fingertips don't touch when you give it a bear hug. Three enormous "stems" rise above rooftops on nearby buildings, and sprouts shoot off to create a green canopy.

One of the best things about the tree is a small knothole at eye level, like the one in the movie, and book, *To Kill a Mockingbird*. Scout found Indian head pennies, figurines carved from soap, and other treasures in her knothole, from Boo Radley. My hollow is home to moss and wet leaves and old, deflated footballs. I'll plant some pansies there next spring.

The other maple was a few feet from our house. Of the two, it was the beauty. It had a massive trunk with arching branches that reached well beyond our rooftop: It's a summer day, and I'm writing in our third-floor office. I look out the window and see a tangle of leaves brushing up against the pane. The trunk, with its shaggy gray bark, was our ground-to-roof curtain. I loved the bark as much as the foliage.

284

One spring, a limb fell off in a rainstorm, leaving an enormous hole. The next year, raccoons moved in and turned the cavity into a palace. The tree was still lush, but it was empty inside and had to go. It came down this summer. I was at work, which is where I wanted to be when the arborists did their business.

We live so close to each other on the East Side that we can exchange ketchup through a kitchen window. Trees are crucial for privacy. They also project strength. I would much rather have a tree in my yard than a bed of daffodils. What could be more calming than sitting on a park bench—or by a window—watching branches bend with the breeze? It's easy to get lost in the majesty of a tree. Trees give us the visual image to think about life's big questions: Why did the light fade early? Why was the fruit bitter? Why did he miss her the whole day through?

Our backyard seems empty now. My kids had a soccer game in Scituate not long ago. I was stunned by the number of trees up there. Losing a tree in Scituate is probably not a gut-wrenching experience. On the East Side trees are precious, even the ones in decline.

This spring, I hope to plant a new tree, maybe a birch. A friend suggested an elm. It would take years to grow to the height of my maple. I won't be around to enjoy its stature. By then, I'll probably be living in a lean-to in the woods, begging the wild, Come in, please. My mind spins with the possibilities: elms, chestnuts, laurels, and anything else conjured by Mother Earth. I'll host them all.

Mayor David

February 2016

The mayor of the East Side has his ramp. An affable and courageous young man named David Goodman, who has physical and developmental challenges and gets about in a wheelchair, can now enjoy kiddushes on the lower level of Congregation Beth Sholom, the Orthodox Jewish synagogue at the corner of Camp Street and Rochambeau Avenue.

Back in May, I wrote a column about how nice it would be to install a ramp for David on the synagogue's lower level, where members attend dinners, festivals, parties, and other events. David appreciated that the upper level was accessible to wheelchairs but was frustrated by the limitations to get below.

For years, four men carried David and his wheelchair down a flight of stairs after Saturday services so he could be with his family—his parents, Jeremy and Marina, and their two other children, Jack and Dina. In time, that situation became too dangerous, and David remained upstairs while family members took turns going up and down the steps to keep him company. That was a tolerable arrangement, but not a compassionate one.

David was born with cerebral palsy, autism, and cognitive challenges. He's a friendly 17-year-old, affectionately called the mayor of the neighborhood by his mom and other admirers because he loves being with people and talking to them. David can read and write, and he also has a great memory. But he can't walk on his own. He needs his wheelchair to live a fulfilling life.

About a year ago, Marina and other members of the congregation launched a campaign to raise money to build a lower-level accessible entrance. Fans of David came forward, and she collected enough to pay for the project.

Contributors included family, friends, big-hearted Providence residents, and a national foundation that helps disabled children and adults. Among the East Siders who donated were Jonah and Rashmi Licht, both doctors; Judy and Jay Rosenstein; Dr. Farrel Klein and Barbara Klein; Dr. Howard Mintz; and Grace Novick. Manocher Norparvar, another East Side resident, donated his time by drawing up blueprints for the project.

In December, the congregation unveiled the new entrance during a Hanukkah party. David was there, along with his family and all the other people who adore him. He was gabbing with everyone, as usual.

"I just want to thank the community for contributing," said Rabbi Barry Dolinger, of Congregation Beth Sholom. "It was a large collaborative effort and a moral imperative. Judaism is largely about learning to care for the other. A congregation that isn't fully inclusive is fully broken."

Goodness can prevail.

CHAPTER 10

....

Driving Peder
March 2016

My son is learning how to drive. Actually he's never been behind the wheel, but he's going to a driver's education class at LaBonte's Auto School, in Seekonk, Massachusetts, to learn about double yellow lines and the blind spot and when to turn on the turn signals. He takes his studies seriously. On the ride home from class one day—I was in the driver's seat, of course—he scolded me at a red light for encroaching on the stop line at a crosswalk. I had no idea what he was talking about.

It's hard for me to imagine that my sons will soon be driving. It seems like yesterday they were zipping around the park in a Mario Go Kart. Those things were dangerous, so maybe I shouldn't worry. I remember once, in my living room, giving my son and his scooter a push—with my foot. The poor kid went flying, landing chin first on the hardwoods: Five stitches at Hasbro Children's Hospital, our second home during the toddler years. Then we progressed to skateboards, which are surpassed only by hoverboards in the crazy-scary category.

Cars are on another level. You could be the best driver in the world, but the guy next to you might be texting his Fantasy Football friends as he's racing down the highway at 75 miles per hour. Make that 100. This is Rhode Island. I work in South Kingstown, and every morning I say a prayer as I exit Gano Street to the Route 95 Racetrack. In seconds, I have to cross three lanes to get to where I need to be: the far left. I dutifully put on my turn signal, but no one slows to let me in. Again, this is Rhode Island. Motorists don't use blinkers, and those who do are universally mocked. I hail from the Midwest, where manners matter.

I can also thank my high school friend Brant for my nervousness about driving. He owned a Triumph. His parents bought it for him when he got his driver's license. It was his first car, and he was proud of it. It was forest green and tasteful, as far as sports cars go. On a sticky summer night, Brant took me for a ride. It was late, and our neighborhood streets were mostly empty. I remember that he was barefoot and wearing jeans and a white button-down, untucked. The top was down. We drove to the edge of our suburb, and I thought he would turn around and go back to what I knew, but instead, he got on the highway. I was terrified. He would speed up, laugh at me for being scared, slow down, then speed up again. This torture went on for a long time. He finally took me home, but I was traumatized, for life. I panic when I'm in a car with a driver who reaches the speed limit—not exceeds it, reaches it. I once gave my son's friend a ride from Providence to a school event in Cranston. In the school cafeteria the next day, she unloaded: "Your mother is the worst driver I've ever seen." Why? Too slow—and in the middle lane, no less.

I don't need Freud to know that I've projected this anxiety about driving onto my kids. First, let me apologize, guys. Second, don't do something just because I don't want you to do that something. Don't go fast because I don't want you to go fast. My kids used to tell me that slowpokes on the road were dangerous, and probably mother hens. "You're going 49 in a 65," they'd shout from the backseat. "Go faster. You're embarrassing us."

At LaBonte's, the driving instructors show a lot of movies. Some of them are about accidents. The images are gory and sad: bloody bodies, mangled cars, roads strewn with possessions—a shoe, an open suitcase, a soccer ball. The movies seemed to make an impression on Peder because he talks about them in some detail.

After class one day, Peder told me that an instructor had scared the bejesus out of the students when he circulated a photo of a car that had crashed after speeding. The driver, he said, did not survive. Speeding, he said, is the biggest cause of crashes. I felt vindicated, but kept my mouth shut and puttered along, on the ride home.

Backyard Dash
June 2016

My neighbors down the street had a party the other day. I was in my backyard gardening when I heard a few people laughing. Minutes later, I heard a lot of people laughing. The crowd had assembled. Oh, joy. Where do I begin? The honk-honk of clown horns. Drumming on what I felt certain was a junior set. "A,B,C,D,E,F,G..." one kid sang, while another burst into tears. Who knows why? Maybe she/he dropped her/his cake on the petunias. The birthday fest lasted all day. I was in heaven.

Most of us live on top of each other on the East Side. Houses were built a century ago when zoning regulations didn't exist or were ignored. That's why you can reach out your kitchen window and touch your neighbor's kitchen window. That's why houses share driveways. That's why a sliver of land on your side is a sliver of land on your neighbor's side.

With this closeness, it's crucial to get along. People who don't like living in cramped quarters shouldn't reside here. They should consider living in communities with sprawling backyards: Loving County, Texas, or Eureka!, Nevada.

Consider my former neighbor, Alice. The details: Fifteen years ago, on a sun-dappled day in August, we moved into our house, on Irving Avenue. Our sons were babies. One morning, I met Alice over our quaint, 4-feet-tall picket fence. We'd chat now and then as the years progressed, but I was busy running after two toddlers and our conversations were brief. Me: How do you get your garden to grow? Alice: Fertilize with old tea leaves. She left cuttings of knotweed in a pail of water in my backyard, and taught me how to trim the small urn-shaped flowers on a Pieris japonica.

Then the boys grew up and started playing baseball—T-ball, AA, AAA, sandlot. Our yard is too small for a game but fine for throwing. One day my husband and sons were playing catch in the backyard and someone from the trio misfired. The ball soared into Alice's backyard. It was a Rawlings, a fine ball.

Rather than knocking on Alice's door, my husband instructed one of my sons to squeeze through a gap in the fence and retrieve the ball. He did. Alice's husband came rushing out of his house, warning us to stay off his property. In all fairness, he was right. Someone should have knocked. But a kid sneaking into a neighbor's yard to get a misbehaving baseball is a harmless deed, and even a bit charming. Film directors seem to think so, too. After all, Mr. Mertle, the gruff-turned-gentle neighbor in the baseball classic *The Sandlot*, gave the ball back.

Things deteriorated after the backyard dash. Baseballs turned into basketballs, which Alice refused to throw back over the fence, despite our pleadings. She kept them. Once a friend's basketball bounced into Alice's yard. It was new, bought that morning. The friend's father wanted it back, please. He knocked on Alice's door and, with help from a police officer he called, retrieved that basketball, as well as a soccer ball, three baseballs, four tennis balls, and a Frisbee.

Noise bothered her, too. She didn't like the sound of boys hanging out in the yard, horsing around in the way that kids do. To convey her displeasure, she would crank up an annoying talk show on her portable radio and sit on a bench in her backyard glaring at Henry, Peder, Eric, Noah, Yaseen, Oren, Theo, Zack, Alden, Aiden, and Jason until they felt so self-conscious, they went inside.

Some things on the East Side annoy me. I don't like floodlights or Billy Joel music past midnight. (Make that any time.) I don't want to hear a TV or a car alarm. Leaf blowers should be banned. So should chain saws that cut down our spready trees. But I love the sounds of life—a crying baby, a yapping dog, the soft chatter on a summer evening. The late-night cheering from the Brown University soccer field up the street is soothing.

Why is it that some people mark off their property with fortress-like fences and others welcome the neighbor's wispy forsythia visiting from the other side? Why is it that some turn their porch lights off on Halloween and others greet the pirates and princesses with pumpkins and Kit Kats? The unexpected surprises and hustle-bustle remind me that the journey starts anew every day. All is not lost. There's reason to hope.

On the Road
July 2016

Okay, so now we're behind the wheel. Correction: My son is behind the wheel. I'm sitting in the passenger seat with a white-knuckle hold on the dashboard, hoping he makes this very sharp turn. He's driving like an old lady—me!—so any collision would not be life-threatening, even if we jump a curb or smash into a ginkgo tree.

Not long ago, my son got his driver's permit. We decided to celebrate. My husband fired up the grill, and we dined on a T-bone. The permit allows him to drive, as long as that piece of paper and another driver are in the car. That would be me, the less-anxious parent.

There was a two-step process to get the permit. First, Peder took a grueling 33-hour class taught by instructors at LaBonte's Auto School in the banquet hall of an old church in Seekonk, Massachusetts. There were lots of lectures about how to navigate a roundabout and the importance of driving with two hands on the wheel.

Then a week or so after the class, my husband took Peder to the state's Department of Motor Vehicles, in Cranston, for his "computerized knowledge exam." He passed. Peder has to wait six months to take his road test, and if he passes that, he will get his driver's license. Until then, he's expected to complete a minimum of 50 hours of driving, including 10 hours at night. Translation: a truckload of driving.

His first practice trip was with his dad. It did not go well. They drove down the long and winding two-lane River Road by the Seekonk River. It's a lovely drive, but not a particularly good one for a beginning driver. Cars were coming toward them—a frightening experience for a new driver. Peder veered to the right, inching toward the curb and the sideview mirrors of parked cars. "Look out!" my husband yelled. The lesson ended. Peder insisted that I accompany him on the next excursion.

I'll admit it: As I climbed into the car for the second session, I had some trepidation. In the wrong hands, cars can be lethal weapons. We decided that the parking lot by the Salvation Army on Pitman Street would be a good spot to practice. I drove there, and then Peder took over. He drove to and fro, making figure 8s with the Subaru. "Should I try parking?" he asked. "Sure," I said. The lot was empty. He did a good job placing the car between two white lines. "Should we give the road a try?" I asked. "Not yet," he said. We swapped seats, and I drove home.

We went back to the parking lot on our third trip, but, on our fourth trip, he ventured into the streets: Up Irving, left on Arlington, down University, over Elmgrove to Blackstone, the mother of all roads. I urged him to go forth with courage. He did a good job, staying well within the speed limit. This being Rhode Island, other drivers came up fast from behind, trying to get him to accelerate. "Ignore them," I said. "But they think I'm going too slow," he said. And then I spoke the words that I hope will remain with him for the rest of his life: "Who cares what anyone thinks?"

Driving is a great way to bond with your kids. It's a time to talk about nothing and everything: that line drive to left field; the impact of the First World War on the Weimar Republic; nature versus nurture; Jupiter on a clear night. It's easy to get distracted. Maybe it was my fault he ran two stop signs. We cruised right past them. I can't say I was too upset. I just wanted to keep driving, deep into the evening light.

Dish-Pan Hands
August 2016

Our dishwasher broke the other day. The control panel with those flat buttons stopped working mid-way through the rinse cycle. Out—just like that. The repair costs were too high, so we decided to buy a new dishwasher at a big-box store that is the highbrow version of Home Depot. We live in a litigious world, so I'll just say that the store's name rhymes with "toes."

I decided against going to a local appliance store because I wanted speedy next-day service. We are a house of four, and only one inhabitant is tidy. She also has wavy brown hair. The thought of washing dishes soiled during three meals, countless snack breaks, and midnight runs to the kitchen terrified me. Sticky food. Greasy pots. Coffee stains in cracked cups.

I acted quickly, hours after the breakdown. I recruited my teenage son to accompany me to the store. I played up how interesting it would be to look at the variety of dishwashers on the market today. I also played the lonely card, as in, "Please don't make me drive all the way to Seekonk solo."

The salesman was pleasant. He showed us the best, the decent, the mediocre. My son whipped out his cell phone and logged onto an app that evaluates appliances. I don't know why he has such an app. I also don't know why he reads *Consumer Reports*. He entered the model numbers and got the skinny on each appliance. He wanted me to go for the reasonably priced GE with five stars, but I didn't care for the clicking capabilities of the handle. "I don't like the way it closes," I said.

"Oh Mom," he said. "Is this going to take all day? I'm meeting Eric." Naturally, I picked the most expensive dishwasher on the floor, the one that looked the most attractive.

The salesman said he would have to order the dishwasher from the warehouse and then someone would call to set up a time to deliver and install it. I figured I'd get a new one in two days—max. I was giddy with delight as I left the store that evening. I felt certain I could manage two days of washing our fine china by hand. I bought a pair of yellow Latex gloves and a bottle of Palmolive.

The first night was tough. I was trembling as I ate my pork tenderloin, mashed potatoes, and peas. I couldn't enjoy my meal. I was too preoccupied with the dirty pots on the stovetop. Whenever my sons took a sip of milk, I thought of white streaks on glass. Why did they have to use knives to cut the butter? Their forks could suffice. Did the salad really have to go on separate plates?

My husband is the chef, so kitchen cleanup is my responsibility. My sons cleared the table and scraped off the detritus. I got to work: Pour a drop of Palmolive on each dish; scrub in hot water; rinse in cold. That was not an efficient way to accomplish the task, but I didn't care. I just wanted it to end.

Then something remarkable happened on the way to the sink. On day two, I started to enjoy myself, even as I took on the breakfast dishes, too. Alone, gazing out the window to my backyard, I let my mind wander—bear left, then right, stop at the fork, peer deep into the woods. The birch sapling was sprouting lime-green leaves. The purple-hued bugleweed was creeping across the flower bed. A squirrel reposed in a patch of sun. I placed the dishes on a rack to dry.

Weeks passed and still no dishwasher—promises "toes"

did not keep. But in the end, I didn't care. A household chore became a meditative journey. I came to appreciate working with my hands. I discarded the rubber gloves. My fingers swelled and dried out. My cuticles bled.

I looked forward to my time at the kitchen sink. When the dishwasher finally arrived, I felt a twinge of disappointment. I did not put the dish rack away. I will use it again. By golly, I will.

Loving Weeds
September 2016

I had a great summer. I spent a lot of time watching my sons play baseball, which I never weary of, win or lose. I visited relatives in our nation's capital, rejoicing in the stifling heat at the Lincoln Memorial. I ate a lot of salmon, fresh from Whole Foods, the one on Waterman, not the uncomfortably cavernous one on North Main. I went to my favorite Rhode Island beach, Goosewing, in Little Compton, although not as much as I wanted to. Baseball beckoned.

And I gardened. We don't have much of a yard. Our house sits on a small lot, so every patch of earth is appreciated. When we moved into "Irving" 15 years ago, gardening was a low priority. Our front yard hosted a stunning kousa tree, but, beyond that, we had nothing but ivy and leggy yews. Two mighty maples dominated the backyard, mostly a patio. A blanket of dirty white pebbles smothered what little land was left.

The boys grew up, and I started to experiment with Mother Nature. Until my marriage, I had lived in apartments. Now and then, I'd minister to a houseplant, but I had no appreciation for the bounty in nature. I could identify the tempestuous tulip and reckless rose—thank you, Eleanor Lavish in *Room with a View*—but that was about it.

Over the years, I taught myself about gardening. I learned how to dig a hole and plant a shrub or a flower that impressed me at the nursery. Light and soil content were of little concern. No wonder my plants died. The maples not only blocked the sun; they also sucked up all the nutrients in the soil. I forged ahead, buying expensive pots of this and that. Still, I didn't have much luck. The sweet woodruff died. So did the hydrangea and the lilies, which I thought were impossible to kill.

This summer, I took a different tack. I abandoned my helicopter gardening for a style that can only be described as benign neglect. I let the weeds be, and then discovered that a weed was not a weed. It was a locust tree trying mightily to get a start in life. It was a Rose of Sharon, or a shade-loving fern, a purple-hued ninebark, or a wax leaf privet.

Suddenly everything was precious. I watered like crazy, and greenery grew. My yard was soon covered with new plants, some a mystery. Leafsnap, an app that identifies leaves, and I became best buds. I snapped photos of my crop and showed them to the botanists at the nursery: What is this? Lysimachis nummularia. At summer's end, I started to transplant my finds to different areas of the yard. A hibiscus found a new home outside the dining room window. The ninebark went under the maple. The barberry bush moved to a back corner.

I wonder what our yard looked like when the last clapboard was nailed to the house a century ago. Did the owners tidy up or let a sapling rise? I hope the latter. Down the street and around the corner lives a homeowner whose entire front yard is a tangle of flowers, shrubs, and, I'm guessing, weeds:

black-eyed Susans; asters; a soft plant with a lavender blossom. Russian sage? Perhaps. Do I need to know what everything is? There's passion in that wildness. Let's hope it's a trend.

The Minors
October 2016

My son Henry is in a band, The Minors. They used to be called The Black Ties—and wore them too—but the new name is catchier. It's a hat tip to music—the minor chord—and to the band's other love: baseball. Henry and two other band members play on the baseball team at their high school. (The fourth member is on the sailing team. Go figure.) The minor league reference in the band's name escapes only those who believe a pop-up is a fruit bar.

Henry tickles the ivories. Will plays the guitar. Casey is on bass. Gabe, drums. They are a jazz band, although they can play anything if they set their teenage minds to it. They first performed at their high school's January Jam but have now broadened their venues to art exhibit openings, Shirley Temple cocktail parties, backyard barbecues, and middle-school graduation parties. I am a devoted roadie.

Not long ago, I went to a performance at an art opening in a renovated mill in Pawtucket. The paintings were okay, but The Minors were the main attraction. "Who are these guys?" asked guests, as they slathered brie on their baguettes. There were requests for encores. As Henry zipped up his portable piano's roomy carrying bag and Gabe disassembled his drums for easy storage in his parents' car trunk, guests lingered for contact information. I think Will handed out business cards.

That gig led to another, and then another. One winter day, band members gathered at Will's house in Rehoboth, Massachusetts, to record a CD. The foursome was joined by high school classmate Isaiah, a light baritone who sings in the relaxed style of the great crooners, Sinatra and Crosby, and who charms audiences with what musicologists call the "conversational style" of singing. Girls swoon in his presence.

After lots of palling around, as teenagers are wont to do, the band got down to business, recording "Jingle Bells," "Santa Baby," "The Little Drummer Boy," "Mary, Did You Know?" and a more secular piece, "My Favorite Things," introduced into our popular culture by Julie Andrews in *The Sound of Music* but propelled into the stratosphere by jazz musician John Coltrane and his soprano sax. The cover photograph, taken by Henry, shows the four in mock horror as they open presents, although it might be the too-busy Christmas sweaters—worn for the occasion—causing the distress. The cover also reflects a new name for the band, The Minor 4, with no apologies to Isaiah, who is on the soccer team, anyway.

Band members brought 48 copies of the "Last Christmas" CD to their high school's Holiday Tea—an annual winter gathering with choral music, musical performances, and delicate cucumber sandwiches—and sold out within minutes. There was a line. I bought three CDs, a violation of the band's one-per-customer rule, but I had connections and used them.

Henry has always loved music. As a baby, he started with spoons, rat-ta-tap-tapping on his highchair, and then he progressed, as a toddler to a keyboard the size of a Subway Footlong. From there, he jumped to his grandmother's spinet and, in high school, to an 88-key portable piano that he kept in his bedroom for late-night jam sessions and transported to gigs, where he glowed as his fingers found just the right keys for a song he made up as he went along.

It wasn't always that way. In elementary school, Henry took piano lessons from a woman who grew frustrated by his lack of interest in learning how to read music. With one hand, she would point to a tiny golf club on straight black lines in *Piano Adventures!* and, with the other, press Henry's finger down on the corresponding piano key, a gesture that he found irritating—and punitive. He quit. At his last lesson she told him that he had no musical talent. A heartless remark, without question, but it did not diminish his love for music. Henry found a new teacher, Ms. Gay, who delighted in and nurtured his ability to play by ear during lessons in the sunroom of her house on the East Side. She told him that music, at its core, is an expressive art, and that Eric Clapton couldn't read music either.

In my dreams, I see The Minors—or The Minor 4, whatever—at a Christmas party in Newport. Guests three sheets to the wind are sipping Scotch whiskey, neat. Striped ties. Velvet shoes. Lucy, a well-behaved golden, brushes against a black taffeta skirt. Henry floats his hands over the keys and whispers, "One, two, three," and the band launches into the exuberant theme song from *A Charlie Brown Christmas*—the one Linus van Pelt plays on his grand, while Charlie, Lucy, Snoopy, and the rest of the gang cut loose on the dance floor. It's the same song I listened to as a child with my four sisters and brother every Christmas. It's so sad and happy I want to cry.

Chef Peder

January 2017

My husband is writing a cookbook. Maybe you've seen the first draft on our kitchen table—or on a bench at the local Y where he swims. "Peder Schaefer Recipes" is in the final stages of editing and should be available soon. It is not fancy-schmancy, just 33 pages of the best meals you will ever eat in your life: black beans and rice, mussels and pasta, chicken curry in a hurry, and more.

The curry dish is one of my firstborn's favorites. (He is also named Peder, and even though his middle name is different—Slaughter rather than Augustus—confusion prevails at home when I shout, "Peder." Inevitable response: "Which one?") Little Peder also likes Big Peder's Norwegian meatballs, which are really his mother's meatballs, and I have little doubt that she inherited the recipe from her mother, Christiane Caroline Sophie Sorensen Johnson, the daughter of Thorvald Sorensen and Emilie Jorgensen of Drammen, Norway.

My husband is the cook of the house. There, I said it. My close friends know he is head chef, but casual acquaintances think I rush home after a hard day at work to stir the pot. Once my boss said, "Thanks for staying late. I know you have to get dinner on the table." I embraced his sympathy and went on my merry way. Those lying days are behind me. I am now making a public declaration that my husband prepares our feasts—seven days a week, 365 days a year.

Cooking has never interested me. My friends believe it has to do with my hyposmia, a partial loss of smell. I can smell the big stuff—fire, tobacco, booze—but the sweet delicacies of life elude me. I cannot smell the soothing aroma of baking bread or the tanginess of an orange. Even garlic is a mystery. Smelling is crucial to cooking, hence my indifference.

Enter my husband, who can smell a peach 100 miles away. He considers his day incomplete if he has not had at least one five-star meal. Food soothes him, gives him purpose. Cooking is also his way of expressing his affection for family and friends. Which brings me to the cookbook, and back to my firstborn.

Little Peder spent four months last fall living in the woods on the Maine coast for a semester of high school. One day, he was sitting at our dinner table slicing into grilled pork tenderloin with lingonberry jam—another favorite—the next day he was hanging out in a cabin with five other teenagers preparing for an outing to a tidal pool. His absence was a shock to our small household that also includes his younger brother Henry. A stillness settled over Irving Avenue, exacerbated by the fact that Little Peder had no cell phone or computer—both banned at the school. Communication came to a halt.

My husband and I had ways of coping. Thanks to Netflix, I binged on, well, whatever. My husband turned to his cookbook. After dinner every night, he'd go upstairs to his office and write. His memory and the Hillshire Farm recipe box he inherited from his mother were his only companions. His introduction was heartfelt:

"My oldest son was going away for a few months and asked me to prepare a cookbook of the meals I typically prepare at home. I obliged." Each entry was a memory, a connection. My husband's goal was to finish most of the cookbook before Little Peder returned for good. He succeeded.

There are dinner meals—chicken cutlets meunière, pork cutlets with capers, grilled fish, broiled sirloin strip—as well as lunch dishes and sauces. Some recipes have catchy names:

Double Play, which is two pasta dishes, one tomato, the other pesto. Other meals are simple like scrambled eggs and rice or pot roast that simmers in Lipton onion soup mix.

And then there are the tributes. My husband thanks his mother and *Vogue* for deviled ham and noodles, and his father, Walter A. Schaefer, for "Walter's Salad Dressing." Eric Dahlberg's grandmother is credited for shaved steak; Kathy Lang gets a nod for bread and her husband, Keith, for cod. Dan's rice pilaf gets a shout-out and so does the now-closed Blue Point on North Main Street for its white sauce on smoked fish. Henry helped with the layout. Anthony Russo, a Rhode Island artist and friend, designed the cover. Former Governor Lincoln D. Chafee, another pal, is recognized for his skill cutting iceberg lettuce. "Peder Schaefer Recipes" should be in bookshops this spring. Look for it. It's a labor of love.

Swimming to Somewhere
February 2017

One of my husband Peder's favorite movies is *The Swimmer*. Burt Lancaster plays a middle-aged man who swims from pool to pool on his way home from a boozy party in an affluent New York suburb. Set in the '60s, the movie is based on a short story by the writer John Cheever. Burt is cheery at first and then realizes after his last dip that his life is a mess. As one reviewer puts it, the story is about a man's journey into darkness. That's heavy stuff, but not why my husband loves the movie. His appreciation is more literal. He relates to Burt's pool hopping.

A few years ago at dinner, our son, also named Peder, told

my husband that he was getting "pudgy." Ouch. Peder had been swimming all summer at the Seekonk Swim and Tennis Club, known to many East Siders as the SSTC, and had intended to stop exercising during the winter. That remark inspired him not to hang up the towel. He decided he would swim off 600 calories a day. Of course, he would have to find an indoor pool. He did not know then that he would have to find many pools, just like Burt.

My husband learned to swim at the Fox Point Boys Club, then off South Main Street. He went once a week with his buddies, most of them from Henry Barnard School, an elementary school. One day, Bud Latham, the revered coach and swimming instructor, approached him: "Son, you can't swim, can you?" It was obvious, but Peder was too proud to admit it. After the group class ended, Bud took him aside and taught him freestyle in 10 minutes. The core of his instruction method was no dog paddling allowed.

After that zinger at dinner, Peder considered his options. The Boys Club, now on Ives Street, has a pool, but it's for kids, not for dads who are putting on the pounds. There is also the Jewish Community Center on Elmgrove Avenue. Their schedule favors morning lap swimmers. Peder is not a morning swimmer. The locker rooms are nice, but the light at the pool is mostly artificial. He likes natural light when he swims.

Then there is the YMCA on Hope Street. The hours are suitable, the light is good, the parking decent. Plus, it's close to Peder's office; he could swim on his lunch break. He settled on the Y.

The calculations came next. His trusty fitness app assured him he was losing 400 calories with every swim. To drop more, he changed his eating habits. Before his swimming days, he'd eat lunch with his boss, Dan, who would order a hearty meal and then complain and discard half of it. Peder would eat his entire calorie-rich meal. He started skipping lunch and swimming instead, which he estimated reduced his daily caloric intake by 200. In his world, this got him to 600 calories, or 400 + 200 = 600.

Other pools also appealed to Peder. He liked the YMCA in Seekonk, known to regulars as the Newman Y. The hours were better on weekends, and he could fill up his gas tank with the cheaper Massachusetts' prices. He also appreciated the Y's warmer water, sauna, and scale to monitor his progress.

Last fall, his routine took a hit. He arrived at the Hope Street Y for a lunchtime swim. The water was cold. Later that day he received an email that the pool was closed until further notice: the boiler was on the fritz. He panicked and then, once again, calmly considered his options.

He stopped by the Nelson Center at Brown University and discovered that he didn't have to sign up for a full year. He could get a monthly membership. A convivial young man took his photo. The facility impressed him: 13 lanes; plush locker rooms; Bergmanesque light (his words); and a majestic ceiling. But he had complaints. The water was too deep. He likes to be able to stand in emergencies. Water polo tournaments interfered with lap swimming. And parking was a problem. There was grumbling.

One evening, a smile returned. The boiler had been fixed at the Hope Street Y. "I'm back home," Peder said. All those pools, all those laps, and he still has not reached his weight-loss goal. Two years ago, he weighed himself on the scale at the Newman Y: 196. He's been as low as 191 and as high as 199. He's determined to take off more, even if he has to hop more pools. His doctor says not to worry, that his weight is fine. Peder wonders: Maybe our son is too skinny.

Georgia's Journey
March 2017

Most writers are terrified by a blank page. Not the Hunters, the father-daughter duo and former East Siders who know how to tell a story.

A few years ago, I wrote a column about Tom Hunter and his book, *Memoirs of a Spaghetti Cowboy: Tales of Oddball Luck and Derring-Do*, which chronicles his days starring in Spaghetti Westerns filmed in Rome in the '60s. It was a best-seller in our house. We received a signed copy from the author, who lived next door before moving to Connecticut with his wife, Isabelle, last year.

Now the Hunters' daughter, Georgia, is joining the family business. Georgia has just published a book based on the true story of her Polish Jewish relatives who were separated at the start of World War II and, through ingenuity and courage, survived to see each other again after a decade apart. *We Were the Lucky Ones* has received rave reviews, with critics and authors calling it "the most gripping novel in years," "extraordinarily moving," and a "truly tremendous accomplishment."

Most writers struggle to get their first book published. The response to Georgia's debut book was so overwhelming she had several bidders. The publisher, Viking, a division of Penguin Random House, is so impressed it has launched a marketing campaign that is taking Georgia, who also lives in Connecticut, to readings throughout the country.

The backstory behind the book is just as compelling as the novel. As Georgia writes in her blog, wewerethe luckyones. com, she was 15 years old when her mother told her that she came from a family of Holocaust survivors. Thus began her journey to unearth her family's history. In a way, Georgia started the project as a student as the Moses Brown School, from which she graduated in 1996. Georgia's English teacher, Ransom Griffin, asked students to research and write about their ancestral pasts. Georgia decided to write about her paternal grandfather, Adolph (Addy) Kurc, who changed his name to Eddy Courts when he arrived in the United States. But some of the details were sketchy. After attending a 32-member family reunion on Martha's Vineyard, Georgia was eager to press on, or, as she puts it, "Write these stories down."

One summer day 17 years ago, not long after graduating from the University of Virginia, Georgia sat down with her mother at their Irving Avenue house and told her she wanted to write a book about Papa's family. Isabelle was thrilled and handed her a black binder—stuffed with photos, letters, and newspaper clippings—that she had put together after her father died in 1993.

Carrying a digital recorder and a moleskin notebook, Georgia spent years retracing the Kurc family odyssey on a 1,100-mile journey through Poland, the Czech Republic, Austria, Italy, and Brazil, sometimes accompanied by her husband, Robert Farinholt, and their now-5-year-old son, Wyatt. The novel is historical fiction but is inspired by the harrowing tales of her grandfather and his four siblings who were flung from Poland to North Africa, the Middle East, and the Americas, enduring unimaginable hardships: a Siberian gulag; brutal prisons; Vichy-occupied Morocco; long treks on foot across the Alps.

Georgia says that 90 percent of Poland's 3 million Jews died in the Holocaust, and of the 30,000 who lived in the Kurc family's hometown of Radom, Poland, fewer than 300 survived. That should make us all cry. The book's title comes from a remark a relative made to Georgia about beating the odds: "It's a miracle in many ways. We were the lucky ones."

Lost and Found
May 2017

McDonald's has been getting a bad rap lately. First, there was that movie about the guy who ate Big Macs and fries for a month and gained a ton of weight. Then my sister in Maryland told me about a woman who found an unattractive creature in her McDonald's salad.

I am here to report some good news about the fast-food restaurant chain, specifically, the one in our own backyard—the McDonald's in University Heights. My husband Peder had an enriching experience there that is worth retelling.

Loyal readers might be aware that Peder is the chef of our house. He cooks all our meals, and for that I am grateful. Moods are directly linked to food, he believes. His words to live by: you are what you eat. It should follow, then, that a chip or a Twinkie dare not pass his lips, but this is not the case. Soon after we were married, I discovered by opening the kitchen cabinet that he had a fondness for Little Debbies, Cheetos, and Pop-Tarts. How to reconcile eating, say, chicken cutlets meunière—his specialty—with junk food was a puzzle, and still is. But we are all mysteries.

I also discovered shortly into the union that Peder had a hankering now and then for fast food, with McDonald's as his top choice. I remember our first encounter with a Happy Meal. It was a dark and stormy night on the New Jersey Turnpike, and we were starving. "A McDonald's is up ahead," he said. "Let's stop." His affection for fast food continues to this day, which brings me to his latest encounter with the Golden Arches.

He was sitting in his office across from the State House when the clock struck noon and his belly called out for nourishment. The meal would have to be quick, for work responsibilities awaited. He raced to the University Heights McDonald's a few blocks away and entered with the intention of getting his usual: a quarter pounder with cheese, mustard and onions, medium fries and unsweetened iced tea, at a cost of $7.69. But on this day, he was forced to improvise when he looked in his wallet and discovered he had a mere $7. Instead, he ordered the two-cheeseburger meal with medium fries and unsweetened iced tea for less than seven bucks. He sat in a two-seater booth next to a window.

He thought about our evening meal—veal marsala—while he devoured his burgers. On the way out, he tossed his empty fries' box and pickle-stained wrappers into the trash can and put the tray on top. Then he stopped at a nearby ATM to replenish his wallet and returned to work. Back at his desk, he reached into his pocket for his phone, but it wasn't there. He panicked. He rushed back to the ATM. No luck. McDonald's was his next stop. So sorry, the workers said, no one had turned in a phone. He went back to work, so disturbed about his loss he was unable to concentrate.

On his way home that evening, he stopped by McDonald's

again. He was wearing his $35 Martian smartwatch. He walked past the dumpster and felt a tickle on his wrist. Could it be? He was close enough to his phone to get a Bluetooth connection that made his smartwatch vibrate. Two McDonald's employees were standing nearby. "I think my phone is in there," said Peder, pointing to the dumpster. He pushed a button on his smartwatch, and Brahms' requiem wafted through the parking lot. His "find phone alert" music was doing its job: alerting him. One by one, the workers removed each crumpled bag, finally coming upon Peder's leftovers. His phone was covered with mustard, but it was intact. He concluded that he had placed his Samsung on his tray during his feast and had accidentally thrown out the phone as he tipped his tray into the trash can.

That night, Peder sent an email to the national McDonald's website, praising the employees who made the daring rescue. A few days later, he received a letter from the owner of the University Heights establishment. "Our goal is 100 percent customer satisfaction," she wrote. "We are glad our employees helped you recover your phone. We have shared your comments with our restaurant team." As a token of appreciation, she included two coupons, one for a breakfast sandwich, the other for a burger. Peder used his breakfast coupon the next day to buy an Egg McMuffin. This time, he kept his phone in his pocket.

CHAPTER 11

....

The Purge
June 2017

The toys are gone. Well, most of them.

The trikes, push buggies, princess houses, slides, scooters, bats, balls, buckets, and other detritus from who-knows-whom have been removed from our neighborhood parks. Not all the stuff. That would be revolutionary. But one baby step at a time. Let us be grateful that we can now enjoy our public land without gazing upon a sea of plastic.

Our city mothers and fathers finally intervened, removing most of the toys that had accumulated over the years. They should be praised for their courage: Hell hath no fury like an angry parent.

Four years ago, I wrote about the plastic in our parks, saying that it was unfair to litter the land with cast-off toys. Parks are open to all, I said, not just families with children. I recalled visiting the East Side parks with my two sons when they were toddlers and how they thrived in the open space with their wit and ingenuity. A grove of hemlocks was a forest. The gentle hill was a mountain. The knotty tree stumps were castles. The only toys we brought to the park were tricycles and buckets for the sandbox, and we took them home at night. Parents didn't leave their toys in the park. It just wasn't done.

The column was not well received by parents. One parent

sent an email calling me an idiot. As a former newspaper reporter, I'm used to criticism from readers, but this was over the top. The discussion was about toys in a park, not politics. The city was clear why most of the toys at Gladys Potter— also known as The Baby Park—Summit Avenue, and Morris Avenue were removed: They pose a safety hazard. Instead, the city intends to create parks that connect children to nature and open and free play, with berms, log retaining walls, rain gardens, and rocks to play on and explore. This is good news. I would suggest fields of tulips, too.

In my earlier column about the plastic parks, I tried my best to be tactful; I didn't want to offend. That's one good thing about aging: You tend to speak your mind. Kindness is still vital, but you realize it's fine to express an opinion that is unpopular. With that thought, let me say this: All the plastic toys should go. Sure, parents can bring toys for their kids to play with during the day, but please take them home at night. Put them in your car trunk. Drive off. The next day, take them out and repeat. If you live close to the park, carry the toys. My husband and I did that for years.

We are lucky to have beautiful parks on the East Side. One evening in March, I sat on a bench in mostly plastic-free Gladys Potter, listening to the branches crackle in the wind. It was creepy, and every now and then I looked over my shoulder, but I loved being there. I thought of that scene in *To Kill a Mockingbird* when Scout, wearing a ham costume, and Jem, her brother, are walking home from a school Halloween pageant through Maycomb's woody park on a dark fall night and hear the crunch of leaves. "Hush a minute, Scout," says Jem. "Thought I heard something." Footsteps? At Gladys Potter, my imagination soared.

Thistle
July 2017

I once read about a woman who despised cut flowers. It's indulgent, she said, to cultivate something for the purpose of ending its life. Suitors who brought her bouquets were met with an icy glare. She sent them on their way, roses in hand. I get her point—let the petals die in their own bed, not on a stranger's tabletop—but the French love cut flowers, and they know how to live. Let us defer to the French on matters of beauty and taste.

I came late to discovering the joy of cut, or loose, flowers. I received roses in my courting days, but they never really impressed me all that much. Calling after a first date or even returning a call—now that was a game-changer. Then I became a gardener and flowers cast their spell. A hastily scrawled sign I spotted one day at the flower shop at Eastside Marketplace caught my attention: "Life is about flowers. Flowers are about life." Agreed.

There are so many places on the East Side to buy flowers: where to begin? I will start at Eastside Marketplace, which made a wise choice moving its flower shop to the entrance. A burst of color greets us and lifts our spirits, especially in the dark days of a New England winter. It's one-stop shopping—milk and daisies cuddling in the cart. My husband and two boys buy flowers there for yours truly. For Mother's Day, my firstborn gave me thistle and golden rod, and my other son celebrated the occasion with white tulips. I enjoyed the bouquets for weeks, and when they faded, I put them to rest under the white birch in our backyard.

Whole Foods, the one on Waterman Street, also has fine

flowers. The store on North Main Street has a robust flower shop, but I'm partial to the smaller store where I go to eat chocolate and cheese at the café tables outside. Again flowers welcome you at the entrance. I can't identify them and don't care to. I just buy what seizes me.

Only the soulless can pass without being moved by these offerings. My son bought flowers for his prom date there. Let me rephrase that: I bought flowers for his prom date there. To be honest, I bought them elsewhere and, in a panic, rushed to the Waterman Whole Foods, but I'm getting ahead of myself.

The story begins with my son's plan to go to a prom. I told him he needed to get flowers for his date. He said, "Oh." I called my sister for guidance. She said, "Take over and buy a corsage." I Googled "corsage." I know the young woman and felt certain that she would prefer a bouquet. I called City Gardens Flower Shop on Wickenden Street. I told the florist to please design something "earthy." I said, "She is not a pink person." A few days later, I picked up the bouquet. The flowers were orange and yellow, with oval-shaped green leaves shooting hither and yon. It was stunning, but it was not a prom bouquet. The prom was that night. I rushed to Whole Foods, where the florist made an elegant bouquet of white tea roses and wrapped the stems in a navy ribbon to match the prom dress. The orange flowers relocated to the kitchen table. The roses danced the night away. I am forever grateful to the Whole Foods florist for her kindness—and humor.

My affection for flowers is making me more observant of the natural world. I've discovered that weeds, or what we've been told by the experts are weeds, flower with the best of them. You can find them everywhere—in your backyard, on a riverbank, in a crack in the driveway. Resist the urge to pluck weeds. Let them be. Some will bring you buttercups, others tiny lavender beauties that look at home in an old honey jar. Two stems are plenty to grace your day.

Holy Moly
August 2017

If you need a tour guide at the Hope Street Farmers Market, the best people to call are Jill Moles and Suzanne McLouth. They'll meet you at the duck eggs and take you from booth to booth, introducing you to farmers, cheesemakers, bakers, herbalists, baristas, gardeners, antique dealers, painters, printers, and even people who make preppy dog collars and gluten-free dog treats. Jill and Suzanne, former East Siders who now live in Oak Hill, in Pawtucket, have been meeting at the market on a regular basis for years. It's the highlight of their week. "It's a godsend," says Suzanne. "It's local," says Jill. "That's important."

If you don't stop by the market at least once this season, you are missing out on an opportunity to experience life as it should be—unhurried and joyous. The market is open on Saturdays and on Wednesdays in Lippitt Park at the end of Blackstone Boulevard. Just look for the cars—sensible and fuel-efficient—and the shoppers carrying unfashionable canvas tote bags. No plastic here, my friends. Even cut flowers are wrapped in paper.

I try to go as often as possible. What makes it special, besides the food, is that you run into people, like Jill and Suzanne who, on this morning, are graciously showing me the grounds and sharing how good it feels to eat vegetables, fruit, and bread that are free of pesticides and other nasty chemicals. "I'm very careful about my food," says Suzanne. "If I don't know where it comes from, I don't want it."

My first stop is Poorboy Sharpening. No, I am not craving a sloppy roast beef sandwich on a submarine bun. I'm dropping off a Sheffield carving knife inherited from my mother-in-law to sharpen it after decades of neglect. I hand it over, handle first, to the craftsmen, with a promise to return after my tour.

Jill is on the hunt for a cucumber plant. The lettuce in her vegetable garden is "all done." It started to bolt, which means, she says, that it has turned bitter. She is also buying Hakurei turnips, a bulbous veggie unknown to me. "They taste like a mix between turnips and radishes," she says. "You can put them in salads, or snack on them like carrots."

Suzanne grew up in the country in western New York. Her father was a doctor. A lot of his patients were farmers. She says she appreciates people who work the soil. She remembers that women planted Victory Gardens during World War II to feed their families. "We're going back to that," she says.

"Vegetable gardens are popping up everywhere." She takes me to the Harvest Kitchen table, where a man is selling jars of pickles. The organization helps young people straighten out their lives. They learn how to cook, and some go on to become chefs.

"Holy Moly," says Suzanne, as she strolls onward. She is thrilled to see a box of squash from Skydog Farm, where produce is hydroponically grown. "Oh boy, this is a treat," she says, and plops down $5. "I was not expecting this today." Jill is enticed by a bunch of Swiss chard, so delicate it looks like a wedding bouquet. "I sauté them in olive oil," she says. "You don't have to add salt or anything. They're good by themselves."

Duck eggs and apples delight, and then we wander to another booth to consult with a master gardener who is giving away seeds: coreopsis, poppy, daisy, larkspur, phlox, and more. Suzanne talks about her milkweed; Jill asks why a zucchini plant fails to produce fruit. (Lack of pollinators.) I pocket two packages of nasturtium.

Along the way, we accept the offerings: feta from Narragansett Creamery, chipotle-flavored sauerkraut from Lost Art Cultured Foods, sweet applesauce from Harvest Farm, and Pina Colada granola from Beautiful Day, a nonprofit in Providence that helps refugees by hiring them to make granola. Jill works with one of the sellers, Maitham, who is from Iraq. The conversation turns to how advanced Scandinavian countries are when it comes to the environment. "See what happens at the market—we talk," says Suzanne.

Two hours whiz by. Jill buys a Yacht Club soda for her son, Nathan—root beer, his favorite. We all promise to exchange plants from our gardens another day. I pick up the Sheffield knife and run my finger down the newly sharpened blade. Now I can slice my apple.

Ed's Daylilies
September 2017

Ed Chetaitis delivers letters and daylilies. The missives are from the United States Postal Service. The daylilies are from his sprawling garden in the Summit neighborhood on the East Side. For a very small fee, he will dig up, say, an Orange Velvet—a big-bloomer with creamsicle-colored petals—and plant it in your yard in a sunny spot, where the flower will thrive and multiply and bring you joy for years to come.

Ed has been our postman for nearly two decades. His route is near the Wayland Square area. Many East Siders know him and adore him. It's hard not to grow attached. He is kind, easy to talk to, and always in good humor. During a blizzard years ago, we made him cookies and hot chocolate. The next day, a thank-you note floated through our mail slot.

I knew Ed was a gardener, but it wasn't until I read our neighborhood blog that I discovered he was a hemeroholic. That's a fancy word for someone who is smitten with daylilies, not to be confused with lilies, although Ed likes those too but not as much. A daylily is from a family of perennials called hemerocallis. A lily—characterized by a single straight stem with whorl leaves—is from the lilium family. People get that mixed up. Ed says they also misspell lily a lot. "One 'l,'" says Ed.

When I think of daylilies, the wild Orange Tiger Lily comes to mind. But there are at least 60,000 varieties of daylilies in the world. Ed has about 150 varieties in his yard on Memorial Road, of which 50 are for sale. He has access to several hundred more varieties at his mother's house in Maryland. Consider these gems: Calico Jack, a creamy yellow bloom with a plum eye; Chicago Silver, a lavender-purple two-tone with a silver edge; and Ruby Spider, a full nine-inch bloom with red petals and a yellow throat that extends halfway to the petals. Don't even ask me to describe Daring Deception or Buttered Popcorn or Bela Lugosi.

Ed started gardening when he was 12. The cancer ravaging his father's body made him too weak to mow the lawn. Eddie took over the landscaping. He planted gladiola bulbs he bought from the Michigan Bulb Company with his 50-cents-a-week allowance and was inspired by what sprang from the earth. He planted a garden at his first house in Virginia, his native state, and when he moved to Rhode Island in 1996 he discovered daylilies in his yard and nurtured them. One daylily led to another. Now there is nary a spot on the property that does not entertain a hemerocallis. Ed even received permission from the city to plant on an easement in front of his house.

Ed's daylilies are all over the East Side, from the Grotto neighborhood to Fox Point. Judith and Kip, my next-door neighbors on Irving Avenue, are some of Ed's biggest patrons, with plantings that include a Little Joy—a blood-red small bloom—and a Happy Holidays to You—a red bloom with a ruffled and serrated gold edge. Word of mouth is working in Ed's favor. One day he found a note taped to the door of a house on his route: "Ed, please call my cell about your daylilies. I've got to know!"

Ed likes being a postman, but he loves growing and selling daylilies. "It's therapeutic," says Ed, who recently returned from the 71st annual convention of the American Hemerocallis Society, in Norfolk, Virginia. "I'll sit on my front porch and see the blooms and sigh. It's a happy sigh. It's a true enjoyment of seeing all the color. There's also a little bit of spirituality to it." Daylilies appeal to him because they are easy to plant, beautiful, and resilient. Neither snow nor rain nor heat will kill them. "They won't die on you," says Ed.

Most of his daylilies pass by the end of August. The petals drop, the leaves curl. This can be a sad time for Ed. The view from his front stoop is colorless. Who can blame him for feeling blue? It's a long time until spring. He does his best to hang in there. May we all.

Purple Toes
October 2017

I grew up during a time in our history when girls dressed like
boys. That's so far from today's look for young people, it's hard
for many to envision, but trust me, we all looked like ragamuf-
fins. Flannel shirts and jeans. Hiking boots in the winter, Jack
Purcell sneakers in the summer. In high school we graduated
to a tad more feminine style with blousy peasant shirts and
burgundy clogs. No one wore makeup. Ever. Fingernails were
cut short, never painted. Pedicures were unthinkable.

Onward to spring of this year, and I am looking at the
toes of my sons' athletic trainer who is wearing flip-flops. Her
specialty is treating students injured on and off the field. On
many occasions, I'd walk by her office and see a linebacker with
his elbow wrapped in ice. Those toenails were painted orange.
"Orange. Wow!" I said to the trainer. "Everyone is painting
their toenails," she said, and rushed off to find an Ace bandage.

A few weeks later, I was sitting in a comfy leather chair
at Angell Nails on Angell Street with my feet in a bucket of
warm bubbly water. A woman was on a stool in front of me,
massaging those feet and skillfully using her pedicure equipment to tidy things up. She asked what color I wanted. I am
a decisive person, except when it comes to grooming and
clothes. Paralysis often sets in. I asked her what colors were in
style. "Bold colors," she said.

My toes were not a mess. In fact, they were rather attractive—short nails, minimum dirt, no calluses. Why was I here?
I recalled a conversation I had heard in my office between
two female co-workers. "I like your sandals," said one woman.
"Thanks," replied the other woman. "I couldn't wear them until

I got a pedi." Her toenails were painted fire-engine red. This must be a Rhode Island fetish: women can only wear sandals when their toes are dolled up. The pressure was mounting.

Angell's shelves offered millions of bottles of polish, from neutrals and light pink to green and black. I panicked. There were too many choices. "Neutral," I blurted out to play it safe. The technician nodded. "Go with something you can see," she said. She explained that she has been painting toenails professionally for years and knows what would go best with my skin tone. "Purple!" she said. I never wear purple, but she was persistent, and the woman with her feet in the bubbly water next to me was taking okra, which I couldn't abide, so I agreed.

Each brushstroke brought a sense of empowerment. I thought about joining a women's group or taking a spin class. I willed myself to love the new look. Artistry accomplished, I transferred to another station to have my fingernails painted, and again, we—uh, I—settled on purple. I paid up and emerged onto Wayland Square feeling well-groomed and complete, until I did not. I thought of the crooner Deniece Williams: *silly of me to think I could ever have you—for my color.* Besides, the nail and toe job made me feel like I was suffocating. Pressured to conform to Rhode Island beauty standards, I had descended into madness.

CVS was open. Hands balled to hide my extravagance, I raced to the makeup aisle and settled on Beauty 360's Advanced Gel Nail Polish Remover Pads. Back in my car, crouched in the front seat, I returned my fingers and toes to their natural state. I tossed the purplish pads in a dumpster. My adventure on the catwalk was over.

Whew! Be who you are.

Benny's
November 2017

The first thing I bought at Benny's was a sled, not the fancy red ones in the storybooks but a plastic sled that was as big as a Buick. It was blue. I took the boys to a hill in East Providence and let go. They barely dodged a grove of white pines. I gave the sled away, but now I wish I had kept it. It'd be nice to have a memento from one of my cherished hangouts.

I felt lousy when I heard the news a few months back: Benny's is closing all 31 of its stores by the end of the year. My initial thought was selfish. Now I'd have to go to a ware-house-style big box store with aisles a mile long, merchandise coated with dust, and employees who would rather be fishing. My second thought was more complicated.

I never set foot in a Benny's until I had a house in need of repair and kids (two boys), and then I went there all the time. I liked the one on Branch Avenue in Providence, across from the North Burial Ground. I also shopped at the Benny's near the East Providence line, down the street from car dealerships and a McDonald's, but it wasn't as fun as the one on Branch. That Benny's was filled with managers and workers who laughed and talked to you like you were their favorite cousin. Customers of all ages and from all walks of life shopped there, and the lack of pretense among them was refreshing. The aisles were narrow, and the merchandise was always within reach. No one had to reach high to get a package of light bulbs. "Where's the laundry detergent?" a woman asked me once. "Next aisle," I said, "by the plastic bins and trash cans."

I bought many things at Benny's. I bought mops, Pine Sol, Comet, Murphy Oil Soap, Windex, Brillo pads, Clorox wipes, and Easy Off. I bought paper towels, paper napkins, paper plates, red plastic cups, a red-checkered tablecloth, and a door mat. I bought a whistling tea kettle and a frying pan. I bought brown towels, a bathroom scale, hooks for a shower curtain, and a shower caddy that holds three bottles of shampoo. I bought Legos, Scrabble, Settlers of Catan, Uncle Wiggily, Rescue Heroes, baseballs, bats, baseball pants, batting gloves, and a coach's whistle. I bought salty peanuts, Swedish Fish, and a box of chocolate covered cherries. I bought air conditioners, a bike pump, and two tricycle bells decorated with galloping horses. I bought a flat-head screwdriver and a sweatshirt. I bought a package of Bazooka Joe bubble gum. Sometimes, I didn't buy anything. I just liked wandering around the place: America at its best.

My last visit was depressing. Many of the shelves were bare or on their way to emptiness. What remained was in some disarray, victims of overzealous shoppers looking for bargains. I didn't recognize some of the employees, which made me wonder if management had dismissed workers early. I wondered where they might land. Home Depot? Lowe's? Rocky's hardware store, which I guess wouldn't be so bad. Not the same energy, but at least the store is small.

I didn't buy much during that visit: a roll of aluminum foil, a football, two pairs of white crew socks. The man in front of me expressed his condolences to the cashier, but I didn't, and I regret that. "Too bad you're closing," I should have said. "I hope everyone finds work." I did keep a souvenir: my shopping bag declaring in red letters "Benny's—our Favorite Store." So true. So long.

Hideouts

December 2017

I've had secret places since I was a kid. On Christmas, I'd hide under the piano next to our Douglas fir, observing the world through a mosaic of blinking lights. I could see my sister's brown brogues, with their curled flaps, clomp across the green rug. I could see the claw feet of our mahogany side table, and our jacks and their red rubber ball. During hide-and-go-seek, I'd hide behind thick coats in closets and prickly yews outside. Old habits are hard to break.

Three decades on the East Side is plenty of time to find hideouts. They are places I go for solitude. Virginia Woolf advocated a room of one's own; I advocate a bench of one's own. Our neighborhood has twists and turns that lead to peace and quiet, even in an urban setting.

One of my favorite hideouts is at Swan Point Cemetery. I started visiting after my mother-in-law Carol died more than a decade ago. Her grave is off North Road, in the section of the cemetery that abuts Oak Hill. I'd brush away dead leaves and sticks, and if the weather was pleasant, I'd sit on the grass. One day, I decided to explore the grounds and ended up at a pond, where I had watched frogs with my sons when they were boys. I sat down on a bench. The water was still. I noticed trash poking from bugleweed near the water's edge. As I got closer, I realized it was a single rose, still in its chiffon wrapping, with a pink bow. The rose was brittle, faded into a pale brown. Someone had probably left the bouquet at a gravestone, and the wind carried it to the pond. Should I take it home? Since then, I've gone to the bench at the pond in all seasons. When it's bitterly cold, I wrap myself in my oversized fake fur coat. I must look like a grizzly bear.

On rainy days, I stay in my car. My hideout for inclement weather is too "weird," as my son says, so I'll leave out details about the location. Let me say this: It is not the long and winding and private driveway of an East Sider's house. It is a public spot, accessible and open to all. One rainy evening, I drove there and parked. I did not cut the engine. I left on my wipers so I could take in the view of the Seekonk River. I sat in my front seat for a long time, watching the current and thinking.

Our neighborhood parks are loaded with hideouts. The bench late at night at The Baby Park on Humboldt Avenue. Behind the forsythia at Brown Street Park. The boulders at India Point Park. I like sitting under a pine in the park across from the Salvation Army on Pitman Street, and on a stormy day the dog park on Angell Street is practically empty of people and pets. It is a tangle of trees and bushes.

Another place for privacy is my backyard. Tucked in a far corner, behind an overgrown boxwood, is a white wicker chair, undetectable from our kitchen window. I like sitting there on summer evenings, shielded on all sides by nature: a dogwood, towering maple, hibiscus. I listen to birdsong and watch the squirrels flirt. One day, I went back there to do nothing. I was startled when I discovered that a visitor was sitting in my chair: my husband. I ceded the hideout to him. Sharing is caring.

CHAPTER 12

....

For the Love of Baseball
December 2017

"Baseball is beautiful, but it's not everything." That seemed like an odd thing for a coach to say at a baseball banquet, especially to a room of teenage boys who probably played catch before they learned how to walk. But Providence Sports and Leadership, which helps young men play baseball at an affordable cost, is not about hype. The coach was telling the players to use the game of baseball to find their greatness.

A parent had to fight back tears.

The banquet was held earlier this month at the Elmwood Community Center, in a room with tall windows framed by billowy pink curtains. Lunch was set out on a long folding table. The mom of one boy, Carlos, brought pasteles with chicken and potato salad, made in the Dominican way, with eggs.

My son Peder, who is 17, joined the program this year. Though he has played the game since he was 3—for high school and regional teams—PSL was one of his best experiences in baseball. The players were devoted to the game—the coaches devoted to the players.

The home field is at Davis Park, on Smith Hill. About 60 kids are in the program. The under-16 and under-18 teams expose players to college scouts throughout New England.

While baseball is the soul of PSL's mission, the program is equally committed to academics. Nearly all PSL alumni attend college, and many play ball.

After our feast, the coaches said a few words, in English and Spanish. Most players are Dominican and live on the South Side, which can be one of Providence's toughest neighborhoods.

Program cofounder Bill Flaherty thanked them. "People say to me, 'Bill, you do all this for the kids,' and I say, 'No, I don't. They do all this for me.'" Flaherty understands how the game gets inside you and never leaves. He played in college and has coached for years.

About a decade ago, while working on a building he owns on the South Side, he looked out a window and saw a man in a crush of ballplayers. He counted at least 40. His heart swelled: "How could he coach all those kids by himself?" Flaherty approached the man, Kennedy Arias, and PSL was born.

They registered as a nonprofit, recruited coaches, and expanded to include winter training, a required community service project, and College Assist, a mentoring program that helps high school students with their academics and college applications.

One of the banquet speakers was Providence Deputy Chief of Police Thomas Verdi, a PSL board member whose son played baseball at the University of Connecticut. The elder Verdi sat with the players during lunch. "You have to work as hard in the classroom as you do on the field," he told them. "We want you to succeed in life, to be somebody." PSL is the state's "best-kept secret," he said, and the most outstanding youth program in Providence.

Why does one youth program succeed and another fail?

Selflessness is a must. The PSL coaches chuckled about how they always answer their phones, even midnight calls from players in distress over breakups with girlfriends. "You put the effort in," said Flaherty, "we'll do the same back to you." Respect, back to you.

Awards for best sportsmanship were handed out, and recipients received a maple bat rather than a trophy. The coaches asked the winners to rise, one by one. Alex Ramirez was singled out for his talent and dedication. He never missed a practice, always walking or biking to the field. If a practice was canceled, he would call up Coach Salcedo to complain.

"I'm not very good at this," Ramirez said nervously, more comfortable on the field than speaking before a crowd. "Thank you, everybody, for helping me get to where I am."

Everyone clapped. They knew. Ramirez will attend the University of Rhode Island next fall on a scholarship, and he will play baseball.

My Puffer
February 2018

As I write, the forecast for tomorrow calls for our first snow of the season. A walloping three inches. This time last year, and probably the year before, we were knee-deep in snow, and I was turning up the thermostat in our house every hour. It was colder last year than it is now, but still, any chill offends. My BFF is the sweltering summer of the American South. Yet here I reside, family to nurture, hearth to protect. I break out my winter survival guide and go forth.

My priority is a decent puffer coat. Wool doesn't cut it.

Apologies to animal lovers, but I need feathers from ducks or geese to stay warm. If a chemist wants to come up with an alternative to down, I'll consider it. But the synthetic fabric on the market today is mediocre; it flattens out much too soon. It's hard to find a decent puffer coat, what with all the knock-offs out there. My coat has to be snug, but loose enough so I can sit comfortably in my dining room—the coldest room in our drafty house.

My first stop was the internet. Big mistake. Puffers selling for up to $2,500 from high-end department stores popped up on my screen, and those were the cheap ones. I found others that weren't as expensive but decided that, in the end, one needs to try on a puffer to find out if it satisfies. I had a stiff drink and went to the Providence Place mall. There were down coats galore, even the showy red Canada Goose jackets, which I scratched off my list because their fur, I am told by my son, is from coyotes. I found a reason to dislike every puffer I observed: too tight, too big, too shiny, too long. I gave up. Back home, I discussed my dilemma, and my son suggested I try his old black Patagonia, covered with patches to contain feathers trying to break free. It fit perfectly. Sold.

My other top priority for the winter is a good hat. This is a problem. For years, I wore an orange hat with flowers embroidered on its rim, but I put it in the wash, where it shrank to an unacceptable size and left the flowers frayed and wilting. Finding a new hat is difficult. I can't bear the feel of scratchy wool against my head or the look of something pointy, with an elfish ball. I need a pillbox style, with a soft interior. I searched but came up with nothing. Hats are mostly oversized and floppy today. My son intervened again, offering his burgundy skullcap with a fleece lining. Not especially stylish, but it will do.

Gloves are also a necessity for the winter months. It's hard, if not impossible, to keep track of a pair of gloves. One falls to a frosty sidewalk; the other languishes, alone, on a cafe table. They will never couple again. I once owned nice gloves. My sister Emily sent me two pairs of soft leather gloves in black and brown for Christmas one year, and I bought a pair of hardy rag wool gloves last winter. All were lost. Not long ago, I searched through our glove basket and found nothing but onesies, and they were all lefties.

Knowing that I would probably repeat my carelessness, I decided to buy inexpensive gloves that I wouldn't miss should they disappear. I thought of the gloves at CVS on Angell Street. They hang on a pole, a vision of practicality and simplicity—forest green with a ribbed cuff; a half-fingered Fagin; cherry blossom pink with rubber daisies on the palm to double as driving gloves. They were all charming and cheap: $3.99 a pair. I bought two.

Fear did not rise up and seize me this season. I didn't have to go far to winterize. What I needed was right in front of me—homespun or at the corner drugstore.

Orchid of Vincennes
April 2018

I'm on a kick to fix things in my house. It started with lamps and then progressed to kid ceramics, kid art, kid magnets, picture frames, ripped clothing, door hangings, torn pillows, dresser tops, side tables, and a shoeshine kit. My kids broke, or disfigured, most of the stuff when they were toddlers; no explanation needed there. Instead of tossing out the remains, I put them in a closet and went on with my life, with the intention of returning to them one day. I'm the type of person who follows through: I do what I say I'm going to do, even if it comes after a long delay. My busted-up stuff was always on my mind. There it sat, in darkness and dust, until the urge to make repairs seized me.

My mother-in-law and her relatives appreciated lamps. I remember walking to the top floor of her house years ago and seeing a dozen lamps in a corner, each one exquisite in its workmanship and detail. We inherited the lamps after she died, but I was wise enough to store them until the teenage years. Boy, that was a mistake. I should've waited until middle age. Teenagers are as clumsy as toddlers. Tables shook; lamps tumbled. Fortunately, they were salvageable. Off to Breeze Hill Lamp Shop in East Providence, where the proprietor worked his magic. A century-old floor lamp with dried flowers in its smoke-stained shade was saved, as was a brass lamp as heavy as an anchor. The art is on display again.

From there, I moved to the medicine cabinet on our third floor. The manufacturer's sticker is still affixed to the door: General Bathroom Products Corp., 2201 Touhy Avenue, Elk Grove, Illinois, 60007. I searched the cabinet up on eBay and discovered that I have a mid-century piece, complete with two fluorescent bulbs on each side and removeable glass shelves, and that it is "exemplary."

My problem: only one bulb worked. I searched that up too and figured out that I could fix it with a power gear fluorescent starter, FS-2, standard, 2-pin, which I bought on Amazon for $14.03. I unscrewed the bulb cover and took out the old starter and installed the new one. It only worked for a day. Undeterred, I called my friend, Val, who fiddled with it for a few seconds and got it to work. High-fives all around.

Then I turned my attention to the toilet. I've always wondered about it since we moved into our house 18 years ago. It's purple, along with the sink and tub. Rhode Island School of Design professors owned our house at one time, and I assumed that they installed the bathroom during the Swinging Sixties. I was wrong. The toilet was running so I lifted the lid and spotted the date of its birth: "1932 Standard." I searched it up.

This was not just any toilet. We were in possession of an Orchid of Vincennes toilet, tub, and sink manufactured by American Standard from 1927 to 1950. Today we would call that color lavender. Back then, it was considered a purplish pink. I know these scrumptious details because I found a website, retro renovation, that helps kooks like me remodel, renovate, and decorate their homes in authentic mid-century style. My bathroom was featured in an old advertisement in a posting about pink bathrooms, which, according to the site, were popular in mid-century America—thanks, in part, to First Lady Mamie Eisenhower, who loved all things pink.

"Orchid of Vincennes was inspired by, and derives its name from, some historic achievement in the ceramic art," the ad said. "The name is a tribute to the high degree of artistry attained by the craftsmen of the potters of old Vincennes in the time of Louis XIV of France." Royalty in the loo. After reading that, I felt enormously protective of my bathroom. I washed the porcelain with lemon juice. I polished the faucets with Quick-Glo. Only one problem marred the set's authenticity: the toilet seat. It was white, a contemporary Bemis. The original had broken long ago. I searched up vintage toilets. "This Old Toilet" popped up. I emailed the owner, asking if he had an original Orchid of Vincennes seat. Get real lady, he thought, but did not utter. Instead, he replied, "See attached memo about substitutions." My new seat—dyed Orchid of Vincennes—should arrive any day. It's been a long, strange journey, for sure.

Dog Tags
May 2018

The thief had wiped her dresser clean, and though deep down she knew she had left her father's dog tags on top, she wanted to be wrong. "I went a little crazy," she says. There was a frantic search. Her secret place. The sugar bowl. Kitchen drawers. Then she had to face it: The beloved keepsake left to her by her father was gone, hustled away in a pillowcase in a break-in that rattled her so much she packed her bags and left to live in another community to feel safe.

Glenda Andes put her East Side house up for sale and is living in an apartment in Narragansett until she figures out what to do next. Today, she is sitting in a Wayland Square café telling her story about losing something so treasured talking about it makes her cry. "Besides feeling disbelief, I feel like I failed my dad," she says. "I couldn't hold on to that one thing."

And what a thing it was: The two dog tags of Robert Andes, a drill sergeant in the U.S. Army who joined the military when he was a teenager and served two tours, one overseas in Germany, the other at a training camp in Georgia for soldiers on their way to the Korean War. Glenda and Robert had a special father-daughter bond, and when he died on April 9, 2009, the dog tags went to her. "They represented his strength," she says. "And they were real."

She grew up in New Mexico but left for college in San Francisco, earning computer science degrees that took her to companies in Seattle and Palo Alto. Two years ago, she moved to the East Side for work and bought a house on Slater Avenue where she could settle in with her Chihuahua mix, Ellie. She liked the subway tiles in the kitchen, and the neighbors were friendly. "All was good," she says.

Two weeks after she moved in, she flew to California for her nephew's wedding. She came home to a terrifying sight: two doors were kicked in. A thief had ransacked the house, taking her laptop and her tablet and a necklace with her father's signature etched on a charm. She was so frightened she couldn't sleep at night. An alarm, cameras, and flood lights were soon installed.

After the break-in, she kept her father's dog tags with her, carrying them in her purse or wearing them around her neck, even to work. In late February, she arrived home after work, fed Ellie, and changed for a trip to the gym. She left the dog tags on the dresser; surely, they'd be safe for an hour, especially on a cold winter night. When she returned, the French doors were "busted through"—again. "I had a sick feeling," she says. She went to her bedroom. The intruder had removed a pillowcase from her bed, "scooping up everything."

Her first thought: "This can't be real." After a frenzied search, she accepted that her precious heirloom was gone. Other keepsakes were missing too: her late mother's diamond earrings; a silver box with relatives' memorial cards; the tags of her beloved Australian shepherd, Freckles. Again, sleepless nights ensued—and sadness over losing something so meaningful to her and so meaningless to a stranger.

Glenda and her father would talk on the phone every day,

visit on holidays, and take vacations with their loved ones together. If she felt lonely, wanted career advice, or had a personal problem, she'd call Daddy. He noticed a lump on his jaw in May 2007. Lung cancer. Doctors gave him 90 days to live. "He decided he would last longer," says Glenda. She was by his side when he died two years later.

Losing his dog tags was devastating. For days she scoured the bushes by her house, hoping the thief had tossed them aside, thinking they were worthless. She searched for the dog tags on Craigslist, in case they had been put up for sale. A week later she moved out. Her furniture is in storage. "I just didn't feel safe," she says. "This is such a beautiful neighborhood, but I can't live here anymore. I had a car stolen in college, but this just feels so different. This is someone getting into your personal space." She knows the dog tags are probably gone forever; still, one can hope: Robert Andes. ER18324776. Blood type O.

Highway Blues
June 2018

I am driving. Again. Down Elmgrove, right on Angell, left on Taber, past Dunkin', then a sharp turn onto 95 South to begin my morning commute to South Kingstown, where I work. Hello Providence skyline! Greetings Big Blue Bug! Who's that greedy lawyer on the billboard? I've been making the trek for nearly six years, and it's not any easier than it was when I started. Patience. I clutch the wheel with my sweaty palms—two hands, always—and I'm off, petrified, anxious, bored.

I grew up in a large city in the Midwest. Correction: I grew up in a small suburb in a large city in the Midwest. I never left Clayton, and neither did any of my friends. It felt odd to venture beyond my borders, and on the rare occasion when I did, all I could think about was going back home to familiar territory.

Work took me to New England, where I fit in nicely with the tribal practice of never leaving one's town, neighborhood, block. I understood when Providence residents said that they had never been to Burrillville, or that driving all the way to Newport was a burden. As a newspaper reporter, I crisscrossed Rhode Island for stories, but in my free time I rarely left the East Side, where I lived in an apartment on Gano Street. Driving to, say, Goosewing Beach in Little Compton was about as far as I went.

Then I got a job at a university in a village called Kingston. Go Rhody. At first the commute wasn't bad. It was different, like the job. New experiences refresh. I'd listen to Rhode Island Public Radio, so by the time I arrived at work I'd know plenty about the day's horrors. I'd come into the office early and leave early to avoid rush-hour traffic.

But things changed, as they always do. I started working longer hours, and the freshness faded. I stopped listening to news reports because they were too disturbing. I turned to music, buying CDs that were favorites, as vinyl records, in my youth: Joni Mitchell, Crosby, Stills, Nash & Young, Eric Clapton, the Allman Brothers Band, Bob Dylan, Leonard Cohen, The Beatles. This brought me back to those unfettered and alive days—thank you, Joni—when my biggest worry was speeding off to Town Hall to scrounge up a story for the newspaper where I worked.

And then one afternoon I hit a big traffic jam. I had left work a tad early when it started to snow. It turns out everyone else had the same idea. By the time I reached Route 4, the flurries had turned into a blizzard. I drove even slower than usual. Five minutes into the journey, the highway turned into a parking lot. Stuck. I tried to calm myself with music, and when that didn't work, I remembered a nautical term from a newspaper story I wrote long ago about a dragger from Galilee who got up at 4 o'clock every morning to scour the ocean bottom: becalmed in a storm. Home three hours later, and I was a wreck. I was so frazzled I couldn't speak.

The road is as unfriendly as ever. Fender-benders cause monstrous delays. So do wild turkey crossings. Road rage is rampant. I'm a slow and cautious driver, which angers native Rhode Islanders, especially those who like to tailgate: "Move over, dear," they bark, edging closer. Switching lanes is a challenge when a Mack truck is bearing down on you.

My alarm rings at 5 o'clock every morning and I remember, The Ride. Nothing soothes the anxiety. The trip is so tedious, so boring, sometimes I can't remember getting from point A to point B, from Nibbles Woodaway on 95 to the Big Red Barn on Route 4. Who knows where the time goes? Gregg Allman got it right. Lord, you got me trapped on this highway. Foolish to be here in the first place.

It's time to get off.

Olive
July 2018

We took care of a dog for a few weeks last year. Dog sitting is the popular term. Her name was Olive, and she was a black lab. She was fairly young—people told me a year or so—but

I'm not experienced with dogs so, truth be told, I had no idea. She was small and compact, with a square jaw. Her fur was soft and shiny, and she didn't shed much. If the eyes are a window to the soul, then Olive was filled with goodness, much like Mother Teresa, also known as Saint Teresa of Calcutta. Olive was Saint Olive of the East Side.

When I was a kid, we had dogs. We were a family of six children, so it was always chaotic. Some dogs adjusted; others did not. There was the shaggy sheepdog (name at a loss); Hans the Schnauzer (jumped out of our station wagon one day and disappeared); and an Irish Setter, Duffy of the Malmar, tall, lean, red-haired. He came with papers, although his boisterous personality did not reflect his pedigree. Duffy walked you. He dug a huge hole in our backyard that remained for years until, one day, my father filled it with dirt and sprinkled grass seed on top.

Tending to a dog when I was a single working woman was out of the question. I was a newspaper reporter and never home. I considered getting a dog when my two sons were toddlers, but another parent told me a puppy was like having a baby. My sons are only 13 months apart, so I wasn't prepared to take on the responsibility of another little one.

That decision did not sit well with my younger son. He spent the best years of his life badgering me about getting a dog. He bought dog books and browsed the internet for dogs we could rescue from, say, swamp country in Louisiana. Whenever a dog crossed his path, he would take the time to pet it and exchange pleasantries: "Hi girl. Hi boy." A tickle behind the ears was his specialty. I felt guilty for denying him such a simple pleasure, but I was envisioning early morning walks in frigid weather and no puffer on the coat rack.

To keep him happy, I agreed to board his friends' dogs. How can I forget Gretchen, the shy beagle who curled up in my lap while I watched a movie, or the Australian Shepherd who escaped from its leash in a park and went after a yapping Jack Russell terrier.

Olive entered my son's life in high school when his adviser brought her to the morning meetings, where students discussed important things like why the forks are so far away from the salad bar in the cafeteria. My son and Olive hit it off. The adviser took note and asked him if he would like to dog sit. Olive was a guest in our house the next week.

Commitment is crucial for the proper care of a pet. One cannot roam the city with The Squad all night if nature calls for Olive. My son agreed to put me in charge.

There was an instant connection. It helped that I was the one who fed her (too much) and took her to the dog park, where she romped in the feathery reeds and sniffed rocks. Her affection intensified so much she started following me around the house, like my son did when he was a toddler. Our bond was rooted in respect (left plenty of room for me on the sofa); unconditional love (waiting for me at the front door after work); and happiness (tail-flapping on the floor after a belly rub).

Our obligatory crack-of-dawn walks introduced me to new neighbors. We all looked like we had just rolled out of bed, grabbed a leash, and stumbled into the street without our morning coffee. There was the teenager, hair askew, with the mutt working on its social skills; Susan with the puppy taking its first steps; and Frank with the wrinkly faced pug that waddled along oblivious to life's cruelties. We'd nod, raise a hand. We all shared a secret.

During Olive's subsequent visits, and there were many over the years, we carried on as if we had never left each other. I read an article once that said dogs communicate with their eyes. Olive sure did. She'd look at me with eyes full of longing—and a tinge of sadness—and I'd retrieve her leash or, better yet, a slice of turkey. She had me every time.

Our last visit was wrenching. Montana would soon be Olive's next home, alongside her owner, who was to start a new job on the prairie. Olive lived only two blocks away, but on that final day my dread of never seeing her again made the walk feel like a slow shuffle around the world. The goodbye was swift. A big hug, then a tug to shut her wobbly picket gate.

In that moment, I wished for words.

Me: How do you feel about moving across the country thousands of miles from your birthplace? Will you remember me?

Olive: I'll thrive wherever I live if I'm loved, and yes.

I've always wondered what people meant when they said their dog was like a member of the family, or why they sobbed when their dog died. Now I know. A dog gets you out of your room. A dog is your best friend forever. A dog loves you no matter what. Thanks for the memories, Olive. See you in heaven.

Acknowledgments

I am grateful to the writers, reporters, editors, friends, and family members who have supported my work over the years: Denise Caterinacci, for never saying, "I don't have time"; Barry Fain, for offering a life-changing opportunity; Hilary Horton, for teaching me how to write true sentences; Emily Lilyestrom, for her wise counsel; Jonathan Saltzman, for his kindness and humor; the squad of boys, for calling me "Liz" and being excellent sources; *The Providence Journal*, for a great adventure; and Jean Plunkett, who edited this book with skill, warmth, and compassion.

I would like to thank Kevin Atticks, director of Apprentice House Press, my copy editor, Natalie Misyak, my design editor, April Hartman, and my managing editor, Claire Marino, for their enthusiasm as they guided me through publication.

My family gets me moving every day. Thank you to my husband, Peder Schaefer, and our sons, Peder and Henry.

About the Author

Elizabeth Rau is an award-winning writer and former newspaper reporter whose work has appeared in *The Providence Journal, East Side Monthly, Rhode Island Monthly, The Boston Globe, Providence Phoenix* and many other publications. She grew up in the Midwest and lives in Providence with her family.

Apprentice House Press

Loyola University Maryland

Apprentice House is the country's only campus-based, student-staffed book publishing company. Directed by professors and industry professionals, it is a nonprofit activity of the Communication Department at Loyola University Maryland.

Using state-of-the-art technology and an experiential learning model of education, Apprentice House publishes books in untraditional ways. This dual responsibility as publishers and educators creates an unprecedented collaborative environment among faculty and students, while teaching tomorrow's editors, designers, and marketers.

Eclectic and provocative, Apprentice House titles intend to entertain as well as spark dialogue on a variety of topics. Financial contributions to sustain the press's work are welcomed. Contributions are tax deductible to the fullest extent allowed by the IRS.

To learn more about Apprentice House books or to obtain submission guidelines, please visit www.apprenticehouse.com.

Apprentice House
Communication Department
Loyola University Maryland
4501 N. Charles Street
Baltimore, MD 21210
410-617-5265
info@apprenticehouse.com
www.apprenticehouse.com

CPSIA information can be obtained
at www.ICGtesting.com
Printed in the USA
JSHW010756030523
40981JS00005B/61

9 781627 204439